BEHIND *the* CANDELABRA

BEHIND *the* CANDELABRA

SCOTT THORSON
with ALEX THORLEIFSON

HEAD *of* ZEUS

This paperback edition first published in the UK in 2013
by Head of Zeus Ltd

Published in the United States of America in 2013
by Tantor Media, Inc.

9 7 5 3 1 2 4 6 8

A CIP catalogue record for this book is available
from the British Library.

ISBN (PB): 9781781856710
ISBN (E): 9781781856703

Printed and bound by CPI Group (UK) Ltd, Coydon, CR0 4YY

Head of Zeus Ltd
Clerkenwell House
45-47 Clerkenwell Green
London EC1R 0HT

www.headofzeus.com

BEHIND *the* CANDELABRA

Introduction

"Too much of a good thing is *wonderful*," Liberace used to say when commenting on a flashy new costume or a wild idea for his act. He loved being known as the most outrageous entertainer in show business and went to outrageous lengths to perpetuate and reinforce that image. Predictably, his passing was outrageous too. From January 24, 1987, the day when front-page headlines in the *Las Vegas Sun* revealed that Lee had contracted AIDS, his illness and death became a media event.

Television reporters camped in front of the Palm Springs mansion where he lay dying, subjecting every arrival and departure to intense scrutiny. Was it true, they ghoulishly asked cornered delivery boys, doctors, and family members alike, that Liberace was dying from AIDS? Lee's staff, under instructions from Lee and others, created an impenetrable wall of denial. Lee had spent his lifetime building what he fondly called "the legend of Liberace." He'd go to hell before he'd see that legend destroyed.

"I don't want to be remembered as an old queen who died of AIDS," Lee told me, clinging to my hand with failing strength when we met for the last time a few weeks before his death.

But Lee, whose every wish had been scrupulously obeyed during his lifetime, would be denied this final one. The zealous Riverside County coroner, investigating the cause of Lee's death, would reveal the truth at a nationally televised press conference. A commemorative service held in Palm Springs two days after Lee died attracted fifteen hundred irreverent curiosity seekers, carloads of press, but few genuine mourners. In celebrity-saturated Palm Springs only two stars—neighbor Kirk Douglas and actress Charlene Tilton—took the trouble to pay their last respects. To avoid another media extravaganza, the time and place of Lee's funeral were kept a closely guarded secret.

February 7, 1987, was a beautiful, sunny, almost smog-free day, just the kind of day Lee would have chosen to make his final curtain call. The service was scheduled for one-thirty in the afternoon and I arrived right on time. But security guards kept all but a select few from entering the chapel, and I wasn't on their list. I stood outside during the brief service. When the mourners came out I realized that they couldn't have numbered more than twenty. I may have been mistaken, but to me they seemed embarrassed at being seen in that place at that time, as though grieving for Liberace was something to be ashamed of. I recognized most of their faces. All of them had been on Liberace's payroll. He referred to them as "his people," as if paying their salaries conveyed ownership. That's the way he was. Lee had millions of devoted fans, hundreds of acquaintances, fanatically loyal employees, but few real friends.

As they filed away I entered the empty chapel and looked around, surprised by the drabness of the room. I saw no floral tributes, nothing to indicate that people had gathered to mark the passing of a remarkable man. As a memento of the occasion, the mourners had been given a simple card that bore a prayer to St. Anthony, Lee's personal patron saint. At its top there were the words, "Liberace; May 16, 1919–February 4, 1987." I looked at it for a while, unable to believe that he was gone. His coffin had been whisked away so quickly, with so little pomp, that there'd been no time to say good-bye.

This isn't the way Lee would have wanted it, I thought sadly. He'd have arranged to bring this final curtain down in a spectacular way. I took a seat in the empty room and bowed my head, imagining the funeral Lee would have planned. I'd been with him during the staging of so many shows that I felt I knew exactly how he'd do this one. The entire funeral would be vintage Liberace, a facsimile of the thousands of performances he'd given during his lifetime. Lee loved an audience and he always left them feeling good. I couldn't imagine that he'd have wanted to do less when he took his final bows.

He'd have wanted to make his entrance in an expensive Rolls-Royce, just the way he made the entrance for his Vegas act. The Rolls hearse would come to a stop center-stage and be bathed in blazing spotlights while soaring trumpets and thundering timpani heralded its arrival. The sarcophagus would be draped in Lee's favorite fur, a $300,000 virgin fox cape with a sixteen-foot train. Then Lee's valet would appear and remove the cape from the coffin, just as he'd removed it so many times from Lee's shoulders. The valet and the cape would be driven off in a miniature Rolls. Lee loved telling an audience that "the damn coat was the only piece of clothing in the world to have its own car and driver."

The chapel would be full to overflowing with all the great Vegas stars and Lee, aided by Ray Arnett, his production manager, would have arranged to keep them entertained. They'd have hired a big chorus and a symphony orchestra. Lee would be resting in a jewel-encrusted, gilded coffin designated by Bob Lindner, the man who designed all his spectacular jewelry. The coffin would be surrounded by a floral display that would put the Rose Parade to shame. Little boys dressed as cherubs would descend from the ceiling and fly across the chapel, just as Lee had so often flown above the Vegas Hilton stage, looking like a phantasmagoric Peter Pan.

Lee loved opulence—flashy jewels, sumptuous furs, luxurious cars, fabulous homes. These were as much a part of him as his trademark smile. He could afford and always demanded the best. His burial service should have been an event, a last hurrah to mark the passing of the man who called himself "the greatest showman on earth." In sad reality, the occasion was sterile and devoid of color. No matter how or why he died, Lee deserved to be ushered out properly, to be mourned and buried with his habitual opulence rather than with secrecy and haste.

Alone in that gloomy chapel, I experienced an overwhelming feeling of regret and loss. It just shouldn't have ended this way. Lee's people had seemed to be in an almost indecent hurry to put the funeral behind them. Six pallbearers, employees of Forest Lawn rather than devoted friends, had whisked the coffin away after the brief service. Then the handful of mourners had scattered quickly, like the fans of a losing team.

Driving home that afternoon, I couldn't still the questions racing through my mind. After all the triumphs, why had Lee's life ended as a tawdry bit of gossip for the tabloids, a footnote to the medical history of the disease called AIDS? Images of Lee flashed through my mind, as diverse as if he'd been a split personality. In many ways, despite our long relationship, he remained an enigma. Who was he, I asked myself—glittering entertainer or petty despot, generous giver or self-gratifying spender, devoted lover or promiscuous thrill seeker? I had lived intimately with Lee as his lover, friend, and confidant. No one knew him better than I; no one else could give me the answers.

The search for answers would be long and sometimes painful. Lee and I had met for the first time in 1977 when he was a fifty-seven-year-old man and I was an eighteen-year-old kid. I've never forgotten that night, seeing my first Liberace show, my curiosity and awe at meeting the legendary entertainer. But that was not the place to start looking for answers. The place to begin is the beginning.

1

On November 11, 1918, headlines around, the globe trumpeted: PEACE! World War I, the war to end all wars, had come to an end. American doughboys were headed home and with them came a new sophistication, a new worldview. A popular song posed the question, "How're you gonna keep them down on the farm after they've seen Paree?"

There would be no keeping the boys who fought their way across Europe "down on the farm." America was poised on the brink of an urban explosion that would be fueled by a technical revolution. Women abandoned their hobble skirts, became flappers, and emerged as a new social force. A booming economy and increased leisure time helped popularize new diversions like movies and radio. Flickering figures on a theater screen and electronically amplified voices coming from crystal tubes right in the living room pushed vaudeville to the brink of extinction. The entertainment industry would never be the same. All these events would have an effect on Liberace's future.

His birthplace, Milwaukee, Wisconsin, was a quiet backwater which didn't respond quickly to the great events at home and abroad. Local farmers and men who worked the Great Lakes shipping trade still counted the weather more important than events overseas. The majority of the people descended from German immigrants; God-fearing, churchgoing, hardworking Lutherans who relaxed on weekends drinking the beer for which their city was famous. In the early years of the twentieth century, Milwaukee was a quiet, conservative community, an unlikely birthplace for the man who would call himself "Mr. Show Business." Lee would never feel he belonged there.

His birth foreshadowed the immoderate man he would become. Lee tipped the scales at more than thirteen pounds when he was born on May 16, 1919, in the suburb of West Allis. His tiny shriveled twin, an apparent victim of Lee's greed in the womb, was stillborn. Lee's mother, Frances, named her enormous surviving infant Wladziu for his Polish ancestors and Valentino for the era's reigning movie idol. But he would grow up being called Wally or Walter, names he detested until, in his twenties, he anointed himself as "Liberace" (his actual surname) on stage and as "Lee" to his friends.

He was the third Liberace offspring, having been preceded by George and Angelina. Brother Rudolph wouldn't be born for a decade. The four of them inherited their mother's short, stocky build, her pointed chin and prominent nose. But their musical talent came from their father. Salvatore Liberace was a classical musician who played French horn with the Milwaukee symphony. Lee recalled sounds as his earliest memories—the lush music of a symphony orchestra pouring from an expensive record player counterpointed by his parents' angry voices arguing over the family budget. Lee told me that the excitable Salvatore and the more practical Frances were ill suited to each other.

Other than music the Liberaces had no cultural interests. Lee recalled no mention of art, literature, theater, ballet, politics, world or national affairs in the household unless they were directly related to music. He would have no interest in these things as an adult. In fact, when he became a superstar, Lee would heartily disapprove of other stars, such as Ed Asner and Jane Fonda, who used their fame to champion a political cause or candidate.

Catholicism was the tie that held the Liberaces together. Frances was devoted to three things: her church, her children, and, most of all, Lee. She adored him. George and Angelina had inherited some of their father's musical ability but Lee, who began playing the piano by ear at the age of four, was clearly a prodigy. His mother would later claim that his talent confirmed her instinctive knowledge that Lee was *special.*

"You never saw a more beautiful baby," she later told me. From the time of his birth she cherished Lee more than the others. As a little boy Lee remembered being happiest sitting on her lap. Frances soon decided he'd be better off sitting on the piano bench, practicing.

"She pushed me from the beginning," Lee recalled, with a trace of bitterness. "I never had a chance to be a kid. George was studying violin and Angie took piano lessons, but they had time to go outside and play. Mom didn't nag them the way she nagged me. It was always, 'Walter, come in the house this minute! You've got to practice.'"

The Liberaces were poor. They lived in a tiny, two-bedroom frame house and they struggled to make ends meet on the penny-ante salary Lee's father made as a classical musician. But somehow Frances always found the money to pay for Lee's music lessons. She was a determined, proud woman who dreamed of a better life for all her children, but especially for Lee.

Later, for publication, Lee would describe his family as "typical, all-American." In private, after a few drinks, he would tell me a very different story, one that sounded more like the soap operas he was so fond of watching. Keeping secrets was impossible in that little house. Lee, who heard his parents arguing late at night, knew his father "played around." But it still came as a bitter shock when Salvatore walked out on the family while Lee was in his teens and began, as Lee said, "shacking up" with a lady who played in the orchestra.

"I never forgave my father for that," Lee confided in me. After Salvatore left home Lee, who could hold a grudge better than most people, didn't speak to his father again until Salvatore was old and sick. Despite Lee's enormous wealth, he would refuse to be held responsible for his father's medical bills. That burden would be shouldered by Lee's far less successful brother, George.

Little Lee had adored his father and tried to win his approval. All that changed after Salvatore walked out. As a teenager Lee later recalled seething with helpless rage every time he thought about the old man. He didn't want to be compared to him in any way, let alone when it came to the one thing that made Lee feel special—his musical talent! After praying over the question of his talent and giving it a lot of thought, Lee managed to convince himself that his musical talent resulted from divine intervention rather than genetic inheritance; in short, it was a gift from God.

After Salvatore abandoned his family to be with the woman he loved, Frances and her children were in a tough situation. First, there was barely enough income to support one household, let alone two. Second, as a devout Catholic, Frances didn't believe in divorce. According to Lee, she couldn't face the potential scandal, the disgrace that would follow the dissolution of her marriage. Frances didn't want the world to know that her husband had left her for another woman. She told her four children to keep the secret from everyone: playmates, neighbors, and friends. It was Lee's first childhood secret—but it wouldn't be his last. From then on Lee's life would be built on a foundation of secrets and half-truths.

One way or another, all four Liberace kids paid a price for their parents' problems. Family members told me that Rudolph often bore the brunt of his mother's anger. Rudy was ten years younger than Lee, barely school-age when the family broke up. In a happier household he would have been the baby and his mother's favorite. But Frances used to look at her youngest and say, "You should never have been born. You're an accident!"

From my own observations, all the Liberaces suffered the whiplash of their mother's anger. She dominated them as youngsters, and she continued to dominate them as adults. On occasion, I actually saw her poke them with her cane to get their attention. Lee lavished public affection on his mother while avoiding her in private. Frances could be a sweet old lady one minute and a merciless nag the next. She frowned on cigarettes and would snatch them from Lee's mouth as if he were a little kid behind the barn instead of a sixty-year-old superstar.

Coming from a broken home was one thing Lee and I had in common. By the time I grew up, society regarded having divorced parents and stepparents as no big deal. Unfortunately, that wasn't the case in Lee's day. His parents' split made him feel embarrassed and ashamed. The situation was aggravated by the appearance of a new man in Frances Liberace's life. Alexander Casadonte, who would eventually become Frances's second husband, was an old family friend. According to an article published in the *Globe,* Frances began sharing her home with Casadonte shortly after Salvatore moved out. Again according to the article, she lived as Casadonte's common-law wife for sixteen years.

When I questioned him about those years, Lee refused to discuss the man who formally became his stepfather in 1943. But other family members told me that Frances did, in fact, know Casadonte well enough, long before she legally married him, to freely borrow money from him whenever she needed to. From their reports it's apparent that Frances did have an intimate relationship with Alexander Casadonte prior to their marriage. But his real place in the family history remains another Liberace secret. While her children were young, Frances kept up the pretense, for the sake of appearances, of maintaining her marriage to Salvatore. Lee said that she warned her children, time and again, not to discuss things that went on at home. Her furtive lifestyle would be the launching pad for Lee's passion for secrecy. As an adult, he would never reveal what actually went on behind the closed doors of his many luxurious homes.

As youngsters the Liberace children were highly competitive rivals who didn't get along. The scarcity of money forced Frances to choose among them. Inevitably, Lee got more than the others: better clothes, the finest music teacher, nicer birthday presents. He felt that the inequity made Angie, George, and Rudolph resent him. But being resented by his siblings was only one problem the youthful Lee faced.

He said he'd always known he wasn't like other boys, but he'd never been able to label the difference. Then, at the age of ten, he began to have crushes on male teachers. It scared the hell out of him. In the twenties and thirties, nice people from proper families didn't talk about sex. Pregnant women stayed at home behind closed doors and children were told that storks delivered babies. Like most boys, Lee picked up his knowledge of sex out on the street. And street talk was damned ugly when it came to gays. Homosexuals were referred to as fairies, fags, queers, or perverts—and these were the nicer terms. The unprintable terms were a lot more graphic. Homosexuality was regarded as a particularly shameful form of mental illness.

Why me? Lee asked himself, feeling like a condemned man. Why am I different? He'd look at himself in the mirror, wondering if his appearance betrayed his true nature. In fact, photographs reveal that he looked more like a choirboy than a potential social outcast in those days. But realizing he was gay devastated him. He had to be crazy, sick, out of his mind, he thought, to be attracted to men. He tried ignoring his homosexuality, denying it. He tried forgetting about sex completely. But no matter how hard he tried, curiosity about the mysteries of sex, and his own sexuality, obsessed him.

In those days no one believed you could be *born* a homosexual. It had to be something that happened to you in early childhood, like measles or mumps; something that could be cured if the victim, helped by a competent doctor, really tried to change. Freudian theory ascribed homosexuality to a boy's overattachment to his mother and hostility to his father. Freud believed it caused the boy to mold his personality on his mother, thereby acquiring feminine reactions and behavior. In Lee's opinion, that set of circumstances described his own background perfectly. He recalled his mother's love as "completely suffocating and damn near incestuous." And his dislike for his father—after he left home—bordered on hatred. If, as the psychiatrists claimed, homosexuals were really created by the circumstances of their childhood, Lee said he had the perfect parents to blame. In the past he'd learned to keep his family's secrets. Now he would keep his own just as carefully.

Frances would never have to confront her son's true nature. Nor would she ever discover that Lee both hated and loved her. He continued to be her favorite. She was always touching him, kissing him, unaware that he almost gagged during those unwanted intimacies. He escaped by playing the piano. No one, including Frances herself, interrupted Lee's practice sessions.

In the morning he attended the Wisconsin College of Music, where he was a scholarship student, before going off to his regular public school classes. He'd be home by three, get in a few hours at the piano, have a hurried dinner, and rush back to school, where he played piano for silent movies shown in the auditorium. Lee had already started to make a local name for himself as a musical prodigy. If he couldn't be *normal,* he decided to make a virtue of being *different.* Perhaps, he thought as he began to achieve local notoriety, some good might be gained from all those long, lonely hours spent practicing.

When he was fourteen years old, Lee was approached by a group of older musicians who had a band that worked local night spots. They were looking for a good piano player. Lee was thrilled. He saw their offer as a chance to earn some real money rather than the nickels and dimes the school paid. By then Lee was sick and tired of being poor. He wanted good clothes, his own car, a better place to live.

Frances, whom I later came to know very well, recalled being furious when Lee told her about the opportunity. She didn't want her baby hanging around older men, playing in speakeasies or even worse places. There was no telling what went on in dives like that, she warned Lee. She had set her heart on seeing him become a great classical pianist, and great pianists didn't get their start playing in honky-tonks.

But, as Lee later wrote in his memoirs, the Liberaces were always broke. They all worked at odd jobs to help make ends meet. When Lee argued that the family needed the money he'd be earning, Frances relented. She gave him permission to join the band on two conditions. First, he mustn't ignore his classical studies. She expected him to practice as long and hard as he had before. Second, she didn't want the Liberace name soiled by Lee's appearances in saloons.

Lee began his career in saloons using the alias Walter Busterkeys. He loved the job, the free and easy atmosphere; he loved escaping his mother's watchful eye. He remembered feeling comfortable with the band and their music from the beginning. The boy who'd cut his musical teeth on the classics discovered an insatiable appetite for popular music. His ability to play by ear served him well during the brief time he could devote to rehearsals.

When he accompanied silent movies the audience concentrated on the film rather than his music. In bars, the audience listened to the music and was intent on having fun. Lee liked that; he liked giving people pleasure. More important, Lee was enjoying himself too. The older band members became his role models. He struggled to achieve their nonchalant attitude toward liquor, cigarettes, and sex. The boozy, smoky atmosphere of the bars and honky-tonks seduced Lee completely. He was playing in a bar when he met his first adult homosexual—and, according to Lee, that man seduced him too.

2

By the time we met in 1977, Lee was one of the most successful entertainers in the world. Along the way he'd come to accept and enjoy his own sexuality. But, he told me, it wasn't always that way. In his mid-teens, being gay made him feel alienated from his family and his peers. He experienced terrible guilt, as if he'd committed an unspeakable crime that must forever be hidden. It was, he recalled unhappily, the worst period of his life.

His homosexuality also alienated him from his church. In the thirties, as I believe it still does today, the Catholic Church regarded homosexuality as a mortal sin. If a gay wanted to stay in the church and partake in all its sacraments, he had to admit that homosexual acts and desires were wrong. Then he would be expected to give them up forever—pretty strong medicine for a teenager with all the sexual desire of his "normal" peers.

Lee, who had no way of expressing his inner turmoil, felt torn between devotion to his church and his own emerging sexual identity. He couldn't stand the thought of not being able to go to mass on Sunday, but he couldn't bring himself to swear an eternal vow of chastity either. Lee told me that he prayed for a miracle, something to alter him so that he could look at girls with the same lust they inspired in other boys.

When his father walked out, Lee had turned to his religion for consolation. His mother's unusual living arrangement didn't keep him from going to confession or taking communion. But he felt that admitting his homosexuality would. According to Catholic dogma, the failure to confess a sin is also a sin—a sin of omission. Lee said he felt he was damned if he did and damned if he didn't.

The only solution to his dilemma seemed to be an all-out effort to transform himself into a heterosexual. Lee tried hard. He would look at a shapely bosom or a rounded female rear and will himself to feel desire. But then his eyes would stray to a pair of broad shoulders or well-muscled arms and the battle would be lost. He couldn't help being attracted to men. Their bodies, their scent aroused him in a way no female could.

He had to face the truth. He couldn't change, no matter how hard he tried. Being gay was as much a part of him as the color of his eyes or his hair. But that idea was unacceptable to the church. Lee felt cut off from Catholicism although he would remain a devout Catholic in his heart and, ironically, one day he would have an audience with the Pope.

By his mid-teens Lee had survived three major traumas: his father's desertion, the discovery of his own homosexuality, and conflicts with his religion. One more serious disappointment lay ahead. Lee had come to the realization that he'd never have a concert career. Even if he could believe in his own genius—and deep down he had some doubts—he knew it would take years to build a name and a following as a classical pianist. By his own admission he was a young man in a hurry. He was tired of being poor, of making do with worn clothes and a two-bedroom house that wasn't big enough for its five occupants. He said that he wanted to get away from his mother and the sad playacting imposed on the family by his father's desertion. He was worn out by the slavery the classical piano demanded, the hours spent practicing until his arms and shoulders ached and his eyes burned.

Lee was a very good pianist, too good not to realize that he'd never be a truly great one in the classical sense. According to him, he'd reached a high level of competence and, after that, no amount of additional practice improved his playing. God had given him perfect pitch and large, powerful hands that easily spanned an octave and a half. Years of hard work had given him excellent technique, but he knew a concert career demanded more than polished skills. God had given him everything, he believed, but the rare spark of genius that would set him firmly above his peers.

Lee told me that the realization was a painful one. Music had been his life, his retreat, his source of happiness in an intimidating world. He admired the great classical pianist Paderewski, a man he would later lay claim to as his mentor, more than any other man on earth, and hoped to be like him. Seated at a piano Lee was neither man nor boy, gay nor straight, but simply a vehicle for the creation of music. Again, I think Lee rationalized his situation. He had to look no further than his own father, still scrimping and counting change to make ends meet, to confirm the fact that he didn't want a life of classical music for himself.

Although his mother never stopped talking about her son's glorious future in concert halls around the world, Lee continued to head in a direction that would help establish him as a *pop* musician. His weekend performances as Walter Busterkeys continued and, in addition, he joined his high school dance band. While playing at school dances Lee first experienced the thrill of manipulating audiences, bringing them to their feet with a wild boogie beat or lulling them into a romantic mood with a love song. Music, he discovered, gave him control. He'd been thinking of himself as a victim, a loser trapped in a world he never made, unable to change his fate. Now he began to see music as a path to popularity and power.

But Frances Liberace couldn't let her dreams go; and, in those early days, her dreams were very different from Lee's. She proudly recounted the story of his concert debut with the Society of Musical Arts in Milwaukee, describing it as a triumph. Lee recalled it as the kind of debut every aspiring young performer endures early in his career. According to him, his performance failed to arouse more than mild enthusiasm on anyone's part, including his own. Frances remained undeterred by her son's lukewarm reception. As far as she was concerned he was going to be the next Paderewski—or else. All he needed was a little more exposure, a little more experience concertizing, which she set about arranging. For the next two years she conned Lee into playing benefit concerts for every charitable organization in need of an inexpensive fund-raising. In the 1930s hundreds of Milwaukeeans had the pleasure of hearing Liberace perform— gratis. It would never happen again. Years later, when his Hilton contract alone was said to be worth three million dollars a year, Lee still laughed about having to give all those free concerts.

He had paid lip service to his mother's dream while privately moving closer to defining the kind of music he wanted to play and the world in which he would play it. Under his leadership, his high school band grew increasingly popular. Determined to pass as straight, Lee admired girls from his position onstage, praying no one would guess that he wasn't dying to date some of the hot little numbers on the dance floor— if only he had the time and the money.

Adolescence can be agony for anyone, but it was a special hell for Lee. Still struggling to deal with his own sexual identity, he had to live through the torture of hearing his classmates making crude jokes about "homos." Every time it happened he recalled dying a little inside. The prejudice against gays seemed more intense than the prejudice against any other minority group. Lee knew he'd be ostracized, or worse, if anyone in school discovered he was a fag. He would go to any extreme to keep that from happening. If it meant lying, he'd do it. If it meant telling "homo" jokes himself, he'd do it. If it meant dating he'd do that too, even though the thought of getting physically close to a girl made him nauseated.

Fortunately, he never had to carry his pretense that far. Everyone knew he was holding down a job, going to the College of Music, and keeping up his high school studies. No one, not even his family, expected him to have time for girls. Lee didn't need to keep up a pretense of normalcy in the honky-tonks where he worked on weekends. No one cared what he did as long as he showed up on time. At first he was quiet and withdrawn in that adult world. He did his job and he did it well. In fact, he soon realized that he was by far the best musician in the band.

Once he felt relaxed and confident, he began to take in his surroundings. Eventually he noticed men coming in together, men who weren't the usual after-work blue-collar crowd. They were quieter and better dressed, he recalled, and, although he couldn't pinpoint what made them different, he felt their difference strongly. It took a while, but the still naive Lee finally realized that they were homosexuals. The revelation came as a pleasant surprise. Knowing he wasn't alone, seeing that other men like him were capable of enjoying their lives helped to relieve his sense of isolation.

Lee was anxious to talk to them. There were so many things he wanted to know. His peers' sex talk didn't extend beyond girls' bodies and what could be done with them. Lee burned with curiosity about his own sexuality. Now he knew there were men who could give him the answers he wanted. But he was far too naïve and unsure of himself to dare approach them.

Frances continued to be upset by her son's weekend jobs, but he ignored her concern. In those dark, smoky bars, he hoped to find the answers to who and what he was. Brother George, who had developed into a competent violinist, often played the same gigs as Lee. His presence helped allay Frances's worries. Lee was seeing a side of life few boys his age get to know. He was growing up fast, but not fast enough to suit him. He later remembered that he didn't like having George constantly around, playing chaperone. Fortunately, George wasn't around the night a football hero from the Green Bay Packers came to hear Lee play.

"I could hardly miss the guy," Lee told me, reminiscing about his first lover. "He was the size of a door, the most intimidating man I'd ever seen. Every time I looked out in the audience there he was, smiling at me. From then on, he showed up wherever I worked. He'd buy me drinks during our break and tell me how much he liked listening to my music. One night he asked to drive me home. That's the night I lost my virginity," Lee told me privately.

The story he told for public consumption was very different. In his book *The Wonderful Private World of Liberace,* published by Harper & Row in 1986, Lee wrote a chapter titled "I Lost My Virginity at Sixteen." In this chapter Lee, who already knew he had AIDS, claimed to have been seduced at the age of sixteen by a stripper. As you will later see in the pages of this book, Lee was determined to the very end to deny and conceal his homosexuality.

The truth is almost every gay has someone like that football player in his past. An older man usually gives a boy his first experience. In the gay community they say, "First you sell it (most young gay men have older lovers who act as mentors), then you give it away (with a sexual partner your own age), and then you buy it" (by having a younger lover). That football player became Lee's lover, an experience that made an indelible impression on Lee.

"I realized," Lee said, "that a strong masculine body next to mine gave me a sense of *security* I'd never known before."

He continued to see his new friend for the next few months, sometimes sneaking out of the house after his mother was asleep. According to Lee sex was a part of the relationship, but not the most important part. He'd never been able to share his deepest feelings with his family and he felt he couldn't trust anyone in the straight world. The football player became Lee's first confidant. He also introduced Lee to other gay men. Many of them came from other cities and they told Lee to look them up if he ever visited their hometowns. Although Lee didn't realize it at the time, he was laying the foundation for his own gay network, a group he remembered turning to for companionship, understanding, and sexual gratification in the years to come when so much of his life would be spent on the road.

Few minority groups are as conditioned to a ghetto mentality as gays. Lee was no exception. He soon learned to depend on his homosexual friends for everything. By his eighteenth birthday, Lee was leading a double life. At home he was still Mama's pride and joy, continuing to study the classical repertoire, to practice every spare moment. But weekends, when he played in bars and strip joints, Lee abandoned all pretense.

Frances continued to push a concert career with every ounce of energy and influence she possessed. The woman was a pit bull when it came to Lee's future. He knew he'd have no peace until he made a serious try for the goal she had set. At the age of nineteen Lee made his last appearance as a classical musician, playing Liszt's Concerto in A Major with the Chicago Philharmonic under the baton of Frederick Stock. Lee felt his talents were ideally suited to the piece. In fact, in the years to come, Lee would toy with the idea that he was Franz Liszt, reincarnated. He would make comparisons, not only to Liszt's technique but to his style, his glitter, his showmanship.

Like Liszt, Lee had huge, powerful hands with a tremendous stretch. They gave him the virtuoso technique a Liszt concerto required. He spent months in dogged preparation for the last concert. When it was over he didn't want anyone to say he hadn't given it his all. If he succeeded, if the critics responded enthusiastically, Lee said he would have taken it as a sign and pursued a concert career. If not, he made up his mind to lead his own life and choose his own future.

By the evening of the concert, Lee told me he knew the Liszt concerto so well he could have played it backward. His performance was received exactly as he had anticipated. He didn't set the concert hall on fire—but he didn't disgrace himself either. A warm wave of applause greeted the end of his performance. The critics were kind, in view of his obvious youth, but Lee hadn't indelibly impressed any of them with his brilliance. He felt a mild depression that quickly passed. And then, without looking back, he returned to the world he loved— the world of saloons and nightclubs.

The year 1940 found him playing two or three gigs a week, making a circuit from Green Bay to Sheboygan to La Crosse and then back to Milwaukee. On the road, Lee said, he made use of the telephone numbers he'd been accumulating. His knowledge of the gay world expanded with each new contact and sexual encounter. In those days most of his lovers were older, a situation that would change in the near future. By his thirtieth birthday, Lee would have developed a decided taste for younger men.

As Lee traveled from town to town, away from his mother and his family, his lifestyle and his music were changing, forming a pattern that would prevail the rest of his life. Lee's classical repertoire was replaced by the music of Cole Porter, Jerome Kern, and the Gershwins. Family and friends would later tell me that Lee, dressed in an immaculate tuxedo, had an ingratiating stage presence, even in his twenties. He was anxious to please, to make audiences remember him. But something was missing and Lee, with his superb showman's instincts, knew it. The way things were going he feared he'd be just another nameless, faceless piano player for the rest of his life, growing old and tired as he drove from one forgettable booking to another. He was just twenty-one but, Lee later remembered, he often felt like a fifty-year-old failure.

Lee didn't like talking about his childhood, his youth, or those early years on the road. There was, however, one story he really enjoyed telling. One night after he'd played his usual set, someone in the audience requested "The Three Little Fishies," a nonsense song that was riding high on the hit parade back then. The song had almost no melody, and it didn't challenge Lee's ability, so he decided to have fun with it. He gave it a standard rendition first. But then, in a moment of inspired genius, he played it as if it had been composed by Bach. The audience responded by applauding as loudly as if he'd just invented the piano.

Lee knew he'd hit pay dirt. He finally had the schtick that would set him apart from every other piano player on the circuit. From then on he closed every performance by asking for requests, which he'd interpret in the style of one or more of the classical composers. Audiences loved his new gimmick. The idea proved to be so popular that he later wished he could have patented it.

In his early twenties, buoyed by local success, Lee decided to leave home. His goal: the bright lights of New York. He felt sure that fame and fortune waited for him on the East Coast.

3

In the early 1940s big bands and swing dominated the music scene. Harry James, Benny Goodman, Glenn Miller, or the Dorseys, and their respective orchestras, could fill a supper club or dance hall for weeks on end. Stand-up comics like George Jessel, Milton Berle, Jack Benny, Eddie Cantor, and Edgar Bergen dominated the live entertainment scene, playing all the best clubs when they weren't working in radio or in the movies. Elegant night spots dotted the Manhattan scene, including the ultra-exclusive 21 Club, El Morocco, Sardi's, and the Stork Club. All the great New York hotels, from the Waldorf to the Pierre, had plush rooms where the nation's greatest performers appeared regularly. The entertainment world bustled with well-known stars whose activities filled the pages of *Variety*. Lee remembered that his arrival in New York, predictably, failed to stir a single ripple of enthusiasm in that world.

At home in Milwaukee he'd been the proverbial big fish in a little pond. In New York the people he contacted about potential bookings said, "Liberace who?" His fame hadn't extended beyond the borders of Wisconsin. Agents and managers had never heard of him, and they failed to be impressed by the long

21

string of credits he'd acquired on the Wisconsin circuit. Lee said he faced the eternal show-business dilemma: he couldn't get an agent until he played local bookings, and he couldn't get local bookings until he had an agent.

For a while he actually went hungry. He unhappily recalled going to Horn and Hardart, a cafeteria chain, and eating tomato soup that he made, gratis, from packets of ketchup and cups of water. After a couple months of near starvation he had two choices. He could go home and listen to his mother say "I told you so," or he could continue struggling with the loneliness, poverty, and hunger that the East Coast offered.

It took guts to stay on—but stay on he did, Lee told me proudly. He finally landed a job in West Orange, New Jersey. It was on the wrong side of the Hudson but he had steady work for six months. Every night after coming back from New Jersey, he mailed out résumés inviting and ultimately begging agents to come hear his music. When he wasn't booked at clubs he supported himself by playing at private parties in the greater New York area. Lee had uncomfortably vivid memories of those parties: the luxurious homes and the self-assurance of the people who lived in them. He'd take a bus or commuter train to his destination and be admitted through the servants' entrance. The handsome tip he received at the end of the evening merely fueled Lee's resentment.

"Most of those people treated me like a waiter or a cab-driver," he later complained, still smarting from injured pride. Lee dreamed of the day when he'd be rich and able to live in a mansion in a ritzy neighborhood. Ironically, years later, when he had a seven-figure yearly income, Lee found that he was uncomfortable in places like Bel Air and Rancho Mirage. His enormous homes were located in more humble areas.

A few families, such as the ultra-rich Gettys, treated Lee well, sending him home in their limousine rather than obliging him to rely on late-night transportation. But people like the Gettys were the exception. From what Lee said, his frustration and ambition played leapfrog as he schemed and slaved to create the career and the life of his dreams.

Lee was playing a club on the Jersey side of the Hudson River when the Japanese attacked Pearl Harbor and America went to war. A cyst on his spine would make him ineligible for service. Had his homosexuality been known it would have excluded him from the draft too, but Lee was so paranoid about concealing his sexual identity by then that I doubt he would have admitted the truth, even to avoid the draft.

The war proved to be a lucky break. It thinned the ranks of Lee's competition. By 1942 the Music Corporation of America, one of the country's leading talent agencies, had lost many of its performers to the war effort. Lee was pleased and surprised when Mae Johnson, an MCA agent, contacted him and signed him to a contract. Thinking all his dreams were about to come true, Lee said he went out and celebrated with a bottle of champagne he could ill afford.

He fully expected to be playing in all the best places within the year. But he soon discovered that his name appeared at the bottom of MCA's booking list. Despite Mae Johnson's personal faith in him, celebrity and security seemed perpetually out of reach. He was on the road week after week, playing the small towns, staying in grimy third-rate hotels, eating in greasy-spoon restaurants. When he played dates in or near New York, Lee made extra money by working as a rehearsal pianist. Those experiences in cold, drafty halls gave him a healthy respect for the dancers and singers, the "gypsies" of Broadway. As he played he watched, judging the individual performers, developing an eye for talent that would serve him well in the years to come when he would choose acts for his own shows.

Lee's work in those rehearsal halls also contributed to his knowledge of the entertainment industry's extensive gay community. Many of the dancers and singers he met were homosexual. He said that his earlier loneliness evaporated as he found new friends, new lovers. With a regular income and an assured social life, he devoted himself to the pursuit of fame and fortune.

Lee hated his first name. "Maybe Walter sounded all right with Pidgeon," he told me, "but it sounded awful with Liberace." Following the example of his idol Paderewski, Lee decided to be booked under a single name. In his opinion, "Liberace" sounded important, unique, *fabulous!*

But abbreviating his name didn't make any difference: MCA still didn't give him the big push he'd hoped for. Although he worked regularly, he was still appearing in the dingier clubs and hotels, playing to an almost exclusively working-class clientele. He didn't realize it then, but they would always dominate the ranks of his fans. However, in those days, Lee's dreams were more grandiose. When, oh when, he wondered, would he finally get his big break?

Throughout the war years, Lee told me, the straight world was even more hostile to gays than it had been during the depression. Every man out of uniform was suspected of being unpatriotic, a draft dodger, a coward, or a queer. To protect himself and his reputation Lee went deeper into the closet, making sure only his closest associates knew his secret. Onstage, he developed a flirtatious patter with the mature women in his audiences. All he had to do was tease them gently, treat them like ladies, and, to his surprise and delight, they responded warmly. Lee discovered that he had a gift for pleasing older women and he began to play to them exclusively. His act was expanding, becoming a combination of patter and piano.

During this period Lee saw very little of his family. He said he returned for visits only when his mother, newly widowed after a brief marriage to Alexander Casadonte, threatened to join him in New York. By the end of the war the Liberace homestead was relatively empty. George and Angie had married, to the first of their multiple spouses. But Rudy still lived at home and he and Lee shared a bed on Lee's rare visits. It was an awkward situation which Lee later said he preferred to avoid. However, his brother Rudy would tell a very different story in the years to come, complaining that Lee had made sexual advances when the two of them shared a bed. Whatever the truth may be, Lee felt uncomfortable at home, distanced from his family by new experiences and new friends. The jealousy that had always been a part of his relationship with his brothers and sister seemed to be aggravated by his growing success.

Two years after Pearl Harbor Lee had achieved modest renown as an entr'acte performer. It was a living. According to him, he was eating, but his soul was starving. He craved recognition. In a continuing effort at self-promotion Lee expanded his practice of advertising his talents via the mail. It was eventually to pay off. Lee loved to tell people just how that happened. One night in 1943, after performing at the Mont Royal Hotel in Montreal, he scribbled out a new group of cards bearing the plaintive query, "Have you ever heard of Liberace?" Few of the recipients recognized his name and most of them failed to respond to Lee's query. But one man, the entertainment director of Howard Hughes's Last Frontier Hotel in Las Vegas, Nevada, took the trouble to call Lee. He offered a six-week contract, which Lee accepted at once.

Lee recalled his shock on arrival in Las Vegas a few weeks later. Back then the city looked more like a cow town than the entertainment mecca it would become. He stared at the cactus-studded landscape, thinking he'd made the mistake of his life, that six weeks in Vegas would be the equivalent of six weeks on the moon. He was feeling thoroughly disgruntled and put upon when the cab he'd taken from the train station delivered him to Howard Hughes's hotel. Lee looked up at the marquee, saw Sophie Tucker's name, and broke into a toothy grin. Tucker was a big star, the kind who could pick and choose her bookings. If Vegas was good enough for Sophie Tucker, he knew it would be good enough for him.

Despite his initial misgivings, Lee was in the right place at the right time, geographically and musically. Vegas, fueled by the public's passion for gambling, was slated for unprecedented expansion. And classical music, thanks to films that romanticized the lives of Chopin, Liszt, and Grieg, was becoming part of the popular idiom. Couples were dancing and making love to tunes like "Til the End of Time," a beautiful melody lifted from the music of Chopin. Lee decided to put a candelabra on his concert grand, an idea he borrowed from that Chopin film. He added a few easily recognized etudes to his act and rode the wave of popularity Hollywood had unwittingly created for someone just like him. His absolute genius as an entertainer took care of the rest.

Lee blossomed in Las Vegas. He negotiated a $750-a-week salary and, when his booking was extended beyond the initial six weeks, he demanded and got $1,500 a week. Over the years, he would play a total of twenty-four different dates at the Last Frontier and his salary would be increased each time. Vegas loved Lee and he loved it back. The wide-open, anything-goes atmosphere of the gambling halls suited his style perfectly. It also suited the needs of a less desirable element of society.

In 1946 a new hotel appeared on the strip. The Flamingo had been financed by Mafia money, and its owners were Al Capone and Meyer Lansky. Their lieutenant and on-site manager was none other than the infamous Bugsy Siegel. All three men were Liberace fans. According to Lee, Lansky and Capone ordered Siegel to get Lee to sign a contract with the Flamingo.

Siegel put in a call to Lee, who was working nearby in Los Angeles, and asked him to come to a meeting in Vegas. He told Lee he was prepared to make an offer Lee couldn't refuse. But Liberace didn't want to have any dealings with the Mafia because, as he later said, "Once you're in with those boys—you never get out."

However, common sense dictated his next action. He agreed to meet with Siegel at the Flamingo. Lee was in a no-win situation. If he agreed to perform at the Flamingo, he'd be delivering himself into Mafia hands. If he refused, he suspected he might wake up one morning wearing cement overshoes. So Lee did what he always did when faced with a difficult choice. He stalled for time by telling Siegel he'd have to check with his agent before signing anything.

After their Vegas meeting ended, Lee learned that Siegel planned to return to L.A. Siegel offered Lee a ride but, knowing Siegel would use the six-hour trip to pressure him, Lee refused, saying he had other business to clear up in Vegas. Then, as part of his cover, he booked a room in a hotel for a one-night stay. That night Lee slept uneasily. By the next morning he'd made up his mind to call Siegel and sign the contract. But the headlines in the Vegas newspaper made the call unnecessary. Lee said that while driving back to Los Angeles, Siegel had been waylaid, and shot and killed in a gangland-style slaying. Had Lee been with him, he would undoubtedly have been murdered too.

Whether by choice or necessity, Lee maintained a friendly relationship with the Mafia afterward. On two occasions, once in New York at an ultra-exclusive restaurant and once in Boston at a pizza joint in the heart of an Italian neighborhood, I accompanied Lee when he met a major Mafia don. Each time, I watched as Lee exchanged warm greetings, hugging the don and kissing his cheek. There was never any question in my mind that Lee had powerful and very dangerous friends.

4

Lee used to say, with uncharacteristic modesty, "I'm just a *piano player*."

In my opinion he was "just a piano player" the way President Reagan is "just a politician." Both men are great communicators; Reagan with the public and Lee with a nightclub audience. From the very beginning, it was Lee's ability to reach out to his listeners that set him apart from his competition. Whatever mistakes he may have made in his private life, he never took a false step professionally.

"An audience can spot a phony a mile away," Lee told me. "If you don't *enjoy* going out there, if you don't *love* what you're doing, they'll know it."

Lee was one of those lucky entertainers who adored performing in front of a live audience. "Onstage," he said, "I know who I am. I'm sure of myself, in complete control." He had the rare capacity of making each individual in the audience feel that Liberace was performing just for him or her. Whether he played to ten people or ten thousand, Lee gave every show the same effort—working so hard that he often lost five pounds during his act.

When I began working with Lee he had an enormous following and played to crowded rooms. But he had bittersweet memories about his early career when he had played to many near-empty ones. As any nightclub performer can tell you, second shows in supper clubs are notoriously dead. Americans just won't wait until ten or eleven for their evening meal. But playing those depressingly unpopular second shows helped shape Lee's act.

"When there are ten thousand people waiting to see you and hear you," Lee told me, "it's impossible to single any one of them out. With a small audience it's natural to feel as if you can talk to them individually."

Lee's act was still in a formative stage in the late forties. It hadn't yet acquired the glitz arid the giant production numbers for which he is remembered. He owned several sets of conservative black tails, a piano, and a few candelabras. These were his only props as, night after night, he entertained the small second-show crowds. Instead of using expensive props and extravagant productions, which he couldn't afford, he made the audience a part of the act. Old-fashioned sing-alongs were one of his favorite ways of pulling them inside each performance so that they became participants in their own entertainment. It was corny, like many of Lee's gimmicks, but it worked.

In my opinion, he was an uncommon man with a common touch. He never lost the ability to relate to the blue-collar working couple, the family who saved for weeks to treat themselves to a night on the town. One of his credos was "Never let an audience wonder what you plan to do. Tell them!"

Every night his show varied, depending on his mood and the feedback he got from the people who came to hear him. He might announce that he intended to play all the Chopin or all the Gershwin he knew, and then add, with a deprecating little laugh, that it wouldn't take more than five minutes. Despite his vast repertoire and his solid grounding in the classics, Lee never talked down to his listeners—he never forgot his own lower-middle-class roots. Stepping down from the stage and shaking hands suited him better than setting himself up on a pedestal.

Lee may have sinned in private but he made a point of keeping his act clean and wholesome in public. Since families could always attend his performances, Lee had access to audiences not available to most other entertainers. When children came to his shows he capitalized on their presence. He'd ask a kid to come up onstage, spend a few minutes teaching him or her to play chopsticks, and then they'd play a duet. It was pure magic, another of Lee's great schticks—listening to a little kid tentatively pick out chopsticks while Lee's nimble-fingered accompaniment made the child sound like a musical genius. Everyone loved it; the children, the parents, and the club managers who saw their revenues blossom. Before Lee permitted a child to leave the stage he gave him or her an autographed miniature piano. Those pianos became coveted mementos of Lee's performances and, along with the candelabra, the piano became his personal insignia.

Before the 1950s Lee enjoyed a secure if unspectacular niche in the entertainment industry. In addition to his Vegas appearances he was under contract to the Statler Hotel chain. Other bookings included the luxurious Fontainebleau Hotel in Miami, New York's famous Roxie Theater, and the Palmer House in Chicago, where he was the favorite performer of entertainment director Muriel Abbott. He'd also done some radio work in New York, but Lee claimed that radio was a sterile medium. Instinctively, he knew he needed to be seen by an audience in order to woo them.

He had what he called a "comfortable career," but he wanted so much more. He told me he dreamed of being a movie actor, of leaving his handprints in the cement of Graumann's Chinese Theater in Hollywood, of winning an Oscar. The newly popular medium of television, with its barely explored possibilities, intrigued him as well. More than anything, Lee longed to be a star. But that seemed increasingly unlikely. At the age of thirty his hair was thinning and his waist thickening. He'd been on the road for ten years and he was still waiting for the lightning bolt of fame to strike. That lightning would finally single him out one night in the middle of a California thunderstorm.

In 1949 San Diego's Del Coronado Hotel, featuring the subdued Beach Bar, was a famous landmark. Like a former beauty past her prime, the old ornate building had an antiquated dignity and served as an ideal vacation spot for families with children.

That year, television executive Don Fedderson was vacationing at the hotel with his wife, Tido, and their children. One evening a severe storm swept up San Diego Bay and the Feddersons canceled their plans to explore San Diego's livelier night spots. They decided to dine in the hotel and spend the rest of the evening at the Beach Bar. The entertainment would be supplied by Lee on the piano and his brother George playing the violin.

The brothers came out for the first show in their customary black tuxedos looking more like morticians than entertainers. Neither the Feddersons nor the Liberaces could know that it would be a momentous night in their lives. Lee, recalling that all important evening in his career, told me how he surveyed the small audience with a sinking heart. It was going to be another quiet, unspectacular night. He sat down at the piano and began to banter with the crowd and when they all felt at home he began a set of show tunes.

Lee had an old-fashioned attitude toward his profession. He not only believed the show must go on; he believed every show and every audience deserved his very best. And that's what he gave those few people on that stormy night: his very best. According to Lee and others, Don Fedderson listened carefully—and he returned to the Beach Bar every night for the rest of his vacation, striking up a friendship with Lee in the process. Television was just a baby in those days, but it was a voracious baby that demanded a steady diet of new talent. Thanks to Don Fedderson, Lee starred in a local television show and that led to his engagement as a summer replacement for "The Dinah Shore Show."

That fifteen-minute, two-month show proved to be so popular that NBC offered Lee a thirty-minute variety show. It premiered in 1953 and lasted three seasons. Those were the days of Uncle Miltie, "I Love Lucy," Jackie Gleason's "Honeymooners," and "The Ed Sullivan Show." By the end of the 1953 season, Lee was part of that exalted company, and he loved it. He proudly recalled being dubbed "television's first matinee idol."

From then on, Lee had it made; no more greasy spoons, run-down hotels, and second-rate clubs for him. He moved to California and built his first home in Sherman Oaks, a town that later made him its honorary mayor. With his developing genius for public relations, Lee had a piano-shaped pool installed in the backyard, a novelty that was soon featured in many national magazines. Overnight, Liberace had become a household name and everything he did was newsworthy. The more extravagant his lifestyle, the more media attention he received. Lee got the message. Offstage, the opulent way he lived would become as much a part of his persona, his legend, as anything he did onstage.

Lee loved being in the limelight and was thrilled by his new celebrity status. California was paradise—until his mother moved in with him. Liberace was an old-fashioned man and he felt an old-fashioned obligation to care for his aging mother. But Frances, who sometimes treated him like a ten-year-old, really cramped his style. She wanted to meet all his friends, to revel in her son's acclaim. But Lee's closest friends were gay, not exactly the kind of men you bring home to mother when you're pretending to be a heterosexual male.

Lee told me that she wanted him to act like the superstar he'd become, to give large parties attended by Hollywood's elite. Frances didn't understand her son or the world in which he now lived. She knew nothing of things like "A lists" or "power lunching." In comparison to Hollywood's true elite—the studio heads, directors, and major stars—Lee was still a very small fish in a big pond. Frances cajoled, pressured, and manipulated Lee just as she had when he was in his teens, trying to get him to do what she thought he should.

Lee needed an escape—and he found one in a rented apartment in North Hollywood. It became his hideaway— another item on his growing list of secrets.

Movie stars seldom experience the kind of overnight fame that envelops a television personality. Lee always referred to the fifties as the "white heat" period of his life. He'd spent years dreaming of, striving for that kind of recognition. Now he finally had it. But Lee would soon learn that sometimes you have to be careful of what you wish for. By the time his first show was canceled, Liberace was a household name. He couldn't go out in public without having someone come up and ask him for his autograph. People recognized his trademark toothy grin and wavy locks wherever he went.

It wasn't long before Lee realized that anonymity had its virtues. He told me that, before his television show, no one had questioned his sexual preference. It had never been an issue as long as he didn't flaunt his lifestyle. He'd been able to quietly patronize known homosexual bars and clubs without attracting undue attention. In the gay vernacular, he'd "tricked around" with a series of lovers, many of them struggling performers too. After ten years on the circuit, he was familiar with gay hangouts in every city where he appeared—and he had frequented them all.

Overnight fame altered his freedom of movement. The "matinee idol" didn't dare risk being discovered in a gay bar or bathhouse. Lee felt absolutely certain that the vast majority of his fans—middle-aged woman, working-class families—would drop him in a minute if they learned who and what he really was. He couldn't risk being found out, having his homosexuality become public knowledge.

Fortunately he'd developed widespread contacts in the gay community over the years as well as building a personal staff, many of whom were gay men. From the late fifties on, Lee would turn to these men when he needed companionship or an evening's recreation. Lee met his gay friends or had assignations with potential lovers in his North Hollywood apartment, a place whose existence his mother never suspected. Although he tried to keep his homosexuality completely hidden from her, other members of the family told me he used the apartment a lot. No one knows if Frances guessed why Lee spent so much time away from home.

By the time Frances had entrenched herself in the Sherman Oaks house, the rest of the family had moved to California too. Lee's enormous success was the catalyst that reunited them. Other family members recall this as the happiest period of their lives. George, a talented violinist in his own right, was an intrinsic part of Lee's act in those days. On the whole, the Liberaces had never done better. Their prospects seemed excellent. But it didn't take long for all the old jealousies to resurface.

According to Lee, George took advantage of Lee's hard-won fame. Angie, although married and raising a family, joined the show as well. On the road, he remembered being under Angie's and George's watchful eyes and at home he had Frances to contend with. He felt he'd sacrificed his personal happiness, his need for a *private* life, for his family. Inevitably, Lee rebelled. Regardless of the publicized image of saccharine familial bdevotion, Lee said he wasn't close to any of them. He resented their constant presence, their interference in his life, and he resented his mother most of all. From the "white heat" years until her death in 198o, he would never feel free of his obligation to her.

Lee was the kind of person who didn't like to dwell on the negative aspects of any situation. Back in the 1950s, his troubling family relationships were easily overshadowed by his booming career. Every entertainer who has given numerous interviews comes to dread being asked the same questions over and over. There was, however, one question Lee never tired of answering. If reporters didn't ask, "How did the outrageous costuming start?" he prompted them.

Liberace's popularity on television led to a flood of offers asking him to do concerts all over the country. One of the most exciting, from Lee's point of view, was an opportunity to give his first concert at the Hollywood Bowl. For those who have never been there, and that included Lee himself back in 1952, the Bowl is a breathtakingly beautiful outdoor amphitheater that seats twenty thousand people. Before the concert date Lee drove out Hollywood Boulevard and up Highland to look the place over. He arrived, paced the stage, feeling an uncharacteristic anticipatory stage fright, and then he walked to the back of the huge amphitheater. It was a long climb to the top.

"From that distance," Lee told me, "the stage looked like a toy. I pictured myself playing a black Baldwin concert grand, surrounded by a symphony orchestra all dressed in black. And I knew I'd fade into the woodwork if I wore black too." Lee made up his mind to break with tradition. Instead of the conventional black tuxedo, he planned to wear a set of white tails on stage. No one could have anticipated the enormous response to that simple decision.

Black entertainers, including the great Cab Calloway, were already appearing in white tails. But Lee was the first white musician to walk out on a concert stage in a getup like that. Television had given him popularity. The Bowl appearance gave him notoriety. Afterward everyone had something to say about Liberace. The critics used so many words to comment on Lee's clothes that they barely had column space to critique his performance. The resulting furor gave Lee millions of dollars of free publicity. If white tails were worthy of headlines, Lee wondered what would happen if he wore something *really* flashy. They say clothes make the man. In Lee's case, clothes helped make the performer.

In the years to come, he would often complain that the clothes had become an insatiable monster, consuming a lot of money and creative energy. But Lee had no idea that he would be creating a runaway show-biz Frankenstein in 1955, when he opened the new Riviera Hotel. His salary would be $50,000 a week, the highest fee ever paid to an entertainer; and, for the first time, his contract specified that he had to top any outfit he'd worn in the past. From then on, all his contracts would contain a similar clause. No problem, thought Lee. He'd been wearing white tuxedos or romantic, Edwardian velvet jackets for a few years. It shouldn't be hard to come up with something a little more spectacular. How, he wondered, would audiences respond to gold lamé, furs, and jewels? Lee was about to find out.

5

When Lee opened the Riviera in the mid-fifties his $50,000 weekly paycheck made him the world's highest paid nightclub performer. His glittering gold lamé tuxedo made him the most talked about. The reaction from the audience was instantaneous and powerful. Some people were offended by the way Lee had dressed, some were amused, some stunned; but no one was indifferent. His fans rewarded his audacity with a thundering round of applause. His detractors stayed and watched the act, mesmerized by the opportunity to dislike, ridicule, and feel superior to the strutting peacock onstage. For some, Lee's appeal lay in the fact that they loved to hate him. But most of Lee's fans, those little ladies from the small towns, adored him for daring to be different.

Today, when rock stars glitter brighter than the Milky Way, it's hard to realize just what an innovator Lee was three decades ago. When they burst on to the scene, the Beatles, who were more daring than most other entertainers, did their act wearing sedate little suits, white shirts and ties, and Dutch-boy haircuts. No one—at least, no *man*—had ever done an act dressed the way Lee dressed. His show required several costume changes, and the costumes grew progressively more outrageous. By the end of that opening night he'd started a revolution that would culminate, decades later, in the incredible flash and glitz of a Michael Jackson or a Prince.

Although Lee was blissfully unaware of it that night, for the rest of his career his costumes would be as important, or more important than the man who wore them. Lee, who so feared having his homosexuality discovered, had unwittingly placed himself in a position where he would appear onstage dressed like a queen, night after night and year after year. Sometimes, after he made his stage entrance, he'd actually hear someone in the audience hiss, "Oh, my God! Look at that *fag*." Those were dreadful moments. Lee's popularity, his success, seemed to depend on his wild clothes, but the clothes themselves could get him in serious trouble. They gave birth to rumors, gossip, and innuendo.

The fifties, like the decades leading up to them, were an intensely homophobic period. Muscle cars and macho men were the order of the day. Although Lee knew that many of Hollywood's most famous and desirable men were gay or bisexual, none of them dared reveal the truth. Lee confessed to me that he began dating women to suppress the growing rumors about his own sexuality. If anyone dared to question his masculinity he needed to be able to flaunt pictures of his latest girlfriend. He had no trouble getting all the dates he wanted and he gloried in escorting well-known entertainers to parties, getting his picture taken with Susan Hayward, Gale Storm, Rosemary Clooney, Mae West, and Judy Garland. He later boasted of having close relationships with many of these women, but Mae West was the only one of his so-called lady friends I actually met. As they say in Texas, Mae was a *hoot!* She and Lee were an unpredictable twosome who enjoyed trying to outdo each other's outrageousness. Mae was one of the few people in the world who had the courage to speak up to Lee—and he loved her for it.

The girl he almost married didn't compare to Mae when it came to nerve. JoAnn Del Rio, a Las Vegas dancer, had good looks and a sweet personality. Undoubtedly the entire Liberace family heaved a sigh of relief as they watched her relationship with Lee progress. For a while, it must have seemed as if Lee would finally settle down to a "normal" life and have a family.

Lee and JoAnn became engaged in 1953 and even set a date for a wedding—a year away. From all reports, Lee liked JoAnn a lot, a first for him when it came to women. He courted her with gifts of flowers and perfume, gifts that foreshadowed the truly extravagant presents he would later give his male lovers.

When it came to JoAnn, the problem was not that he didn't like her; it was that he still loved men. After Lee's death, JoAnn's father was reported to have claimed responsibility for ending the engagement because he knew Lee was gay. But Lee told me he never planned to walk down the aisle, with JoAnn or anyone else. His engagement served to squelch the rumors about his sexuality—period!

Many homosexual men enjoy relationships with women. There are a few who even come to love them, as friends or as temporary sexual partners. Not Lee! He had to forcibly control his dislike and distrust of most of the women he dated. He complained that all of them were too demanding, an opinion of females that he'd formed in childhood. When I asked if he'd ever had sexual relations with a woman he told me he'd had a couple of experiences, but complained that the way women smelled revolted him. While dating JoAnn publicly, he confessed that he continued to have secret dates with young men. By the end of 1955, JoAnn Del Rio was just a footnote to Liberace's history.

A man in Lee's position—famous, wealthy, a star—never lacks for companionship. When he felt lonely he had only to ask one of the gay members of his staff to get him a companion and one would soon be delivered to his doorstep. The older Lee got, the more younger men appealed to him. In that regard, he was a Dracula who never wearied of the taste and touch of youth. By his fifties he preferred dating boys in their teens.

There have been rumors that Lee had an affair with Rock Hudson early in their careers. But Rock wasn't any more Lee's type than Lee was Rock's. The supposed affair never happened. However, the books I've read about Hudson's life reveal startling parallels to Lee's. Both men had been abandoned by their fathers and dominated by their mothers. As adults the two of them devoted a great deal of time and energy to creating a fictional personal history for public consumption. Neither man could deal with anything distasteful—an argument, the illness of a parent, getting rid of a lover—and both used others to do their dirty work.

Most important, they both had giant egos; they were stars and the rest of the world (friends, lovers, family) damn well better not forget it. That alone would have negated any possibility of those two having a relationship. Men like that cannot tolerate equals. Had Lee and Rock actually met, I think they would have disliked each other on sight. They were much too much alike to fulfill each other's needs and too egocentric to want to try. Such an encounter would have been more the clash of rutting stags than the true meeting of minds. In the years we were together, Lee never mentioned knowing Rock. Although hundreds of celebrities came to Lee's shows, Rock never made an appearance. The two men moved in completely different circles, socially and professionally.

Lee's closest associates were gay men who worked for him. When Lee needed companionship or a sexual encounter he called men he knew and trusted. In turn they'd call a friend, or a friend of a friend, until they found someone who could deliver the kind of kid that appealed to Lee. Then a meeting would be arranged. For Lee, it was as easy as snapping his fingers, and almost as risk free.

The growing sexual permissiveness of the late fifties and sixties had a profound effect on the gay community. Promiscuity, which had been somewhat suppressed, became socially acceptable. Having multiple partners was both pleasurable and chic. Bathhouses, pickup bars, and clubs that existed for the sole purpose of arranging sexual encounters between strangers all thrived in that "anything goes" atmosphere. Lee, who had an insatiable sex drive, took full advantage of the developing situation. He admitted to spending more time thinking about sex during those years than he spent thinking about his act. And he preferred to have a *variety* act—onstage and behind closed doors.

The homosexual community was ideally structured to satisfy all his desires. Gays make up one of the largest subcultures in the United States and, because the majority were "in the closet" then, each gay man had his own network to rely on. Lee never used male prostitutes. He was an intensely romantic man who preferred the thrill of the chase rather than the cold reality of a cash transaction. Young men eager to make a connection with a big show-business personality usually jumped at the chance for a date with him. He used his success, his fame as foreplay. If they pleased him he would keep them around for a while—a week, a month, a year or two. If not, he would send them on their way with a gift. In the gay community money seldom changes hands for services rendered. It's more a matter of exchanging favors. Lee could be very generous to friends who granted him favors.

During those first years of fame, he became even more skilled at leading a double life. The matinee idol dated glamorous women and then headed for his Hollywood apartment to meet a homosexual lover. Onstage he smiled sweetly and flirted with his fans. In private he built an enormous and expensive collection of pornography that he shared at all-male parties. Although the family never discussed Lee's sexual identity, they had to know he was gay. His mother may have known too. But she undoubtedly thought there was nothing wrong with her son that the right woman couldn't cure.

Frances herself played an unwitting role in Lee's carefully crafted public image. She often attended his performances and he proudly introduced her as "My mother, Mrs. Liberace," thereby negating Alexander Casadonte's existence. Lee's publicity people churned out endless stories about the *first* lady in his life, his mother. But having a mother like Frances could be difficult.

Touring abroad gave him an occasional break from his problems. He said he felt safer, more free to be himself in countries where his name was not yet a household word. In the mid-fifties he was invited to play the famed London Palladium and he jumped at the offer. The Palladium is to stage acts what Nirvana is to Buddhists. To be asked to perform there signaled Lee's arrival as a star of international magnitude. He would have other, greater thrills, but that first show at the Palladium ranked right up there with his first appearance in the Hollywood Bowl. London, he said, sounded like heaven. Before he returned to the States it was to feel more like hell.

Lee's enthusiastic British audiences were very much like the ones he attracted in the States—mostly middle-aged, working-class housewives. He enjoyed a huge box-office success in Britain, but the critics united in attacking him. One columnist for the *London Daily Press* launched an all-out war, describing Lee as a "deadly, sniggering, snuggling, giggling, fruit-flavored, mincing, ice-covered heap of mother love." "Fruit," of course, was the colloquial expression for homosexual.

For the first time in his career Lee was publicly branded as gay and it devastated him. He imagined himself stripped of his fame, success, wealth, and power—all the things he'd worked so hard to achieve. Seeing the *London Press* article made him feel naked in front of the world. His entire career had been jeopardized. Lee burned with impotent rage for days. In Vegas, where he had connections, he'd have known exactly how to handle the situation. He'd have used his influence, his power, or his dangerous friends. But in London he felt helpless. So he struck back in the only way he could. He sued.

Lee didn't care what the lawsuit cost in time, effort, or money. Money was surely no obstacle to the highest paid performer in the world. In the past he'd used his wealth to attract friendship and love. In England he used it as a tool to buy vindication and revenge. Lee made up his mind to *prove,* for all time, that he wasn't gay, even if it meant bringing another woman into his life. This time she would be far better known than JoAnn Del Rio.

Sonja Henie had been the world's premiere figure skater in the 1920s and thirties. She'd parlayed ten world championships and three Olympic gold medals into an enormously successful show-business career. Blonde, blue-eyed, she had an attractive figure and, more important, a celebrity name. Sonja was seven years older than Lee and her fame was waning when they met. I think mutual need drew them to each other. Together, they generated more publicity than either one could separately. The aging skater merited a lot of space in movie magazines and tabloids when she became the woman Liberace spent his evenings with. Lee used his romance with Sonja as proof of his sexual preference.

Lee's acquaintances describe Sonja as a motherly type; but Lee told me they had an affair. If he was being honest—and with Lee you could never be sure—it would be his last relationship with a woman. After the London court case came to an end Lee never again felt the need to camouflage his true nature by dating ladies. In 1959 Lee was completely vindicated and his name cleared. On June 9, 1959, the *New York Daily News* ran an article under the headline I'M NO HOMO, SAYS SUING LIBERACE. Before the year ended Lee was completely vindicated; his name and reputation were freed of any blemish.

Lee's lawyers had managed a miracle. They'd actually convinced a judge and jury that black was white. Lee was awarded a $22,500 settlement. He gave every penny of it to charity. Never mind how much he'd spent during the three-year legal action; Lee had been officially, in a court of law, cleared of any suspicion of homosexuality. He'd have gladly spent a fortune to achieve that goal. In 1987, after Lee's death, there were reports that the *London Daily Press,* feeling they'd been had, was considering suing Lee's estate to get that money back. From 1959 on Lee turned to the courts whenever he failed to get his way by other means. His lawyer soon found that handling Liberace's considerable legal affairs provided a lucrative livelihood. Given Lee's stubbornness, his power, and his money, he usually got what he wanted by simply wearing his opponents down. When Lee and I finally confronted each other in a court of law, the bitterly contested case dragged on for five years.

In the coming years Lee's vindication in the British courts would have one penalty. As America's social climate became increasingly liberal, other gays came out of the closet. Lee felt compelled to keep his silence. "I can't admit a thing," he said, "unless I want to be known as the world's biggest liar."

After winning the case Lee went on to an escalating series of triumphs. ABC signed him for a TV variety show that ran in 1958 and 1959. He was in even greater demand as a live entertainer and set new attendance records wherever he appeared. The money came rolling in faster than even he could spend it. He sold his Sherman Oaks property and bought Rudy Vallee's fifty-room house in the Hollywood Hills. Lee also acquired a mansion in Las Vegas, another one in Palm Springs, and a place in Malibu overlooking the ocean. He had the power he'd always wanted. And he'd finally distanced himself from his family. According to Lee, it hadn't been easy.

At the beginning of his "white heat" period, his family had made an all-out effort to become indispensable to him. George was an intrinsic part of Lee's early act and Angie went on the road with her brothers too. Lee promoted her to his manager and, from that position of responsibility, whether true or not, Lee told me that she convinced him that George was taking advantage of his position as favorite brother. Lee never knowingly permitted anyone to take advantage of him. Whether he was right or not in this instance, he dropped George from the act. When Lee's income plummeted under Angie's stewardship, he dismissed her as well. The turmoil capped the Liberaces' already troubled relationships, resulting in a prolonged period of estrangement during which Angie worked at other jobs while George's career sagged.

Meanwhile, Rudolph, the youngest of the Liberace children, passed away. He left behind a widow, Isabel, and four children. Lee drifted away from Rudolph's widow and children just as he drifted away from George and Angie. He couldn't turn his back on his mother as easily, but he did the next best thing. He moved her into the Hollywood mansion and then spent most of his time elsewhere. For the first time in his life, at the age of forty-five, Lee felt relatively free of his family and, based on what he told me, from what he regarded as their never-ending demands. His life seemed to hold endless happy possibilities; he had everything to live for when a bizarre accident almost ended everything.

In the fall of 1963 Lee was playing the Holiday Inn in Pittsburgh, part of his regular circuit. He felt sick after the opening of the engagement and got progressively worse with each succeeding performance. On November 22 he woke up late in the afternoon, as was his custom. A cold sweat bathed his body when he got out of bed to turn on the television, running through the stations searching for one of his favorite soap operas. That particular day all the network shows had been cancelled in favor of a steady stream of news programming. Lee soon learned that President Kennedy had been assassinated in Dallas.

Lee wasn't political in any way. His first thought was "What a tragedy," but his second was "Thank God, I won't have to go on tonight." Lee had never felt sicker in his entire life.

The country came to a halt that day as grieving, stunned Americans sat in front of their television sets watching the tragedy unfold. Millions would forever mark that date in their lives by where they happened to be when they got the news. An entire nation sat, transfixed, as they watched a stunned Jacqueline Kennedy, in a suit stained with her husband's blood, setting an example of dignity and courage.

But Lee was too ill to feel anything except his own growing discomfort. He was planning to spend the next twenty-four hours in bed until one of his people—he was too ill to remember which one—told him the show would have to go on after all. The Holiday Inn's entire showroom had been booked weeks in advance for that particular night, and the group that had booked the room wanted to see Liberace despite the day's tragic events.

Lee was astonished. He couldn't believe anyone would want to go to a show the very day the president had been shot. But Lee was a trooper. Shaking with weakness and fatigue, he dragged himself out of bed and laboriously made his way to his dressing room to prepare for his act. By then the performances depended on costumes as much as they did on piano playing. That night Lee attempted to make his normal lightning quick changes in a makeshift dressing room in the wings while the singer, Claire Alexander, entertained the audience. Lee didn't remember how much of his act he managed to complete but, during one of his changes, he collapsed. His powerful will couldn't drive his failing body back onstage.

"I can't go back on," he told Ray Arnett, his producer.

Ray, who'd been with Lee for years, knew something was terribly wrong. Lee lived for his act and his audiences; he'd never missed a performance before, let alone walked out in the middle of one. A simple case of flu wouldn't be able to sideline him, Ray thought. But he had no idea just how sick his boss really was. It was a day for ill omens and unpredictable events; a day in which the stars seemed malevolently misaligned.

Lee had been felled by the most bizarre set of circumstances. During his act he worked under blazing lights which caused him to sweat profusely. Consequently, his costumes required frequent cleaning. Before arriving in Pittsburgh one of his costumes had been cleaned with tetrachloride. Sweating heavily on opening night, Lee absorbed the deadly chemical through his pores. Lee wore that costume for part of each performance on all the ensuing evenings, absorbing more and more of the lethal chemicals. By the time he collapsed, his kidneys had shut down completely.

The doctors at St. Francis Hospital diagnosed his ailment as uremic poisoning. Their prognosis sounded ominous. Waste fluids had already collected in Lee's tissues. His feet and legs were already swollen. If the swelling couldn't be halted before it reached his vital organs, Lee would literally drown in his own body fluids. Kidney dialysis, a relatively new treatment, was the only thing that could save him. Lee, expecting to die, began spending money from his hospital bed. "What the hell," he told me later, "you can't take it with you."

He ordered jewelry from Tiffany's, furs and many other things he hadn't yet gotten around to buying. He also made arrangements to give away many of his possessions. It must have been weird in that hospital room, as he bought things and gave others away in frantic haste to squeeze the last ounce of pleasure from all the money he'd earned.

His worst fears were realized when the first dialysis treatment failed to improve his condition. The doctors told him he'd die if they couldn't get his kidneys working again. But they didn't dare administer another dialysis treatment for thirty-six hours. During those hours Lee's life would be hanging by a thread. He was given the last rites.

Said Lee, "I knew prayer was the only thing that could help me, so I began to pray harder than I ever had in my life."

Barely conscious, he directed his prayers toward St. Anthony, whom he described as the patron of the underdog. Sometime during the thirty-six hours between treatments, Lee woke to find a nun dressed all in white seated by his bed. The nun, whom he assumed to be one of the nursing sisters at the Catholic hospital, told Lee that he mustn't waste his strength worrying because of his illness. She assured him that he was going to live.

Twelve hours after the second dialysis Lee's kidneys began to function again. Afterwards the doctors told Lee they'd almost given up hope for his recovery. In their opinion he was a living, breathing example of a miracle. He owed his life, not to their skills, but to divine intervention. As soon as Lee was feeling better he asked to see the wonderful nun who had given him so much faith and courage. He could describe the woman in detail, but none of the nuns in the hospital fit his description, none of them wore all-white habits.

Six weeks after he'd been taken to St. Francis, Lee was released, weighing twenty pounds less than he had on the day he'd been rushed there by ambulance. He looked like a new man. More important, he had a new view of himself and his position in the scheme of things. Despite the church's position on homosexuality, Lee firmly believed he wouldn't have been spared if being gay was the sin Catholic dogma held it to be. He believed he'd been saved because God, and most particularly St. Anthony, looked on him with special favor. As for the mysterious nun, nothing could convince him she wasn't God's messenger.

Knowing God loved him filled Lee with peace and well-being. He'd done things the church regarded as sins—sodomy, homosexual acts with multiple partners—but God had spared him anyway. From 1963 on, Lee, believing there was no sin too great for God's forgiveness, would stop at nothing in his pursuit of pleasure.

6

When I first met Lee in the summer of 1977 I was an eighteen-year-old kid who thought, like most eighteen-year-olds, that I had all the answers. Living with Lee would eventually teach me I didn't have any of them. I was born in La Crosse, Wisconsin, a couple of hundred miles from Lee's birthplace in Milwaukee, a coincidence he often remarked on. Like him, I am also the product of a broken home and, like him, I am gay. My mother suffered from manic-depression, a chemical imbalance that resulted in emotional problems, and, consequently, most of my early memories are unhappy ones. She married three times but her illness prevented her from settling down with any of her husbands for the long haul.

I have two sisters, Annette and Carla, and one brother, Jimmy, plus four half brothers and sisters: Gary, Wayne, LaDon, and Sharon. Wayne and Sharon grew up with their father, Nordel Johansen, while Gary and LaDon lived with my father, Dean Thorson. Those of us who stayed with Mother had a rough life. There were times when she'd disappear for days, leaving us to fend for ourselves. Once, when we'd been left with nothing to eat, I begged our landlady for food. She gave us peanut butter and jelly sandwiches and called the authorities.

When the police came, we children were turned over to a welfare agency and Mom was hospitalized. For the next year we lived first in St. Michael's Orphanage and then in the La Crosse Home for Children. After her release, Mom reclaimed us and headed for California to make a new start. But she was far from cured. She spent a great deal of time in California state hospitals and we spent most of our childhood moving from one foster home to another. One of them, the home of Rose and Joe Carracappa, was memorable for the love and kindness they gave. Unfortunately, my stay with them would be all too brief. My mother soon reclaimed me, and the round of brief stays with her, and then in foster homes, continued. It was a hard, loveless life most of the time. But kids survive. We went to school and did our best to support each other along the way.

Back then the state paid foster parents three hundred dollars a month to care for a child and that didn't cover any luxuries. Foster kids soon learn to earn their own spending money. I worked at odd jobs from the age of ten. By my thirteenth birthday I'd grown tall enough to lie about my age and hold down part-time jobs.

Somewhere along the way I picked up an intense love for animals, maybe because I trusted them more than people. The happiest memories of my youth began when I bought a dog and a horse with money I'd saved. Leonardo was a two-hundred-pound St. Bernard and, like me, in bad need of a home. Beauty was a half Shetland, half Arab horse that no one seemed to want—except me. It didn't matter that my current residence had no place to keep animals; I just had to have them to love and care for—or I'd shrivel up and die.

I was fourteen then and living in a state-run home awaiting permanent placement, while the animals were in a boarding facility. Finding a permanent place for us to be together seemed like a hopeless task, but I decided to try phoning all the ranches and stables listed in the yellow pages, asking if they could take a foster kid with a horse and a dog. Halfway through the listings, I called the Pacheco Ranch, owned by David and Marie Brummet. They amazed me by saying they'd be willing to consider my proposition. The next day I hitched a ride to their two-thousand-acre spread in Marin

County. With its green rolling hills and five hundred horses, Pacheco looked like paradise.

For a year and a half the Brummets were my family. I went to school, worked on the ranch, and began to put down roots, thinking I'd stay with the Brummets until I was old enough to be on my own. We shared an almost idyllic life until David Brummet was told he had cancer. His illness forced him to sell the ranch, and I was homeless again. When my welfare worker told me I'd be placed in another group home I offered an alternate plan. My half brother Wayne Johansen, a man fifteen years my senior, lived in the San Francisco area and I'd lived with him before, briefly. Wayne agreed to take care of me again. Our tie was tenuous but I grabbed at the lifeline he extended.

The next few months were difficult. Wayne made his living as a bartender, and had a wide acquaintance with California's gay community. When I'd stayed with him before, some of his friends who were gay upset me with their propositions. Returning, with the infinite wisdom of my fifteen years, I knew more about myself and felt I could handle the gay environment.

After a couple of fumbling, adolescent sexual encounters with girls while living on the ranch, I admitted feeling equally attracted to men. In my brother's home, I would have a chance to explore that attraction. Defining my sexual identity in the mid-seventies didn't traumatize me the way it had Lee in the mid-thirties. San Francisco gays had come out of the closet and built a strong political base. They were in the process of becoming a power to be reckoned with in those gloriously naive pre-AIDS days.

I didn't think that being bisexual was a fate worse than death. In fact, after I recognized it, my bisexuality didn't seem like much of an issue. I accepted it the way I accepted being blond and blue-eyed, as part of the package called Scott Thorson. I had my first sexual encounter with a man while living at Wayne's in San Francisco. That man is still my very good friend and trusted adviser, a part of my support system.

On the ranch, I'd decided to be a veterinarian. But I knew that goal would never become a reality if I permitted myself to become trapped in the gay lifestyle. Wayne and I came to a mutual parting of the ways, and I moved into another foster home and, eventually, to Southern California. As soon as I was settled I went job hunting and found work as a veterinarian's assistant with a Dr. Tully, who had an office in the San Fernando Valley. He specialized in cropping dogs' ears. I learned a lot of practical, everyday remedies from him, but cropping ears and taking care of poodles wasn't very exciting work for an adventurous kid. By then I had decided I wanted to train animals. On the advice of a contact at Walt Disney Studios, I called Shumaker Animal Rentals.

Mr. Shumaker invited me out to Sunland to see how he and his crew did things. He had a big place where he kept forty dogs. One look and I was hooked; I thought I'd found my life's work. From then on I went to Sunland every weekend, acting as an unpaid gofer. One day Mr. Shumaker phoned to tell me an employee had quit without notice. Shumaker was preparing to go on location with thirty dogs to film *The Pack,* starring Joe Don Baker. He said the job was mine if I could be ready to leave in two days.

I loved working for Mr. Shumaker, learning how to make up the dogs with Vaseline, mud, and phony blood so they'd look crazy-mean. Learning how to handle them, train them, and care for them seemed like a worthwhile life's work. For the next year and a half I worked for Shumaker off and on. Despite my unhappy start in life I felt things were working out for me—my goals were set and, although I knew they'd be tough to achieve, I thought I was on my way.

My personal life continued to revolve around a few gay friends I'd made while living in northern California. It was through them that I met a man I will call Bob Black. Black was about twenty years older than I, extremely good-looking in a blond, Nordic way, nicely dressed, well-spoken, and easy to talk to. During our first conversation he told me he was a choreographer-dancer who'd worked on various TV shows. I was attracted to him and intrigued by his show-business background. We met often during the next few months, building a friendship that lasts to this day. In July 1977, he asked me to go to Las Vegas one weekend to catch a few shows. Black owned a sporty Mercedes 450 SL and the idea of driving it cross-country appealed to me. Black also promised to take me backstage and introduce me to a few of the celebrities he knew.

I loved Vegas on sight! The neon glitter and nonstop nightlife were intoxicating. Bob and I went to see *Hallelujah Hollywood* our first evening in town. The next night we caught Juliet Prowse's act and afterward Bob took me backstage to meet her as he'd promised. Liberace's show at the Vegas Hilton was last on Black's agenda. I'd heard of Liberace for the first time a few weeks earlier when I'd seen a magazine article about him. From what I read, I didn't think I would enjoy his performance. But Black, who knew Lee's production manager, was determined to see the show and go backstage afterward to renew old acquaintances.

The Hilton showroom holds twelve hundred people and it was packed that night. Lee's obvious popularity took me by surprise. The guy couldn't sing, I thought; he couldn't dance, and he was over the hill! So how the hell did he draw such a crowd? Black had enough pull to get us an excellent table just as the house lights dimmed. From the moment Liberace appeared onstage in his mirrored Rolls-Royce, I was spellbound. The man seemed to be having such a good time that I couldn't help being caught up by the fun. His humor sounded so fresh and spontaneous and he did such a terrific job of poking fun at himself that I got the impression he was ad-libbing all the way. The Chinese Acrobats of Taiwan performed while he changed clothes, and each time he returned to the stage his costumes were increasingly outrageous. It was pure camp and great fun.

Midway through the act Lee introduced his protégé, a man I will call Jerry O'Rourke. The two men came out dressed in identical silver outfits, wearing the same jewelry. Their hair had been teased into identical, high pompadours and sprinkled with sequins. To me they looked like a matched pair of queens. Whether it was true or not, they appeared to me to be lovers. I looked around at the audience, wondering what all those middle-class, middle-aged women were thinking. Did they assume what I did about the relationship between O'Rourke and Liberace? Seeing nothing on their faces other than adulation and admiration, I couldn't help nudging Black. "Doesn't Liberace realize he and O'Rourke look like a matched set of queens?" I whispered.

Black just grinned.

Jerry and Lee were seated at white, back-to-back concert grands adorned with enormous matching candelabras. They played beautifully, but I thought Jerry was the better pianist—he certainly had the most difficult parts of their duets. They exited to thundering applause.

After the show Bob took me backstage where we were met by Ray Arnett, Lee's producer. Arnett greeted Black like an old friend, gave me a very warm hello, and escorted us to the dressing room where Liberace and Jerry O'Rourke were seated at a table, eating. I sensed a chill in the air as soon as we walked in, as if we'd caught the two pianists in the middle of an argument. But Lee turned on the charm when Ray introduced us.

Liberace looked larger than life onstage: youthful and bubbling with energy. I was surprised to find myself towering over him as we shook hands. He was only five feet seven but he had large bones, a barrel chest, and he carried himself with the assurance of a big man. Jerry, who didn't seem happy at having his meal interrupted, ignored us and continued eating. Liberace ignored O'Rourke's behavior and took us to the bar at one end of his dressing room where Ray Arnett poured drinks all around. He and Black talked about the "good old days" on Broadway. While they were chatting I could feel Liberace's eyes on me; appraising, friendly, questioning. I was six feet three inches, slender and blond—not a bad-looking kid but certainly not worth the once-over he was giving me.

Lee finally turned to the other men when Arnett asked if it would be all right if he invited us to Lee's home for brunch the next day. "I'd love to see all of you," Lee said, looking at me again. "Make it about three in the afternoon because I need my beauty sleep." He winked at me as he walked us to the door, explaining that he had to get ready for the second show.

The whole experience had an unsettling effect on me. I'd been feeling peculiar vibes the entire time we were in Liberace's dressing room. Later that night I told Bob Black I didn't want to go to Lee's the next day. "He makes me uncomfortable," I said, remembering Lee's scrutiny. "I don't have any idea what that old queen is all about, and I don't think I want to find out."

7

Bob Black and I arrived at Lee's home on Shirley Street at three in the afternoon. I expected something impressive but nothing could have prepared me for the property's opulence and glitz. Inside and out, it was a palace. Ornate wrought-iron gates set in an eight-foot wall swung silently open to admit the 450 SL as we drove up. From then on it was fantasy time. The grounds were decorated with statues of cupids and nymphs, large urns, gurgling fountains, and enough flowering plants to stock a nursery. The house itself was a block long, topped by a steep mansard roof.

Ray Arnett, our genial host of the previous evening, waited for us at the entrance. He was dwarfed by twelve-foot mahogany doors decorated with carved cupids and angels.

"Welcome, gypsies," Arnett said, smiling broadly as he ushered us inside. Nothing in any of my experience prepared me for what I saw next. Now I knew why Black had insisted on coming. The huge entry hall, much bigger than the living room in my current foster home, was guaranteed to make a first-time visitor gasp. Marble floors, mirrored walls, a curved stairway with clear Lucite banisters that looked as if it had been suspended in midair, and gushing fountains vied for the viewer's attention. Millions of dollars' worth of antique furniture, crystal, priceless china, objets d'art, fresh flowers, paintings, crowded every available surface. Obviously, Lee was into conspicuous consumption. I was impressed—very, very impressed.

While I tried to get my bearings and take it all in, a pair of carved doors at the end of the hall opened and Lee strolled out with three dogs at his heels and one in his arms. He'd been wearing heavy stage makeup the night before. Now, he was casually dressed in a short terry-cloth robe but still wearing cosmetics. A light foundation failed to conceal the shadows under his eyes. Their glacial blue was accented by mascara and eyeliner. But even the carefully applied makeup couldn't conceal how tired and debauched he looked.

Lee welcomed us warmly, apologizing for his informal attire, and we followed him into the living room. It was huge and even more ornately decorated than the entry. A mirrored concert grand with a Lucite top, Lucite music stand, and Lucite piano bench took up one end of the room. It would be a couple of years before I knew enough about interior decorating to recognize the incongruities of Lee's decor. But a cheap pillow, looking out of place on the piano bench, captured my attention. Overstuffed sofas covered in tufted raw silk flanked a marble-mantled fireplace. Crystal chandeliers, ornate gilded furniture, urns on pedestals, priceless porcelains, cluttered the room. Crocheted pillows were a strange contrast to the decorator sofas, inexpensive paintings clashed with walls covered by French silk moiré, blown-glass souvenirs cheapened priceless commodes. Years later I would know that the theme was palatial kitsch.

I'll be damned, I thought. Liberace not only *looks* like a queen, he *lives* like one.

Lee led the way to the sofas and sat down, still holding the one dog while the others sniffed at our heels.

"To the ovens," Arnett said, flinging his arms wide and gesturing down at the animals. Lee grinned in response. Obviously the dogs were an old sore point between the two of them, one that had eroded enough to become a standing joke.

"They're my family," Lee said, noticing my interest in his pets. "And this," he added, indicating the one in his lap, "is

Babyboy." His nasal tone softened as he stroked the ancient poodle. "Babyboy is very old. He's blind and deaf. I'm his seeing-eye person." By the time Lee finished, his voice had risen an octave and he was using baby talk. But at least I knew we had something in common—we both loved animals.

I studied the old poodle, noticing that its eyes were opaque and running badly. "I think I can get you something that might help him," I said, explaining I was a veterinarian's assistant. "Dr. Tully sees a lot of poodles with problem eyes. He can usually make them more comfortable."

Lee beamed. "That would be wonderful!" he said. "Nobody's been able to help my poor Baby and I hate to see him suffer."

Our conversation was interrupted by the appearance of a man Lee introduced as "Carlucci, my houseboy." Carlucci, a small man, looked nothing like my idea of a houseboy. He wore conspicuously tight jeans, a shirt open to the navel, and a thick gold chain around his neck. He had a narrow face, a beaked nose, dark olive skin, and eyes that darted about with lively curiosity. I later learned that he'd been a maître d' before being discovered by Lee and becoming a member of Lee's household.

Carlucci placed a tray of hors d'oeuvres and a large pitcher of Bloody Marys on the mirrored cocktail table. I expected him to leave at once, like any well-trained household help, but he lingered long enough to look me over very carefully. Between his perusal and the way Lee had studied me the night before, I was beginning to feel like a yearling at a thoroughbred auction. Black and Arnett had been talking about show business and I escaped the uncomfortable once-over I was getting by turning my attention to what they were saying.

Arnett was one of the friendliest men I'd ever met. Short, slightly overweight, with sparkling eyes and a quick smile, he oozed good humor. I liked him immediately. Like Bob Black, Arnett had been a Broadway hoofer, a show-business gypsy in his youth. He was one of Lee's old guard, an associate from the early days before Lee developed his glitzy stage show. Arnett explained that he'd started as a dancer and choreographer for Lee's shows and worked his way up to production manager.

While the other men talked I could feel Lee studying me again. Each time I caught him looking at me during the cocktail hour and the brunch that followed, he'd glance away quickly, as if he didn't want to meet my eyes. The intense covert scrutiny made me very nervous. I couldn't figure out exactly what was going on. If a guy stared at me like that in a bar, I'd figure he was coming on to me. But Lee obviously had a live-in companion and he had to know I was involved with Black. As far as I was concerned, all the bases were covered.

After we finished eating, Lee took us for a tour through the house. The upstairs held a large studio-rehearsal room and a generous bedroom with its own bath. I wasn't surprised to see Jerry O'Rourke in this spare room. He acted preoccupied, as if meeting us again was either the world's biggest bore or the biggest imposition. He and Lee barely looked at one another and I could almost feel the temperature in the room dropping. Apparently our visit had interrupted another quarrel.

Although Lee and Arnett exchanged meaningful glances as we left Jerry's room, Lee seemed unaffected by the awkward moment. He led us from room to room, proudly describing how he'd created this showplace from three ordinary houses. "I like to rescue things that no one else wants—houses, dogs, people!" he declared. "Anyone can buy a palace. It's more fun to create one yourself."

Again, I couldn't help being impressed. Obviously, Lee and I had been moving in different circles. Certainly none of my friends could afford to either buy or build a palace. In addition to the living room and dining room, the downstairs held a room that Lee proudly called his Moroccan room. It featured a peacock-blue tiled floor covered with Persian rugs, mirrored and tiled walls, a soaring glass roof, and more Lucite furniture. The decor combined potted plants in wicker baskets, assorted candelabras, and antiques. Matched sculptures of pantalooned harem boys, each carrying an electrified candelabra on his head, flanked a mirrored bar. A breakfast table had been set with priceless oriental porcelain, as though Lee were expecting a second group of brunch guests. The room's pièce de résistance was a stuffed peacock on a mirrored stand above the bar.

"I do all my own decorating," Lee said, grinning with self-congratulatory pleasure and waiting for compliments. Being dutiful guests, Black and I obliged, remarking on his extraordinary taste.

The rest of the house held a fully equipped casino, two kitchens, a breakfast veranda, and servants' quarters. As we walked from room to room I counted an astonishing number of pianos. At the time, Lee owned a grand total of seventeen, divided among his various homes. I kept on expecting him to sit down at one of them for an impromptu performance, but he seemed intent on giving us the history of each room and of the objects in it. The pianos seemed no more important to him than the rest of the decor.

Lee had saved the most outrageous for last. He paused before his bedroom doors and then flung them wide. I couldn't restrain an awed whistle. The room, carpeted in the deepest pale blue plush, was larger than most homes. You could have held a football scrimmage inside it. An enormous canopied bed covered by an ermine spread, with a large stuffed bear propped against the headboard, dominated one wall.

"How'd you like to live like this, Scott?" Lee asked. "Not bad, huh?"

Three gilt-framed portraits of Lee, one of them an almost life-sized photograph taken when he had an audience with the Pope, hung on one wall. Two cream-colored brocade sofas, an antique desk and chair, and several dressers barely dented the available floor space. A cocktail table held a malachite phone, an art deco bronze, two three-foot-tall gold candelabras, several cigarette boxes (one in malachite), assorted antique porcelains, and a cheap glass ashtray from a Vegas hotel. I later learned that Lee took special pleasure in taking mementos from the hotels where he appeared. Pilfered ashtrays, towels, and stationery became treasured objects to be displayed in Lee's many homes. In the future, when I would remind him that he could have any number of those things if he just asked, he grinned like a bad little boy and said, "Yeah, but it's more fun my way."

The room's most notable feature was a facsimile of Michelangelo's Sistine Chapel frescoes painted on the ceiling. Looking up, I saw that Lee's own face beamed down at us from amid the other cherubim and seraphim.

Lee next ushered us into his bathroom, a pleasure seeker's paradise. I couldn't imagine ever using a place like that to go to the toilet. A gigantic oval tub circled by marble pillars stood in the center of the room. Hot and cold water came from gold fixtures in the shape of swans. There was enough marble on the ceiling and floor to restore a Roman bath. Lee swelled with pride as he explained how he'd designed the room. Clearly, his philosophy of decorating was *spend, spend, spend.*

Last, Lee showed us his closet. Suits, sports jackets, and dozens of robes took up one long wall. The voluminous closet also held many of his costumes. I'd never seen so much lamé, so many furs, sequins, and rhinestones. Up close, the overall effect of those clothes dazzled me even more than they had when Lee wore them onstage.

Grinning, Lee pulled a few outfits off their hangers, spreading them on the floor. "I support the entire Austrian rhinestone business," he laughed. Then he added, "Too bad you're too big, Scott, to try a couple of these on." Lee obviously enjoyed showing us his possessions. And I had loved seeing them the way I might have enjoyed seeing things like that in a museum. But it was hard to believe that one man had so much.

At the end of the tour Lee seemed suddenly tired, as deflated as a punctured beach ball. It was time to leave. Black and I thanked him for his hospitality and we headed toward the front door. On the way out Lee caught my arm and pulled me aside. "I want you to call me as soon as you get the medicine for Babyboy. Here's my unlisted number," he said, slipping a piece of paper into my hand. "Don't forget! I'm counting on you."

I put the paper in my pocket, expressed my thanks, and then Bob Black and I were outside in the afternoon's fading light. We climbed into the 450, the wrought-iron gates opened, and our visit to fantasyland was over. As we headed into the late afternoon traffic, I thought I'd never see the place again. My life, my job, the real world, were waiting for me in L.A. With the benefit of hindsight, I wish I'd stayed there.

The entire afternoon at Lee's had a weird quality; the man, his home, his strange houseboy, his relationship with Jerry O'Rourke, were all too complex for me to decipher. I'd sensed strong emotional undercurrents all afternoon that made me feel like I'd stumbled into deep water. Despite the display of wealth, the house had an unhappy, unhealthy atmosphere. I made up my mind to mail Babyboy's medicine and then forget all about

Liberace and his bizarre household. But when I got home, I even forgot to mail the medicine.

Two weeks later I put on the slacks I'd worn to Liberace's brunch and realized the piece of paper with Lee's phone number was still in one of the pockets. I'd forgotten all about my promise to send some ointment for his dog's eyes. The next day, I called to apologize. Carlucci answered the phone and he recognized my name immediately. "I'll get Lee at once," he said, adding, "he's been hoping to hear from you."

When Lee came on the wire I apologized for taking so long to get in touch with him. "I'll mail Babyboy's medicine today," I assured him. "You should get it in a few days."

"Oh, no!" Lee exclaimed. "I don't want to wait that long. Why don't you get on the next plane and fly up here at my expense."

"Hey, it's really not that important," I replied.

Lee interrupted, an odd note of urgency in his voice. "Let me decide what's important," he said. "Scott, you'd be doing me a great favor if you'd fly up here this afternoon."

Naïve I may have been, but not naïve enough to believe Lee wanted to see me that desperately just so I could give him some ointment for his dog's eyes. I was almost certain he'd try to put the make on me if I came to Vegas—and I didn't know how I'd react when and if he did. Lee, the man, didn't attract me. However, the glitz and glitter of Vegas did. I saw no reason why I shouldn't make a quick trip at Lee's expense. But I made up my mind to drive up in my own car so I'd have some degree of independence.

"Come straight to the Hilton when you get here," Lee said, "and ask for Ray Arnett. And, Scott, thanks a lot. I can't tell you what this means to me."

The drive took five hours. It was dark when I arrived at the Hilton. The last time I'd walked through these doors Bob Black had been with me. Now I was walking through them alone, feeling sophisticated, worldly, and in complete control of the situation. There's nothing to worry about, I told myself; you can give the man the medicine, see a few shows, and have a blast. I was determined to make the most of the unplanned trip.

Ray Arnett met me in the lobby acting even friendlier than he had before. He told me that Lee was onstage at the moment but that he couldn't wait to see me again. In the meantime I was his guest. Anything I wanted—a room, a meal, drinks, gambling—were all to go on Lee's tab. That suited me fine.

"But first," Ray finished, "Lee wants to say hello."

I followed him through the hotel, past the casino, down a maze of hallways, until we arrived backstage. On our way through the wings we passed Jerry O'Rourke. He gave me what I felt to be an unfriendly look, which I ignored. We found Lee in the makeshift dressing room in the wings that he used for quick changes.

"Here's your friend," Ray said happily.

Lee beamed at me. "Hello, Scott," he said, reaching for both of my hands. "I knew I could count on you." Lee introduced me to Bruce, his valet, who was busy fussing over Lee's incredible costume. "I've got to finish the show," Lee explained, "but I want you to stay right here and wait for me. Bruce will keep you company." Then Lee was gone, his rhinestoned outfit flashing fire as he headed back on stage.

Throughout the rest of the early show Lee was in and out of the dressing room, making unbelievably fast changes. He seemed very up, almost hyper, a far different Liberace from the man I'd met two weeks ago. I didn't have time to wonder why he seemed so happy, because Bruce kept up a constant stream of chatter.

I remembered Bob Black telling me that many men in show business, from the most macho leading man to the humblest dresser, were homosexual. But I'd dismissed his remark as idle gossip. Now I began to realize Black had not been exaggerating. I eventually learned there would be a gay connection, however tenuous, in most of Lee's activities.

Between the two evening shows Lee invited me to his formal dressing room. "I always eat between acts," he explained, "but I seldom have such pleasant company." He smiled at me and those cool blue eyes suddenly lit with genuine warmth. Walking at his side, I intercepted a dozen curious glances in my direction. Again, I caught O'Rourke watching us from the wings, looking angry.

Carlucci was waiting for us in the dressing room. He seated Lee, tucking a napkin under Lee's chin solicitously as he prepared to serve us. Carlucci continued to cluck and fuss like a mother hen throughout the meal, telling Lee to eat more of this and skip some of that. It was an astonishing performance, made more so because Lee seemed to follow the directions without thinking. Lee kept our conversation very light, telling me he was grateful I'd gone to so much trouble to help Babyboy. "People have been advising me to put the old dog to sleep," Lee said. "But I could never do something like that! He's my oldest friend."

Then Lee asked about my family, my background, how I knew so much about animals. I gave him a thumbnail sketch of my life, telling him about my mother's illness, the many foster homes I'd lived in, and my dream of becoming a vet or an animal trainer. Lee listened intently, his eyes brimming with an emotion I couldn't read. I remember thinking I'd misjudged him. He had seemed remote and preoccupied at the brunch two weeks earlier. Face to face and one on one, Lee was warm, sympathetic, and very likable. I couldn't help responding to him.

When it was time for him to return to the stage, I followed him out to the wings. Bruce greeted me like an old friend and we visited throughout the show. Each time Lee came into the dressing room to change costumes he seemed happier and more energetic. Obviously, performing charged his batteries rather than depleting them. After the second show ended, Lee asked me to join him for a midnight supper in the Hilton penthouse.

"It takes me a while to unwind after doing two shows," he said apologetically. "I'll probably talk your ear off." He changed into street clothes but left his makeup and jewelry on. We rode the elevator to the penthouse in silence. Lee seemed preoccupied while I continued to ask myself what I expected to gain from this trip to Vegas. So far there'd been no opportunity to see other shows or even to play the slots. It had been Lee, Lee, Lee all the way.

The penthouse was only slightly less luxurious than Lee's own home—however, even my untutored eye could see it had been done in better taste. While Lee and Carlucci talked I walked to a window. Vegas glittered beneath me, more alive at two in the morning than it would be at two in the afternoon. Behind me, Carlucci fluttered around his master, fixing drinks and preparing to serve us. But Vegas—seductive, glittering, sleepless Vegas—held my complete attention.

8

Lee removed his stage jewelry and handed it to Carlucci, dismissing him with a curt nod before we began to eat. The houseboy gave us a sad, almost wounded look before he stalked out the penthouse door. Two o'clock in the morning seemed like a weird hour to have a meal, although Lee assured me that it was part of his normal routine. Normal or not, I felt disoriented, as if I had jet lag. But he appeared wide awake and full of nervous energy. He ate quickly, greedily, saying little. When he finished he walked over to a sofa and, patting it, indicated that he wanted me to sit beside him.

"Alone at last," he said, grinning at his use of the old cliché. Then his face grew unexpectedly somber. "Scott, I feel I can trust you and—I have to talk to someone. I've gotten myself into an awful mess."

Not knowing what to say, I just nodded.

Lee lowered his head to his hands. "It's Jerry, my protégé," he said, his voice beginning to rise. "I've created a monster, a *monster!* I gave that boy everything—discovered him—made him a part of the act—put his name up in lights! Arid what thanks do I get?" As Lee spoke, he became terribly agitated.

Suddenly tears began to pour down his face as though a tap inside him had been turned on full force. I moved closer and patted his shoulder. As I later learned for myself, Lee had a habit of putting things in the worst possible light when he was upset with someone.

That night, he wept for what seemed like an eternity. When the emotional storm passed he told me a story of a relationship gone awry. Jerry had been with him for three years and the last year had been a nightmare. According to Lee, Jerry was drinking heavily, getting in fights. One night in Tahoe he'd taken an expensive Mercedes, a car that belonged to John Ascuaga (the owner of the Nugget Casino in Sparks, Nevada), for a joyride. Pursued by the police, Jerry wrecked the car and wound up in jail. Lee, afraid the press might find out what had happened and ambush him as he walked into the jail, had fearfully gone to bail Jerry out. Although Ascuaga, an old Liberace friend, refused to press charges, Lee told me it had taken all his influence to keep the incident out of the courts and out of the papers.

"Jerry is ruining me," Lee moaned, "ruining my image. I can't stand bad publicity. My fans. . . ." His voice trailed off.

"Why don't you fire Jerry?" I asked, not knowing Lee always relied on others to do his dirty work.

"I can't," he moaned. "I signed him to a contract and it has six more months to run. How can Jerry be so thoughtless, so ungrateful, after everything I've done for him. He's a *monster*!" Lee moaned.

His shoulders hunched. Stage makeup streaked his face. He looked shrunken, vulnerable, and very alone. Although I didn't know why he'd chosen me as a confidant I couldn't help feeling sorry for him. Here he was, the biggest star in Vegas, and yet, when the curtain went down, I could see he was completely alone. Logic told me that if he had any *real* friends, anyone he could trust, he'd have confessed his problems to that person rather than to a comparative stranger.

"I hate my life," Lee said, looking through red-rimmed eyes. "Do you know what it feels like to have no one you can trust, no one you can talk to?"

I nodded, thinking, damn right I do; I hadn't known a completely safe, secure day in my life.

"Can you imagine how isolated I feel? I never know if people like me for *me,* or if they like me because I'm *Liberace.* I'm surrounded by takers. They've all got their hands out. Gimme, gimme, *gimme!"* Lee wailed. "Everybody wants a piece of my action!"

Funny. I'd been feeling sorry for myself, just eighteen and on my own. But I didn't feel half as sorry for myself as Lee did. His sobbing finally slowed and he seemed to be getting control of himself.

"You've been good for me, Scott," he said, sighing deeply before he squared his shoulders. "I feel better already, just getting that off my chest." Suddenly his expression brightened. The man was an emotional chameleon. "I've got the most wonderful idea," he said. "How would you like to go to work for me?"

"Doing what?" Lee's question really took me by surprise.

"You could be my secretary," Lee said.

"But I don't type!" I answered honestly.

"Hell, Scott, I can pay people to type. But I need a companion, a bodyguard, someone to keep Vince off my back, someone I can talk to the way I've talked to you tonight."

I didn't know what to say. Lee obviously needed a friend but I suspected he wanted a full-time lover even more. I wasn't sure I could fill that bill. We hardly knew each other. He was so much older and not terribly attractive in my eyes. Loneliness seemed to be the only thing we had in common. It could provide a strong bond, but would it be strong enough to bridge the huge differences in our ages and experiences? Could I really be the friend he so obviously needed? Knowing he believed it possible was incredibly flattering.

While I tried to weigh the pros and cons, Lee added, "I'll pay you three hundred dollars a week and all expenses. You'll be my right-hand man. Please, Scott, say yes."

That tipped the scales. Being the kind of kid who spent every penny he earned and then some, I was perpetually broke. I'd just bought a new car but it really belonged to the bank, and I had no savings; just a couple of part-time jobs that didn't pay near what Liberace was offering. What the hell, I thought; I had everything to gain and nothing to lose. There'd be no worrying about where my next meal was coming from, no more living from hand to mouth in homes where I was often an unwelcome stranger. With Lee I'd have a place to live, a chance to travel, and no financial worries, no worries at all as far as I could see. The more I thought about it, the more the offer seemed like the answer to all my problems as well as some of his. The fact that Lee would probably demand a sexual relationship was the only drawback to his proposition. He just didn't turn me on. But I felt sure I could live with that part of the bargain. After all, Lee was almost sixty. How big a sex drive could he possibly have?

"Okay," I said. "I accept. When do you want me to start?"

"As soon as you can," Lee declared happily.

We agreed that I'd fly home later that day, pack up my belongings, and return to Vegas immediately. By the time we finished making the arrangements Lee had left his earlier misery behind. I should have been prepared for his next move—but it took me by surprise. One minute we were talking, and the next he grabbed me. Whatever doubt I had about his sex drive vanished immediately. Lee wanted sex then and there! But physically, I couldn't oblige.

My car was in the hotel parking lot and I could have—probably should have—headed back to L.A. But realizing I had no place to go, no prospects to compare to the future I'd just been offered, kept me from leaving. Instead, I got up and said, "Hey, this is way too sudden for me."

Lee got to his feet too. "Scott, don't worry about it," he said. "I understand." Getting up, he straightened his clothes and ran his fingers through his hair. Then he walked over to the bar and poured himself a drink, which he sipped while our conversation limped along. It was four in the morning and I'd been up almost twenty-four hours. Stifling a yawn, I said, "I'd better see about getting a room."

"Don't be ridiculous!" Lee replied. "You're staying here with me. Don't worry. I don't have any ulterior motives. I just can't stand being alone." Then he laughed. "I *promise* to stay on my side of the bed."

I agreed to stay, reluctantly, not trusting him at all. We undressed and lay down on opposite sides of the king-size bed. I tried to stay awake, thinking he might try something the minute I fell asleep. But that night Lee was as good as his word. Within minutes, he was snoring noisily. Completely exhausted, I sank into a restless sleep. But the next morning Lee's patience ran out. It was put-up-or-shut-up time.

That afternoon I flew back to Los Angeles in a daze. The sensible part of my mind said I had to be crazy to consider becoming Liberace's companion. I could see that he was demanding, dictatorial, and used to getting whatever he wanted whenever he wanted it. But the loneliness, the vulnerability, he'd revealed touched me deeply. His need for companionship, for someone to care for, struck a chord inside me. I knew just how he felt because I felt the same way too.

Lee had driven me to the airport in his piano-key station wagon, looking like someone who'd slept ten hours instead of five. Before my flight was called he removed a diamond ring from his own hand and placed it in mine. Then he gave me three crisp hundred-dollar bills. He winked and said, "I want to be sure you come back. I have a feeling we're going to be very good for each other."

I dreaded breaking the news to the Carracappa family, whom I'd been living with for the last few months. They were genuinely good people and they'd always had my best interests at heart, ever since the first time I'd stayed with them when I was seven or eight. But I was eighteen and legally of age. I no longer needed anyone's approval when it came to what I wanted to do with my life.

As I feared, my new plans horrified Joe and Rose Carracappa. "You'll be making a big mistake," Joe said sternly. "I worked for that old fag in his Hollywood house a few years ago and it's not a fit place for a young man."

"You don't know him like I do," I replied, remembering how lost and unhappy Liberace had seemed the night before. The more Joe and Rose argued against my going, the more determined I was to leave. Like most young adults, I felt certain I knew what was best for me. The Carracappas, who had no legal hold over me, finally gave in. I would go with their love if not their blessings.

The next day I returned to Vegas, Lee's ring on my finger and his three hundred dollars nestled like a talisman in my wallet. The argument with my foster family had solidified my resolve, my feeling that I'd made the right decision. Lee and Carlucci met me at the airport and I took it as my due, not realizing that Lee never met arriving guests. To my surprise, Carlucci seemed even happier to see me than Lee.

When we arrived at the house Jerry was there, looking upset. I'd been hoping he'd be gone before I arrived. The incredibly awkward situation I'd gotten myself into finally hit me. I'd be sharing the house with Lee's former companion, a man who saw me as his replacement and had every reason to hate me. The optimism that had shielded me from my foster parents' concern disappeared instantly. Jerry was a handsome, dark-haired man about ten years my senior with a mature, powerfully muscled body. The expression on his face told me he resented my presence. In the coming weeks I would find out how much.

Lee and I hadn't talked about where I'd live in the mansion but Carlucci, obviously acting under his master's orders, carried my bags down the hall that led to Lee's bedroom. I hadn't bargained for that. Although I expected to share Lee's bed when he wanted me, I thought I'd at least have the privacy of sleeping in my own room.

Lee had his arm around my shoulders as we walked through the double doors. "I'm so happy you're here," he said. "Just seeing you makes me feel better." A sweeping gesture of his hand encompassed the room. "From now on, I want you to feel this is your home."

Home. My home, I thought, testing the words in my mind. Except for those months at the Brummets', I'd never felt I had a home. I suspected there'd be a price to pay for this one, but I was smart enough to realize that everything worth having had its price.

The next weeks revealed how large the price would be. Liberace kept a very strange household. Carlucci seemed to be in charge of every phase of his master's private life. He monitored Lee's spending, his intake of food and drink. He laid out his clothes in the morning, ran his bath, and even tucked him into bed at night, oblivious of my being in the bed too. Although Lee took Carlucci's ministrations for granted, it startled the hell out of me that first night when Carlucci walked into the bedroom. Acting as if I wasn't there, he fussed with the bedcovers, making sure Lee was comfortable and had everything he needed.

"Does he do that every night?" I asked after Carlucci left the room.

"Sure," Lee replied, as if Carlucci's actions were perfectly ordinary. With Carlucci in the house, Lee and I had no privacy. We only escaped his mothering when we left the house to go shopping or go to the Hilton where Lee was appearing nightly. Shortly after my arrival Jerry's valet moved into the spare bedroom with him. Having the two of them in the house kept me on edge. Passing me in the hall, they'd glower and shoulder me aside, seeming to take what I felt to be delight in intimidating me. Before long I found myself believing every word Lee said about Jerry. During the weeks that we lived under the same roof, Jerry acted like a monster as far as I was concerned. Much later, I realized that unhappiness motivated his actions. Lee had hurt Jerry the way he would one day hurt me.

Four years earlier Lee had discovered Jerry in New York. Jerry was playing in a piano bar at night and, according to Lee, driving a diaper-service truck during the day to support his wife and children. Lee was instantly smitten with Jerry's dark, sultry good looks and his talent. The fact that Jerry was married and a father did not deter Lee or even give him pause. He wanted Jerry to be in his act, and once Lee decided he *wanted* anything, his pursuit was relentless.

Lee offered Jerry a lucrative contract, a chance to appear in the best clubs, to be featured in Lee's shows. All he had to do in return was leave his wife and children at home while the show toured. For an aspiring entertainer an opportunity like that comes once in a lifetime, if at all. I guess Jerry couldn't turn down a chance to make more money than he'd ever made, a chance to become a star. Lee used his money, his fame, his success, to sweeten the deal. Early in their relationship Jerry's wife came west to try to save her marriage. Lee, still smarting years later from what he perceived as a rejection, was outraged because Jerry actually had the *nerve* to sleep with his wife.

Poor, naïve Mrs. O'Rourke didn't stand a chance of keeping her husband. She couldn't match what Lee had to offer—a chance at fame and fortune. Lee could really turn on the charm. Most of the time he reserved those high-voltage performances for the stage, where he literally wooed his audiences. When wooing a potential companion, he oozed the same potent appeal. Lee was one of those people who *knew* he could buy affection, or at least a reasonable facsimile. Potential protégés were inundated with costly gifts—cars, furs, jewels. Lee left no dollar unspent to get what he wanted.

But I didn't know all that during my first weeks in Vegas. All I knew was that Jerry scared the hell out of me. I found myself in an untenable situation that I was totally unequipped to handle. By the time I'd been with Lee for a month I felt certain that moving in had been the mistake of my life. I couldn't stand the lifestyle of the other men in the house. Like most guys my age, gay or straight, I'd had a few lovers. But, at eighteen, I wasn't sophisticated. During the brief periods I'd spent in northern California, I'd been disgusted with the promiscuity I saw in the gay community. To see similar behavior in Lee's home made me sick because I was getting to know Lee as a very sweet guy, a real homebody who doted on his dogs; a man who loved to putter around the house, to cook, to shop, to spend quiet days at home. Despite the glitzy, overdone decor, Lee had a real gift for creating a warm, comfortable home. And he went out of his way to make me feel at ease in it.

But I couldn't deal with the pressure of living under the same roof with Jerry and his roommate, dealing with what I took to be Carlucci's interference. Late one night when Lee was relaxing in the Jacuzzi, unwinding from his performance, I told him I'd be leaving. "I'm terribly sorry," I said, "but this has been a mistake. I just can't take your lifestyle. Carlucci's always watching me. Jerry dislikes me. I feel like I have to watch my step every minute when he's in the house. It's not up to me to tell you how to live. But I can't take it here."

"Then I've failed you," Lee said, beginning to weep loudly. "Your happiness means more to me than anything in the world, Scott—more than my own. The first time I saw you, when Black brought you backstage, I couldn't take my eyes off you. I felt something grabbing my guts, something that said this kid is one in a million. It killed me, those two weeks hoping and praying you'd call. And when you did, I can't tell you how happy it made me. You see, Scott, I love you."

I gulped. That was the first time in my entire life that someone had said, "I love you." When I was little I used to imagine my mother taking me in her arms, hugging and kissing me, and saying she loved me. But it had never happened. Not with her and not with anyone else.

"I love you, Scott," Lee repeated. "Does that mean anything to you?"

I didn't know what to say, didn't know if I could trust him, didn't know how to react. But something inside me that had been frozen for a long time began to thaw.

9

Lee spoiled me, just as he undoubtedly spoiled his previous lovers. Although I hoped he'd ask Jerry to move out, that didn't happen. As a substitute for meaningful action, Lee sent me flowers daily. My tiniest whim was his command— clothes, jewelry—and all I had to do was admire something and it was mine. He even cleaned up after the dogs when they had an accident, a job that would be mine as soon as the "honeymoon" ended.

Our sexual relationship caused problems from the beginning. I'd completely underestimated Lee's sex drive. He may have been over the hill but he wanted sexual encounters as couple of times a day. Ironically, he often had physical difficulty in fulfilling his desire. Lee used amyl nitrite as a stimulant, to heighten his sexual experiences, and he urged me to use it too. Amyl nitrite comes in little ampoules or "poppers," like smelling salt, and it has an odor like rotten eggs. On Lee's insistence I tried it once, hated the smell, and refused it from then on. Lee continued to use it heavily, but he stopped asking me to join him. In our first months together he cared about me enough to put my feelings and wishes ahead of his own.

He showered me with affection and presents. But the gift of his love proved more seductive than anything else. In the end I couldn't resist it. The night he confessed that he loved me, I'd already started caring for him. When we left for Tahoe a few weeks later, I'd learned to love him. It was the last thing in the world I'd expected to happen. I'd made a bargain with Lee, a deal for sex and companionship in exchange for financial security; and I'd done it with my eyes open. Now, for the first time in my life, I stopped worrying about my future and my welfare and concentrated on someone else's happiness. Although Lee was forty years my senior, there were times when he seemed like a lost soul. I made up my mind to devote myself to him, to make him laugh, to lighten all his burdens—lofty plans, but typical I guess for an eighteen-year-old with his head in the clouds. At the time I didn't realize how difficult a task I'd set myself, or how many people would bitterly resent my attempting it. But I soon learned that Jerry wasn't the only person who would be unhappy with my role in Lee's life.

Lee had a three-week booking at the Sahara Tahoe and he always took his entourage on such trips. It was my first opportunity to meet the group Lee called "his people." He introduced me around and made certain they understood how important I was to him. The most influential of them all was Seymour Heller, who worked through AVI (American Variety International) as Lee's West Coast agent and manager. Heller was a small man in his mid-fifties, balding, with a permanent frown etched on his face. When we met at the airport he gave me what I took to be a cold, appraising look before congratulating me on joining Lee's organization.

Heller was one of Lee's few close heterosexual associates. He did a marvelous job of pretending that the young men who moved in and out of Lee's life were employees rather than sexual partners. Lee helped the deception by putting his lovers on his payroll, giving them jobs and titles. During my years with him I was variously described as a chauffeur, bodyguard, and secretary-companion. My predecessors had been called valets, protégés, yard boys, or houseboys, depending on their individual talents. Some, like me, wound up in the act.

It struck me that Heller was jealous of his privileged, influential position in the Liberace camp. His thirty-year employment had been interrupted only once, in the early sixties, when, according to Lee, Angie had temporarily taken over his job. The experience must have made Heller insecure. Businesslike and pragmatic, Heller made the ideal foil for Lee. Heller played hardball when negotiating contracts, while Lee played the smiling, agreeable, "anything goes" entertainer.

But when he carried his role too far Lee admonished him, saying, "Put the hatchet away, Seymour!"

Ray Arnett, Lee's production manager, was Heller's opposite, a jovial pixie liked by everyone. I felt as comfortable in his company as I felt uncomfortable around Heller. Arnett was also part of Lee's old guard. After joining the act in the fifties he'd quickly become indispensable. Arnett was a real talent with the imagination and flair of a Busby Berkeley. He and Lee made a terrific team. Between them, they dreamed up the outrageous ideas that audiences had come to expect of a Liberace show, and then Arnett saw to their staging.

Lee played a variety of dates, from the luxurious rooms of Vegas, Tahoe, and Miami Beach to theaters in the round and enormous stadiums. Arnett was in charge of tailoring the act to suit each site, choosing the props that would work within the physical limitations of the differing locations. Well-equipped stages like those at the Hilton or the Sahara got the full Liberace treatment, from the mirrored Rolls to the "dancing waters" and the Chinese Acrobats. Theaters in the round got a streamlined version of the act. When Lee played stadiums with limited facilities he simply used a piano, a candelabra, and a couple of costume changes, just like the old days.

Arnett functioned as a focal point for Liberace's entourage and he handled his taxing, multifaceted job with dedication and good humor. He was completely devoted to Lee and described him as the easiest of bosses, a man who seldom lost his temper or threw his weight around. Lee knew mishaps could derail the best plans and he never complained when things went awry. On the road, he was a total professional, as undemanding and hardworking as any neophyte performer. Arnett backed and supported Lee all the way, reflecting Lee's style and grace as a performer.

Liberace's musical support group consisted of Bo Ayars, his conductor; Chuck Hughes, the drummer; and Ralph Enrico, who played bass and guitar. These three men, all heterosexual, were never admitted into Lee's inner circle. The entourage also included Lee's dresser; Jerry's dresser; and Jerry himself, whom I'd come to regard as a major problem. In the past Jerry had always traveled with Lee in first class. After my appearance he was relegated to flying coach with the musicians and dressers. It didn't improve his attitude.

Others who worked for Lee on a regular basis but didn't travel with him included his attorney, Joel Strote, a relative newcomer to Lee's employ; Lucille Cunningham, his accountant; Bob Lindner, who designed Lee's jewelry; Anna Nateece, his furrier; and Michael Travis, who made his costumes. In addition, Lee kept domestic staffs in each of his several homes.

Lee played the Sahara Tahoe for several weeks every year. During our stay we lived in the hotel's "entertainment house," the luxurious quarters the Sahara kept for VIPs, complete with a chef and housekeeper. The rest of the entourage stayed in the hotel proper. When we were alone, free from the dual burdens of Jerry's anger and Carlucci's interference, I got to know a new and thoroughly delightful Lee, a man with a corny sense of humor who loved to be teased, to have me make fun of his superior status. At night when he prepared for his performance, I joked that he was better dressed than Queen Elizabeth.

"But I am an old queen," he quipped back. Lee had a good sense of humor and could tell off-color jokes by the hour.

Our quarters overlooked the lake and we spent many quiet, relaxed hours on the patio. Lee would sit staring at me, just as he had when we first met. It made me uneasy until he explained that he couldn't get enough of looking at me. "I'm memorizing your face," he said, "so I can picture it perfectly when we're not together."

Lee needn't have bothered: we were together all the time. Afternoons we sailed Lake Tahoe's beautiful turquoise waters. During those early autumn weeks we shared everything, exchanging information about our unhappy childhoods as well as talking about our hopes for the future. Lee said he wanted to make me a part of the act, having me drive the cars he used for his entrances and exits. "I want you with me all the time," he said, "onstage and off."

74

He spoke of his love for children and how saddened he was at never having his own. He even talked about adopting me, a topic that he'd bring up many times in the years to come. "I want to be everything to you," Lee said, "father, brother, lover, best friend."

If I so much as frowned, he would be by my side instantly, asking what was wrong. He had an even temperament while I was a little like my mother, unhappy one minute and smiling the next. If I seemed at all dissatisfied Lee said, "Please don't be depressed. When you're sad I'm sad."

It was overwhelming stuff for a kid who'd spent his life unwanted by anyone. I loved Lee for caring that much. He filled an enormous void in my life. When he asked me to cut all my ties with the past, I did it gladly. I'd have done anything in the world to make him happy.

Lee and I discovered a mutual love of cooking. He planned all our menus and, when we had time, dismissed the chef so we could prepare our own meals. Lee liked simple food made with the best ingredients. He taught me to make a killer of a spaghetti sauce that included Italian sausage that he made himself. I still make the sauce for my friends today.

Basically, despite the glitz of his lifestyle, Lee was just an ordinary guy who enjoyed everyday pleasures. He was a big movie fan who liked to relax in front of the television with a big bowl of popcorn. In Tahoe he screened many of his television shows for me, laughing when I thoughtlessly commented on how the years had changed him. "You make me young again," he said happily.

We saw very little of Lee's people during that Tahoe stay. Lee wanted our time alone to be uninterrupted. He did, however, agree to join Jerry and the valet one evening when they were going to see Lawrence Welk's show. Although I didn't care for the idea, Lee insisted I accompany him. As I feared, it proved to be a bizarre outing. Jerry seemed to be flaunting his friendship with the valet, perhaps in an effort to make Lee jealous. But Lee acted as if he was oblivious of any of the undercurrents flowing around him.

Another night Lee took me to meet his brother George, who was working locally as a lounge act. Although we were in Tahoe for several weeks, it was the only time they saw one another. The playboard advertising George's appearance billed him as "george *LIBERACE.*" Seeing it really upset Lee. "Hell," he fumed, "I made the name what it is, and now they all take advantage of it."

It was my first exposure to Lee's complicated and often contradictory relationship with his family. I couldn't help wondering how George felt, playing a small lounge when his younger brother was so successful. When I met him after his performance George proved to be a quiet, gentle man who walked softly in his brother's shadow. Lee told me George had made a small fortune in his lifetime, but that his many wives had taken it all. The brothers treated each other with a distant, uncomfortable politeness, and the evening turned out to be far from a joyous reunion. It gave me some insight into the complexities of Lee's relationships and how little I really knew him. I would later come to know most of the Liberace family quite well. Like all families, they had their share of problems getting along with each other. However, despite Lee's often voiced complaints about this one or that one, I found all of them to be devoted to him. They did their best to protect him and his reputation, right up until the day he died.

While we stayed in the entertainment house I couldn't help worrying about how our relationship would be perceived, not realizing that Lee's homosexuality was an open secret in the show-business world. Like other gay entertainers, he was protected by the people who worked for him or with him. They would never risk their lucrative jobs by talking to the press. Even if they did, the press wouldn't publish their stories. The entertainment world is a closed fraternity—and the media are as much a part of it as the stars.

Back then I was scared to death the staff would catch us in a private moment. Lee didn't share my concern. His sex drive was at an all-time high and it made him reckless. He had a dread of growing old and ill and insisted that contact with me made him feel young again. He'd suffered an impotence problem before we met and had a silicone implant that made him semierect all the time. Lee never admitted his problem to anyone, not even to me—and I never questioned him. I felt it was a sensitive issue that he would discuss if and when he felt the time was right. But various members of his inner circle had learned about the surgery. They whispered and giggled, assuming it had been done to enlarge Lee rather than to deal with a legitimate medical problem. Sadly, Lee preferred to leave people to draw that sick conclusion rather than tell them the truth.

In our first months together Lee's weaknesses and faults made me feel even closer to him. He wasn't a vain man in the usual sense. He didn't regard himself as a musical genius and he wasn't in love with his own appearance. But he was very protective of the Liberace image and would go to any lengths to maintain and perpetuate it. A major part of that image was his full head of thick, curly hair.

Lee had started balding in his thirties. By his fifties he'd lost almost all his hair. The first time I saw him getting out of the shower without a wig, I hardly recognized him. He looked like a nice, middle-aged man with a too-big nose, an ingratiating smile, and a bald head. Lee had a paranoid fear when it came to letting anyone see him that way. He didn't even swim, although all his homes had pools, because he was afraid his wig might come off underwater. When Lee turned the care of his many hairpieces over to me, it was the ultimate compliment. It signaled that he now trusted me with his life.

By the time we left Tahoe, Lee and I were well on our way to a very solid relationship. He confided that he felt he was getting too old to start over again, that he wanted ours to be the final relationship of his life. "I saved the best for last," he said.

10

After three weeks in Tahoe we returned to the chaos of our strange Vegas household. It seemed we'd no sooner walked in the door than Carlucci picked up where he'd left off: trying to be a part of every facet of Lee's life. The size and scope of Jerry's bouts of anger escalated. He and his roommate, the valet, continued to make me feel ill at ease.

Lee faced a three-month hiatus before his next booking and I made up my mind to use the time to sort out our lives. I've been told I was the only one of Lee's lovers to insist on playing more than a passive role in his life. But I wanted him to be happy, and I didn't see how that was possible unless I changed the way we lived. Gays have no choice when it comes to their sexual preference. We are what God, or fate, or our environment, or whatever higher power you hold dear has made us. But we do have a choice when it comes to the life we lead and the people we associate with. I felt that our present lifestyle was intolerable and unhealthy, that having so many men living under one roof would lead to serious trouble. Yet Lee continued to tolerate what seemed to me to be an intolerable state of affairs. He turned a seemingly deaf ear to all my pleas to change the status quo.

I was disgusted, baffled, angry, afraid Lee still cared for Jerry enough to want to keep him around. All I knew was that I couldn't continue sharing a home with my lover's protégé—and the protégé's roommate. It was just too bizarre. Once again I told Lee I'd have to leave and once again he broke down and wept, but I was beginning to be leery of tears that came so easily and conveniently. Lee was a consummate actor and Camille his favorite role. He played the part again and again during our years together. I never did learn to ignore his tears; knowing my weakness, he cried when he couldn't get what he wanted any other way.

Jerry, however, seemed immune to all Lee's blandishments. Tears, anger, coldness, had no effect on him. Saying he had no place to go, Jerry simply stayed on in the Vegas house on Shirley Street. So Lee did what he always did when he needed someone to play the heavy. He called in Seymour Heller. Their discussion foreshadowed future discussions they would one day have about me. According to Lee, they agreed that Jerry must be made to understand the jeopardy of his position. Lee didn't want to risk rejecting Jerry and having him take his revenge by telling the world that Lee was a homosexual. In the past Lee had gone to great lengths to protect his name and his reputation, to keep the secrets of his homosexuality from the world. He was prepared to do so again—and he wanted to be sure Jerry knew it.

Carlucci was given a leading role in the plan to get Jerry to move. First, Carlucci and Lee found a house for Jerry and, according to Lee, secretly made a deposit on it. Then Carlucci, acting under Lee's orders, packed Jerry's belongings. Jerry came home one afternoon to find his bag and baggage neatly stacked outside by the front door.

Carlucci had the responsibility of asking Jerry to leave. Lee, who had been through this particular situation in the past, arranged to be out of the house when it happened. He seemed to be afraid to deal with Jerry face to face. But Carlucci suffered no such fear. Matter-of-factly, he told Jerry he had two choices: he could leave the house under his own steam, or be removed bodily. Anyone who knew Lee knew he had some dangerous friends. Jerry did the sensible thing and left quietly.

By then four months had passed since my arrival in Las Vegas. Lee had been brooding the entire time, trying to figure out how to rid himself of his live-in protégé. When Jerry finally departed it happened so quickly and completely that I felt as if someone had waved a magic wand. Once he'd gone Lee went about systematically removing all traces of the life he and Jerry had shared. He stripped Jerry's bedroom and bath down to the bare walls, disposing of the furniture and repainting and papering. He went through the house, gathering every item they'd bought together so Carlucci could get rid of them. Clearly, Lee wanted no reminder of Jerry in the home we now shared. It was a frightening display of Lee's ability to shut the door on unhappy memories. A voice in my head warned that one day I might receive the same treatment, but I blithely managed to ignore it.

We redid those empty rooms together, shopping with a vengeance. Lee loved to spend money; the more he spent, the better he seemed to feel about himself. Roaming through stores with him, knowing we could buy anything that took our fancy no matter how foolish that fancy might be, was a blast—the ultimate ego trip. That shopping spree would be just the first of many. For Lee and me, they soon became a way of life. In the future, I would develop a taste for flamboyance, for the good life, that rivaled Lee's. Like him, I would come to believe that "too much of a good thing is wonderful." It would come close to ruining me for life.

When Jerry's rooms were redone Lee decided to visit his other homes. We drove to the Cloisters in Palm Springs first. It was even bigger and more luxurious than the Vegas house. The Cloisters had been built in 1925 as a thirty-two-room hotel. When Lee first saw it, fifty years of hard use had transformed it from a resort into a flop joint. He was terribly proud of having seen value and worth in a structure other people wanted to tear down. Lee liked to think of himself as someone who saved things no one else wanted: buildings, stray dogs, even people like me. However, little of the original hotel structure, other than the bell tower, remained after Lee finished what he called "remodeling." He loved the rebuilt Cloisters, all fifteen thousand square feet. Its most notable features were two small chapels; one in the garden had stained-glass windows and the other, adjacent to the master bedroom, contained a large sculpture of St. Anthony. While at the Cloisters Lee occasionally invited gay priests to say a private mass.

He liked to boast what a bargain his two chapels had been. His statue of St. Anthony had been covered with several layers of dirt and paint when he found it—and he bought it cheap. Restorers discovered a valuable sixteenth-century wood carving under the layers of grime. The stained-glass windows in the outdoor chapel came from churches that were being torn down. Lee purchased them for little more than the cost of carting them away. He loved a bargain, the feeling of having bested a seller, even more than he loved walking into an expensive store and flaunting his personal wealth.

The Cloisters, although less formal than Lee's other homes, was just as much a jumble of flash and trash as the house on Shirley Street. A priceless bronze sat alongside furniture Lee found in Watts. Cement garden sculptures from Mexico stood next to authentic marbles from Italy. Lee laughingly described as "homey" a dining table that seated forty, which he'd bought from the estate of William Randolph Hearst. Lee loved the clutter and waxed poetic as he told how he acquired each individual piece. The history of those inanimate objects was as dear to him as incidents in the lives of children are to their parents.

Of all his homes, the Cloisters was my favorite. It had an Olympic pool where I swam laps. Lee, of course, never joined me. But he'd sit in the Jacuzzi smoking and having cocktails by the hour. The caretaker family—Hermine, Joe, and their son—watched over the Cloisters in Lee's absence and waited on him when he was there.

Lee's mother lived in her own house behind the Cloisters and I met her for the first time on that trip. Lee didn't talk about his family very much. He'd been visibly uncomfortable during our brief visit with George in Tahoe. I'd learned that George and his current wife, Dora, lived in Sacramento and that Lee had never visited them there in their home. Sister Angie lived in California too and, again, Lee told me he rarely had time to go and see her. But Mama Liberace was another story. Lee felt a strong sense of obligation toward his aging mother.

She struck me as a bright-eyed, warmhearted, lively woman, obviously devoted to and very proud of her son. We no sooner were in her home than she began to complain about how seldom she saw Lee. He gave her what I presumed was his standard excuse—he was working hard, always on the road. But, Lee added, he never forgot her in his prayers. He worked hard at looking and sounding like a dutiful son but he seemed very uncomfortable in the role. He embraced his mother as though she were all sharp edges instead of a plump, matronly woman, just made for hugging; and his eyes always slid away from hers when she looked at him with parental love and concern. In my opinion, she made him nervous.

I never did figure out what Frances Liberace made of me and my presence in Lee's life on that visit because we soon left for Hollywood, where Lee owned a mansion high in the hills on Herold Way. It was the first truly opulent residence he'd purchased and he had a special fondness for it. The house, originally built by Rudy Vallee, perched on a two-acre ridge crest. Like Lee's other homes, this one was filled with pianos, including one that had reputedly belonged to Chopin. Lee never played any of them. I was learning that he performed only for money, not for pleasure. Once or twice, at special parties, he played briefly for his guests. The rest of the time those pianos just took up space. They were part of his image but not of his life. Lee told me he'd spent enough time practicing as a kid to last a lifetime.

Gladys Luckie, a delightful black woman, cared for the Hollywood house. Compared to some of the other servants, Gladys was a breath of fresh air. During our brief visit, we thrived under her care. Gladys confided that she'd been stranded in that beached whale of a house for months on end. Lee rarely came to stay anymore and, as far as Lee and the faithful Gladys were concerned, it was the old story of "out of sight, out of mind." She'd been left alone on that lonely hilltop with a broken-down station wagon for transportation, consigned to a lonely existence. I felt very sorry for her and very conscious of the difficulties of her position.

Gladys and I seemed to be on the same wavelength. I made up my mind to get her to Vegas if I could. That meant dismissing Carlucci but, after getting Jerry to move, anything seemed possible. Lee agreed with my plans in principle but left implementing them to me. I talked to Gladys about coming to work for us in Vegas and she agreed, reluctantly. I think she was tired of being taken for granted. When we returned to Las Vegas I used my position as Lee's favorite to discharge Carlucci.

Lee's people soon realized I intended to be more than a boy-toy. Evidently, I intimidated some and made others jealous. Angie began to call me to find out what her brother was doing. But when I reported her calls to Lee, he said, "Don't tell her a damn thing. My life is none of her business!"

Seymour Heller and I continued to have a somewhat adversarial relationship. Whether true or not, I even heard he had the police run a check on me. Accountant Lucille Cunningham's reaction was typical of Lee's straight employees' reactions to me. I dropped by her office one day to discuss the payment of some bills—a subject she regarded as her exclusive territory—and she turned on me in a fury.

"You really think you're something, don't you?" she said. "Well, let me tell you, Mr. High and Mighty, Lee's had a string of boys like you. Has he told you about Bobby or Hans or the male stripper who used to live with him? We called that one 'the country boy' because he was such an ignorant hick! I've seen them come and I've seen them go. You won't be any different. One of these days Lee will tell Seymour Heller to get rid of you and then you'll be out on your ear too!"

If Lucille had been a man I'd have taken great pleasure in decking her on the spot. I knew I wasn't the first man in Lee's life, but he'd said I would be the last. Occasionally one of our gay friends would allude to someone from Lee's past, but Lee would scowl and the subject would be dropped immediately.

"How dare you talk to me like that?" I said to Lucille. "What Lee does in his private life is none of your business!" I stormed out of her office full of righteous anger. But driving home, I couldn't help wondering if I was living in a fool's paradise.

11

Life with Lee would never be completely normal, but it did normalize to some extent once Gladys Luckie took over the Vegas house. I unwittingly became her favorite when, on learning she'd gone without a raise for years, I insisted Lee double her paycheck. Although my concern surprised him, he agreed at once. Gladys had been deeply hurt by her virtual exile in the Hollywood Hills, but she was too loyal and devoted an employee ever to broach the subject of salary herself. And Lee never worried about the nuts and bolts of daily life, especially details as mundane as someone else's salary. In all honesty, he didn't have time.

When Lee worked Vegas he gave two two-hour shows, seven nights a week. He wasn't a kid and performing took all his energy. By necessity our lives revolved around his needs, his schedule. He'd get up between two and four in the afternoon, shower, shave, and dress for the day, often in one of his favored jumpsuits. A late afternoon breakfast was usually followed by a shopping trip. Lee craved shopping the way an addict craves a fix. He felt the day was incomplete if he didn't purchase something. Buying his own groceries and browsing in supermarkets would do if nothing more seductive and costly loomed on the horizon. He could wax ecstatic over imported cheese, fresh vegetables, prime beef. "Oooh, fabulous!" he'd say in his benevolent whine when something pleased him.

By seven we'd be at the Hilton, getting ready for the first show. Lee liked to get there early because he did his own makeup, in part to protect the secret of his baldness. He didn't want some talkative makeup artist telling the world that Liberace's luxuriant locks were phony.

He used the hour and a half between the eight o'clock supper show and the midnight cocktail show to rebuild his energy. It was our private time—and heaven help anyone who made the mistake of intruding. We'd have a light meal and afterward Lee would take a catnap, leaving instructions to be wakened fifteen minutes before he was scheduled to go onstage. Once he nodded off I'd slip out and wander through the casino, gambling or just having a quiet drink by myself. It was the only time in any given twenty-four hours while I shared my life with Lee that I could count on being alone.

My first visit to Lee's dressing room with Bob Black had been a rare exception to Lee's hard and fast rule of no visitors between acts. In the years since, I've often wondered why he permitted two strangers like Black and myself to come backstage. Was he hoping that someone like me would come along? I'll never know. Inviting us to the house the next day was even more out of character for Lee.

He saw people in his dressing room after the last show, friends from out of town, visiting celebrities, people he couldn't avoid seeing. He preferred playing host in his dressing room to inviting guests to his home. Describing him as an intensely private man doesn't seem adequate. Once he left the theater he didn't want anyone around him other than his lover. A "cross at your own risk" line divided his public from his private life. Even close associates like Arnett knew better than to drop in on Lee unannounced. If anyone called, fishing for an invitation, Lee made it instantly clear that they wouldn't be welcome. He had a standard routine when Heller, who was Jewish, telephoned unexpectedly.

"You can't come over tonight, Seymour," Lee would say with ill-concealed glee. "I'm cooking pork for dinner."

We usually got home between three or four in the morning. It might have been the crack of dawn to most people but for Lee the workday had just ended. We'd have a snack, watch movies, play with the dogs, or sit in the Jacuzzi smoking and having drinks until he unwound enough to go to sleep, usually about seven in the morning. The routine had been established long before I arrived on the scene and, although I often felt isolated and missed having other people around, Lee refused to alter his restrictive and reclusive life-style.

Despite the crazy hours we led a very sedentary life. That came as an unpleasant surprise to me. I'd been expecting a private life that in some way matched the glitter and excitement of Lee's onstage performances. But nothing could have been further from the truth. Lee had no hobbies, played no sports. He lived for his hours onstage and his lover at home. The routine was perhaps well suited to a man in his late fifties—but it soon bored the hell out of me. I cared for Lee deeply, but no single person can satisfy another's every need. I craved other conversation, other viewpoints, the company of people my age. But if I voiced those desires, Lee would either call me a kvetch or accuse me of not loving him enough. Since he insisted I be with him every minute, I sometimes felt like a prisoner in paradise.

True to his word, Lee made me part of the act when Jerry left. Even though I would participate in the show hundreds of times, seeing the house lights dim always got my adrenaline flowing. The stage would be completely dark when Ray Arnett, standing unseen in the wings, said, "And now ladies and gentlemen, the star of the show, Mr. Showmanship, Liberace, the man who is famous throughout the world for his candelabra . . ." At that moment a spotlight would illuminate a single golden candelabra that seemed to float, disembodied, in velvet darkness. After a meaningful pause Ray's voice continued, *"And his piano* . . ." Then another spot would reveal a piano, not your everyday concert grand either. Lee's stage pianos always glittered with gold leaf, mirrors, or rhinestones.

The full orchestra would begin to play, a rose-colored spot would play over the wings, and I'd drive Lee onstage in his mirrored $250,000 Rolls-Royce. I wore a white chauffeur's uniform liberally sprinkled with rhinestones, a white peaked cap, knee-length white boots, and full stage makeup. Lee loved the outfit. "You look like an Adonis," he said the first time I wore it. "My own blond Adonis."

Lee would continue to sit in the car after his entrance, his demeanor as regal as a king's, until I opened the door and helped him out. His most outrageous costumes were reserved for his entrances. They generally included floor-length coats or capes with long trains, many of them adorned with priceless furs. Lee spent half a million or more each year on his costumes, in part because he had to rotate them and could never wear at any engagement what he'd worn the previous year. He also owned the many cars he used in the act and most of the stage props. Set pieces, the least costly part of the production, could usually be rented.

After stepping from the Rolls he'd walk to the edge of the stage and give his audience a brilliant smile. "Well, look me over," he'd say. "I didn't get dressed like this to go unnoticed!" One of his favorite coats was virgin fox with a sixteen-foot train. "Think how long it took to get the pelts," he'd joke when he wore it.

Lee could play a crowd even better than he played the piano. He'd look for someone wearing conspicuous diamonds and then, holding his own bejeweled fingers up for display, he'd jibe, "I didn't have to do anything to get mine. What did you have to do to get yours?"

It was his standard introductory patter and the audience never failed to respond by laughing in all the right places. Once his rapport with them had been firmly established, Lee would turn toward me, saying, "I'd like you all to meet my friend and companion, Scott Thorson." I'd take a bow, salute, and drive the Rolls offstage. As far as I was concerned, Lee might as well have announced that we were lovers. To my amazement, his fans never seemed to draw the obvious conclusions.

Next, Lee's valet would make his entrance and remove Lee's coat. I'd appear again, this time driving a Volkswagen that had been modified to look like a miniature Rolls. The valet would put the coat or cape in the car and I'd drive off while Lee explained that *his* was the only coat in the world to have its own car. It wasn't sophisticated, but it worked. I'd exit to appreciative laughter.

After the opener, Lee would get around to playing the piano. By the 1970s the music was almost an incidental part of his act. The real show was Lee himself, his clothes, his cars, his outrageous stage persona. He rarely played more than five minutes at a time before saying, "I have to slip into something more spectacular." That never failed to elicit a laugh and applause.

Early in his career, Lee's costumes were made by Frank Acuna, a superb tailor. By the time I joined the act they were being created by Michael Travis, one of Hollywood's most gifted theatrical designers. Travis, who looks more like a matinee idol than someone who works behind the scenes, made a great contribution to the success of Lee's act in the seventies and eighties.

The two men met through Ray Arnett, who was a long-term friend and associate of Travis. Travis's credentials were outstanding. He'd worked for the Bell and Firestone television shows in New York during the fifties and moved to Hollywood in the sixties to do "Laugh-In." Stars such as Dionne Warwick, Diana Ross, Neil Sedaka, and Wayne Newton were on his client list. More important, Travis had a genius for the spectacular that matched and complemented Lee's. The first costume he created for Lee was a silver-blue chauffeur's livery trimmed in mink, which Lee wore in 1976 when the mirrored Rolls became part of the act.

Six months later Travis had, as he puts it, "ascended the throne"; from then on he made all Lee's costumes. The two men had a terrific working relationship based on trust and respect. When it came to costumes they were on the same wavelength. Lee never quibbled about the cost of his costumes, his sole specification being that they be more eye-catching every year. The virgin fox coat with the sixteen-foot train, made at a cost of $300,000 by noted furrier Anna Nateece, was the most spectacular to date of Travis's ideas. But he had an even more fabulous number on the drawing board for the 1987 season. The pièce de résistance was to be a cape the size of a stage curtain, adorned with an electrified candelabra embroidered in gold. The scenario called for Lee to open the act wearing the cape. At the strategic moment the hem would have risen slowly until the garment became the stage's back curtain. The costume would have been a fitting climax to the highly successful collaboration between Travis and Lee, but, tragically, Lee didn't live long enough to wear it.

Like all stage entertainers, Lee faced his share of hecklers. I've never seen anyone handle them better. If his patter was interrupted he'd walk to the stage apron, his toothy smile never faltering. "Hey, who's running things?" he'd ask. "You or me?" If the interruption continued he'd put on his Jewish mother routine, scolding, "Don't be a kvetch." If that didn't end the problem, Lee would raise the third finger on one hand and, still grinning, look directly at the heckler, asking, "How do you like the ring on *this* finger?" By then the audience would be roaring with laughter and ready to lynch anyone who interrupted the act again. Lee would get them laughing even harder by saying, "Oops! I really didn't mean to do that." He could do no wrong onstage.

He made ten or more costume changes during a regular performance. Acts such as the Chinese Acrobats, Barkeley Shaw and His Puppets, or the Ballet Folklórico kept audiences amused while they waited to see what outrageous outfit Lee would wear next. He'd come to refer to his million-dollar wardrobe as "a very expensive joke"—although sometimes, I suspect, he thought the joke was on him. I'm sure he had no idea what would happen on the night when he wore that set of white tails at the Hollywood Bowl. The next thing he knew, he traveled with fifty-four trunks full of costumes and a full-time employee to care for them.

Lee was justifiably proud of his ability to pick outstanding performers to be part of his show. He felt particularly proud of having introduced Barbra Streisand to Las Vegas. Streisand had just done *I Can Get It for You Wholesale* on Broadway but, according to Lee, her reputation hadn't traveled beyond the Greater New York area back then. In the early sixties Barbra had yet to achieve the celebrity and glamour of her later Hollywood years. Lee described her as an average-looking girl, given to wearing high-necked, drab dresses.

"But she had the voice of an angel," he said. "The first time I heard it, I got goose bumps."

He brought her to Vegas as part of his act. When the hotel's entertainment director saw her rehearsing, he complained to Lee. "What the hell will our audiences make of a girl with a big nose and a neckline up to her chin?"

Lee just laughed. "They don't know what to make of me either, and it hasn't hurt me a bit!"

After seeing Barbra onstage, Barron Hilton came to Lee in a fury. "I want that girl *out!*" he said. Hilton was a powerful man, accustomed to having his way. But he'd more than met his match in Lee. "If she goes, I go too," Lee said quietly. Hilton, not wanting to lose his most popular headliner, backed down.

Lee's instincts were dead right. Vegas audiences fell in love with Barbra's magical voice. Her later glamour was just frosting on a very talented cake. After the Vegas appearance Lee took her to the Sahara Tahoe. While she was performing there, she got the offer to star in *Funny Girl* on Broadway. The rest is show-business history.

Many performers who never worked with Lee were influenced by what he did onstage. In the fifties when Elvis Presley made his first Vegas appearance—which laid a giant goose egg—he sought Lee's guidance. Lee gave him a gold lamé jacket, the start of Elvis's glittering wardrobe, and some succinct advice on how to woo an audience. "Don't be a phony," he warned the young Elvis. "The audience can spot a phony in a minute. You've got to give one hundred and ten percent every time you go on stage."

Although Lee didn't understand rock 'n' roll, had no feel for it really, he was a staunch Elvis supporter. Then, near the end of Elvis's life, Lee told me he went to see an Elvis performance and came home close to tears. "Elvis was just going through the motions," Lee remembered sadly.

That would never be said about Lee. Sick or well, happy or sad, he put his personal problems behind him the minute he stepped onstage. He gave everything he had to every audience he faced. Whether Lee appeared with the Young Americans or Streisand or the Rockettes, the heart of the act was always Lee himself. In the 1960s his Riviera show was called *Come As You Are*. The production revolved around the fictionalized story of Lee's life, narrated by the then-famous horror-film hostess Vampira. It was a crazy concept but Lee loved it. "The wilder the better," he used to say. Over the years he made entrances flying across stage in sequined hot pants looking like a superannuated cherub or popping out of an enormous replica of a Fabergé egg while dressed as a bunny.

Lee went for laughs and seemed to delight in poking fun at himself. When the act called for him to dance with the Rockettes famous high-stepping chorus line he said, "I'm no good—but I've got guts!" He and Ray Arnett created a new act every few years, but certain tried-and-true schticks never varied. Flashing diamonds on every finger, he'd tell an audience to "Look all you like. After all, you bought them." At the end of the act he'd walk to center stage, grin confidingly, and say, "I've had so much fun tonight, that honestly, I'm ashamed to take the money." Following a perfectly timed pause worthy of Jack Benny he'd add, "But I will." It was pure corn, but he made it sound fresh night after night.

It's almost impossible to describe his genius to people who never saw him perform. He closed every show by leaving the stage, walking between the tables, and singing, "I'll Be Seeing You." People would line up to shake his hand and I was always surprised by the many macho types who waited patiently until Lee got to them. Time and again the men would say, "My wife made me come—and I thought I'd hate your act. But you're the *greatest.*"

Lee never used security people or police to build a wall between himself and his fans. I often saw crowds surge toward him and felt certain he'd be trampled, only to hear his voice saying, "If you'll all back off, I'll shake hands with everyone."

Unlike many other celebrities he didn't want to be protected by a phalanx of police or security when he dealt with the public. He claimed the protectors would cause more panicked pushing, shoving, and general pandemonium than the most eager fan. Lee spent ten minutes after each show talking to people, signing autographs—as he called it, "paying his dues."

By the time I joined the act Lee was coming dangerously close to revealing his homosexuality on stage. Wearing one of his most glittering costumes, he'd comment, "This is one of my sport coats. But don't ask me *what* sport." Part of his magic was the ability to make people like him, to accept him no matter how he looked or what he did. His middle-aged, conservative fans lapped up his performances like contented cats drinking cream.

Lee was the only major entertainer I can think of whose entire career depended on live performances. He never understood Streisand's refusal to appear in nightclubs after she became a superstar. He'd done television and made lots of records—he even made a few movies—but he lived for his stage act.

"You can't tell what an audience is thinking when you do television or work in a recording studio," he explained. He might have added that you can't feel their adoration either. The approval of a room full of living, breathing, applauding fans reaffirmed Lee's sense of worth. His psyche demanded a steady diet of that kind of feedback. He loved what he did and felt so serenely confident of his ability as an entertainer that he never exhibited a trace of apprehension or stage fright, even when things went wrong. He was unflappable—the eye of calm in the center of the backstage hurricane.

One night disaster seemed inevitable. After an absence of several years, Lee was debuting a new act at the Riviera Hotel. Everyone associated with him wanted him to have a dynamite opening. A new set, the most expensive and elaborate of Lee's entire career, was being trucked up from Los Angeles, where it had been built to order. But the truck ran into a snowstorm on its way. One hour before the eight o'clock curtain the set had yet to arrive. Pandemonium reigned backstage.

Arnett and Travis paced the floor, more nervous than expectant fathers, wondering how in the world to handle the sudden emergency. When they couldn't delay any longer they went to Lee's dressing room to advise him of the impending disaster. To their amazement, Lee was so relaxed that he'd fallen sound asleep. After being told he had no set and hence, no new act, Lee just smiled and said, "Don't worry. It will all work out." He'd started his career with a piano and not much more, and he wasn't afraid of opening that night the same way. And the audience gave him an enthusiastic reception after being told of the problem.

Once Lee knew a particular line or joke worked, he refused to change it, no matter how much pressure the club owners applied. Some of them complained bitterly that he had been using the same opener for years. "I'll change it when I stop filling rooms," he said.

The act worked, night after night and year after year. The costumes and the props and the sets changed, but the patter grew by accretion, like a pearl. Lee built his own career without the backing of a powerful agent, studio, or network. He knew, better than anyone else, what audiences wanted from him. He listened to people like Ray Arnett or Seymour Heller but, in the final analysis, he made all his own decisions.

Lee told me that he and Heller were often at loggerheads because Heller wanted him to work more than thirty-two weeks a year. Heller, who, by contract, got 10 percent off the top of every dollar Lee earned, would present Lee with a proposed schedule, often one that would have kept Lee working steadily for months. Lee would glance at it, say, "I'll do this, this, and this—forget the rest!" and toss it back.

If Heller argued, Lee just said, "I'm not going to be the richest piano player in the grave."

Lee alone decided when and where he'd perform, which contracts to sign, how much he wanted to be paid. He'd sit through a business meeting while Heller explained the pros and cons of a particular deal. When Heller finished Lee would spell out the terms he was willing to consider. If the terms Lee insisted on didn't bear any relationship to the contract under discussion, that was Heller's problem. Lee didn't negotiate. He knew his worth.

By the early 1970s he was getting a minimum of $150,000 a week. Net dollars were always more important to him than working conditions. He played the same stadium in Hershey, Pennsylvania, three nights every year, despite a dressing room that consisted of a locker room redolent of dirty jocks and gym socks, where the only privacy was supplied by army blankets hanging on a clothesline. Many other stars would have refused to do a show under such conditions. Lee never balked at things like that. But his normally placid demeanor exploded into anger when he was opposed.

He was the boss and his people knew it. Heaven help those who didn't! I remember an associate director on the "Tonight" show who made the mistake of treating Lee like your average, garden-variety celebrity instead of the uncrowned king of the world of live entertainment. First she asked Lee to submit a list of subjects he wanted to discuss with Johnny Carson, and then she told Lee what time she wanted him to show up for the taping. Lee reacted to her somewhat cavalier treatment by failing to submit the required list and by arriving at the studio two hours late!

Another time, when Lee was making an appearance on Dean Martin's show, he flatly refused to participate in a skit that called for him to take a pie in the face. The writers had to be called in to do some frantic rewriting in order to satisfy Lee. He wasn't being deliberately difficult. He simply knew what he wanted. He didn't mind having people laugh *with* him, but he'd be damned if he'd put himself in a position where they'd be laughing *at* him! And he wasn't used to taking no for an answer.

That extended to our relationship and, in particular, to the way many of his employees reacted to me. When, after we'd been together six months, I mentioned that I was still having trouble with some of his staff, Lee called a meeting. "The most *important* person in my life," he told his people, "is Scott! His job is to make me smile, to keep me happy." And I did—for five more years.

12

I wish I'd known Lee before he became a success. Once his stage act had been defined and polished, once he'd achieved international stardom, his drive, energy, and ambition had no way of venting themselves. The man was a bundle of energy with no place to go. He didn't know how to sit still, relax, and smell the roses, even during his vacations. Lee was a workaholic who seemed to lack the inner resources to keep himself amused and happy.

His loyal staff protected him from having to deal with the real world. In fact, Lee lived a sheltered existence, free from almost every worry. He didn't read the papers, was blissfully ignorant and uncaring when it came to politics or events of national concern. He avoided confrontational situations, using Seymour Heller to act for him.

When we went home after a show Lee locked himself away from the outside world. No one came to see us without express prior invitation. His need for privacy bordered on paranoia. Even members of his inner circle, old and trusted friends like Ray Arnett, were restricted to a limited number of invitations to Lee's home each year. After Lee's performances ended and we went home, the world narrowed down to just Lee and me.

Christmas was the sole exception to his demand for total privacy. He began planning and talking about the holiday at the end of October and from then on it took on gigantic proportions. Few children, even those young enough to believe in Santa Claus, looked forward to the holiday more than he did. Although he considered himself to be a religious man the spiritual aspects of the season paled in importance before the opportunity to *spend*. Christmas gave him the perfect opportunity to exercise the power he had over the lives of people who worked for him; to reward or punish each individual by the size of the gifts he gave to each.

By late October he was hard at work making lists of everything he wanted to buy, literally hundreds of items he planned to purchase personally. At one time he'd used the services of a professional shopper and gift wrapper to send out countless gifts to people in the industry. But that deprived him of the fun of doing it himself. The most dedicated shopper would quail in the face of the task Lee set for himself. But he was no ordinary shopper. He transformed shopping into a quasi-religious experience, a reinforcement of his power. He reveled in spending, gloried in it, devoted a large part of his waking time and energy to it.

Early in November of our first year together Lee asked me to pick up a check for $25,000 at Lucille Cunningham's office. The money wasn't intended for gifts—just decorations. When I remarked that it seemed like an enormous amount to spend on tinsel and baubles, Lee didn't blink an eye. He made it clear that the $25,000 would go for decorations and incidentals in the Palm Springs and Vegas houses, not for any of the presents he planned to buy. I knew, firsthand, how generous Lee could be. But nothing I'd experienced in our life together up to that point prepared me for the next few weeks.

Lucille Cunningham and I had already established an antagonistic relationship, so I wasn't surprised when she balked at the size of my request. "You're just like all the rest," she scolded, "out for what you can get. You just tell Lee he can't afford to give you that much money!"

I couldn't help grinning. Lucille knew very well that no one *told* Lee anything. But she felt duty bound to try to control his spending and, since she knew he wouldn't listen to her, she tried to do it through me. "It's not for me," I explained, knowing she probably wouldn't believe me. "Lee wants it for Christmas—and you know how he is, Lucille."

She fussed and fumed but, like the rest of us, Lucille didn't dare say no to a Liberace request. I had the check in my wallet as I drove back home.

Lee gave me carte blanche when it came to readying the houses for the holidays. That money was mine to spend any way I liked as long as I turned Shirley Street and the Cloisters into a Liberace-style fantasy. I wanted to surprise him, to give him the most beautiful holiday house he'd ever seen, so I asked him to move out while I went to work. For anyone else that might have been an inconvenience. But he still owned his previous Vegas home, called the White House for its pristine white exterior and interior. The White House was fully furnished, ready for immediate occupancy. Lee packed a bag and left, leaving me to my job.

He kept an entire truckload of decorations from previous Christmases in storage and I had them delivered. Meanwhile I packed up most of the objets d'art that cluttered the rooms, emptied the casino of all the gambling equipment, and put everything in temporary storage. I felt like one of Santa's helpers who had stumbled across a treasure trove as I began opening the stored crates of ornaments. There were thousands of lights; a dozen reindeer; a life-size nativity scene complete with wise men, shepherds, and a zoo full of animals; fourteen-carat gold lamé cloths to put under everything—a king's ransom of goodies plus all the things I bought. For the next five days I did nothing but unpack and put up decorations, going without sleep a couple of nights to get everything done in time for Lee's scheduled return.

That year we had eighteen huge Christmas trees, more than 350 red and white poinsettias, table decorations, greenery, wreaths—enough candles, lights, and tinsel to stock a department store. Getting everything done required a huge expenditure of effort and unbelievable expense. I spent every one of those $25,000. Looking back, it's hard to imagine doing all that for one fifty-eight-year-old man's pleasure.

It was fun at first but, by the end of the third day of doing nothing but put up decorations, I'd decided that Lee and I were out of our minds. The experience of readying the Vegas house, plus the one in Palm Springs, was pretty far removed from the spirit of "peace on earth, goodwill toward men." It was damn hard work. Putting up one tree is great, especially when children are around to help. But the only children who would see the house that year were Seymour Heller's, and they celebrated Chanukah rather than Christmas. Putting up eighteen trees is pure torture. It's like being forced to eat one rich meal after another, hour after hour, day after day. The senses soon reach saturation and the mind goes into overload.

Lee, however, wouldn't have had it any other way. "Too much of a good thing is wonderful!" Whether it was sex, cars, pianos, costumes, clothes, or Christmas, he lived by those words, overindulging his way through life. When he came back I'd successfully transformed the Vegas house into a winter fairyland. Outside in the glaring Nevada sunshine it might have been 70 degrees, but inside Santa reigned supreme. Lee walked through the rooms, oohing and aahing over everything. "Fabulous!" he exclaimed gleefully, "it looks *fabulous!*"

Heaven help anyone who suggested a booking during the holiday season. Lee would have been outraged. He had too much to do—shopping for dozens of people and wrapping every single gift himself. By the time he finished, hundreds of presents surrounded the bases of the eighteen trees.

As a foster kid I often dreamed of the kind of Christmas I would have liked. But nothing in my wildest fantasies prepared me for Lee's extravaganza. The holiday culminated in a traditional Christmas Eve dinner, followed by the ritual opening of all those gifts. The people Lee worked with, from the stagehands on up, were invited. It was the only time during the year that most of them saw him socially. A few old friends from his early days in show business were invited too. We were a motley crew at best. Joel Strote, Lee's attorney, and Seymour Heller, his manager, didn't strike me as the sort of men who enjoyed mingling with the stage crew.

Lee's family came too. George and his wife, Dora, flew down from Sacramento, Angie and her husband flew in from God knows where, and Frances came from Palm Springs. To my surprise Lee's sister and brother were not accompanied by their children. Nor were Rudy's widow and children present. With the exception of Seymour Heller's wife and children, family groups were conspicuously absent from the party.

That first Christmas George and Angie seemed somewhat estranged. As I watched them treating one another with a formal politeness, I remembered the story Lee had told me about their past problems. Fortunately, Frances seemed unaware of the strain between her children. Despite Lee's constant complaining about his mother, I thought she was a delightful lady—outspoken, full of life, and fun to be with.

The tension between family members was only one of the undercurrents evident when the people closest to Lee gathered in one room. They were always jockeying for position, fighting to get close to him, to get the smile or nod that meant he approved of what they said or did. But, despite the stress and strain, Lee made the party work. He had such a good time that everyone else followed his lead. Gladys had prepared a traditional turkey-and-trimmings dinner for thirty to forty people and it was wonderful. That first Christmas I half expected Lee to sit down at the piano and play carols, even though I'd never seen him play at home before. But he didn't offer and no one asked. Sing-alongs were part of Lee's act—not his holiday traditions.

The two months of preparation had been aimed at the moment when we began opening presents. From beginning to end it took four or five hours. Each gift had to be admired, held up, or passed around. Most of the time Lee's generosity had no parallel. Arnett, Heller, and Bo Ayars, Lee's conductor, received extravagant gifts. Angie, Frances, and Dora received furs and jewelry. More practical gifts like color televisions and VCRs were given to lesser employees. Torn paper and trashed ribbons piled high while Lee presided over the ceremony like a jovial genie.

That first year he gave me two diamond rings, a black mink coat, a white mink jacket, a coyote and leather coat, a sapphire cross, a gold watch wreathed in diamonds, lots of clothes, a Maltese puppy named Georgie, a schnauzer named Precious, and a basset named Lulu. I was overwhelmed, inundated with expensive goodies and barking, untrained dogs. There was no adequate way to thank him. I have been told, by people who were with Lee for decades, that his generosity to me was unparalleled in his relationships with other lovers.

But Gladys, who'd worked even harder than I to make the party a success, got a token gift. I didn't understand Lee's hit-and-miss generosity then, and I don't now. The pattern repeated year after year and Gladys was usually one of the people he shortchanged. One Christmas I put my foot down and insisted that he give her a fur coat and some jewelry that had been slated to go to Angie, who already had more furs and jewels than she could possibly use.

Lee's spending was equally erratic when it came to charity. He was the perfect example of the old saying "Charity begins at home." I don't recall him giving to any nonprofit organizations other than the one he later established himself. The almost obscene scope of our holiday extravaganzas took place in stark contrast to the fact that Lee's generosity rarely reached the genuinely needy. It bothers me now, but that first Christmas, when I was just eighteen, I threw myself into the orgasmic event without a care. Gifts were piled so high in front of me that I couldn't see over them.

That holiday seemed to open a floodgate of spending that never closed during the years we lived together. Lee continued to give me valuable presents, often for no reason at all. "Spoiled rotten you are!" he exclaimed gleefully, "and I love it."

Lee was constantly giving me jewelry and clothes, and enough never seemed to be *enough*. I soon learned to copy his wildly flamboyant style, but no matter how far I went I could never top Lee. I still feel sort of awed embarrassment remembering a typical incident. We'd just closed at Warwick, Rhode Island, and five of us had to catch a plane to New York for a meeting at Radio City Music Hall. Since Lee felt the way I dressed reflected on him, I wore a navy blue suit, a white shirt, and fourteen—count them—fourteen gold chains around my neck. But Lee took one look at me and said, "I think you need one more." He delayed our departure long enough to buy another one which he placed around my neck with immense satisfaction. I looked more like Mr. T than a model for *Gentleman's Quarterly* but Lee was enormously pleased with my appearance.

I've never figured out why he bought me so many things. Of course he could afford it, and he cared for me and wanted me to stay with him, but that doesn't fully explain the hundreds of thousands of dollars he spent on me. Once, when we were out walking, I admired a passing car. A few days later Lee had a custom Camaro delivered to the Hilton. When I asked why he'd purchased the car, he said it was because I'd admired a similar one. Without thinking I told him the car I'd actually been admiring had been a Rolls-Royce. Within a few days a ribbon-wrapped Rolls was waiting for me on the floor of the Hilton Casino. If Lee was trying to buy my love and loyalty, he was wasting his money. I was deeply committed to him because he cared for me as no one ever had before.

13

To my knowledge Lee never invested in stocks or bonds or other aspects of the financial marketplace. He bought, decorated, and sold houses instead with an extravagant disregard for cost. When we began living together he owned the property on Herold Way, the Cloisters in Palm Springs, a condominium in Malibu, and the two houses in Las Vegas. Lee loved to invest in real estate for two reasons. First, property was tangible, something he could see, touch, live in. Real estate, particularly luxurious real estate, held a powerful appeal for the man who'd grown up in that drab, tiny house in West Allis. Second, and perhaps even more important, buying houses gave Lee an excuse for exercising his dual passion for decorating and for spending vast amounts of money.

Every time Lee bought another piece of property, there'd be unhappy rumbles from his business manager, Jay Troulman, and his accountant, Lucille Cunningham. But he shrugged aside all their well-meant advice. "If I'd have listened to people like that," he said, "instead of following my instincts, I'd have gone broke years ago."

After bringing Gladys to Vegas, Lee put the Herold Way house on the market and sold it for $1.2 million. He gleefully confessed to having paid $80,000 for the house when he bought it years before. With the large amount of capital thus freed, he wasted no time buying a house in Tahoe. We were appearing in Sparks, Nevada, at John Ascuaga's Nugget (an annual booking) when the deal closed. Every night after the last show we'd pile into the car at two in the morning. I'd play chauffeur and drive the sixty miles back to the house while Lee slept. Once we got home we'd both catch a few hours sleep, getting up before noon to go shopping.

Lee wanted to finish the decorating before his six-week Sparks engagement ended. Spending money was a fever in his blood while he worked on the house, a desire even more compelling than sexual hunger. He just couldn't stop buying things. After four weeks on that schedule, I gave up—totally exhausted—and told Lee he'd have to shop by himself. He was shocked at my refusal to continue with what he considered a *fun* project. Not even appearing onstage energized him the way spending money did. He was forty years my senior but he had incredible energy.

He often hired decorators, only to fire them because he enjoyed doing the job himself. Lee knew what he wanted— excess, excess, excess. After becoming successful enough to indulge himself, he jumped from project to project. Our years together marked the zenith of his spending. His next major purchase was a five-story building on Beverly Boulevard in Beverly Hills. He renovated and refurbished the first four floors of offices, installing huge aquariums to add the luxurious Liberace touch. The parking lot was repaved and glamorized by the addition of large trees in planters. But Lee hadn't bought the building because he wanted to rent out office space. He intended to turn the entire fifth floor of the building into a penthouse for his personal use. And he had only a four-week hiatus from work to do it.

We spent the entire time shopping, spending more than $100,000 a week for the entire four weeks in a mind-blowing demonstration of his personal wealth. The fifth floor, which had been a disaster, was transformed into a magnificent private hideaway. The sad thing is that Lee rarely spent time in his various homes after he finished decorating them. We occupied the Tahoe house only when he worked there, three to six weeks a year. The penthouse was a terrific place but Lee treated it more like a hotel suite than a home, rarely living in it for more than a few days at a time.

Lee also purchased four condominiums in Vegas, just for the sheer pleasure of decorating them. Later, in *The Wonderful Private World of Liberace,* he told his readers that he'd been commissioned to decorate those condominiums as models. Like many of the statements he made in the book, it wasn't so. Lee bought those condos and decorated them for the fun of it. Of all the properties purchased during our relationship, his favorite was my little house in Vegas. We spent a great deal of our free time there.

When Lee and I had been together for a year he said he wanted me to start investing my money. For Lee, that meant buying a house. At the time I couldn't afford much. I bought a little tract house at 933 Larrimore Street in Las Vegas—six rooms crammed into fourteen hundred square feet—and Lee helped me make the down payment in exchange for my giving him a third mortgage on the property. I made all the mortgage payments from day one, but that proved to be a drop in the bucket compared to what we actually spent on the house. Lee insisted on redoing it in his customary opulent style. I paid $58,000 for the property but we ran up a $40,000 bill for structural changes, $25,000 on landscaping (which included using cranes to lift huge palm trees over the roof so they could be planted by the new Jacuzzi in the back), and $40,000 on furniture. When the job was done Lee loved that house more than any of his mansions and took more satisfaction in it.

When we were in Vegas we'd go back to his mansion after a show, pick up the meal that Gladys had prepared for us and head straight for my place. No one, other than Gladys, knew where we were and she was the only person in Lee's entourage to have my phone number.

Lee seemed to enjoy playing hooky from the demands of his fame. In my home, he played at being a hausfrau. He cooked and cleaned and fussed over me like a bride. My best, happiest memories of him come from the time we spent there. Pushing a vacuum, dusting furniture, fixing lasagna, Lee and I pretended to be equals. But the pretense never lasted long. Sitting in the Jacuzzi as the sun came up, he'd say, "I wonder what the poor people are doing?"

The longer Lee and I were together, the more I understood his sense of isolation, his need to have a confidant and full-time companion. From Heller to Frances to Angie to George, he felt that everyone's motives were suspect because everyone had something to gain from their association with him. For years his wealth had sequestered him, made him suspicious of even the best-intentioned offers of friendship. Before long I found myself caught in the same trap. Suddenly I was Mr. Popularity, pursued by my own relatives and even some of my former foster families. They all wanted to meet Liberace, be invited to his homes, go for a ride in his limos, hit him up for a loan or a job. One afternoon one of my sisters telephoned and in the course of our regrettable conversation, suggested that I get Lee to buy her a diamond ring. Little did she realize that Lee, who monitored many of my phone calls, was listening on another phone. After I said good-bye he came racing into the room. "Now you know what I've been going through for thirty years," he said triumphantly. "See! You can't trust anyone. They all want something!"

Lee exercised complete control over my life. He told me what to wear, where to go, who to see once I got there. There were times when he acted more like a father than a lover. Once, when we were in Fort Lauderdale, he had the hotel manager move us to a new suite because he couldn't see the beach where I planned to sit in the sun for an hour that afternoon. Another time, Seymour Heller offered me a ride from Las Vegas to Los Angeles so I could take care of some personal business. When Lee heard about the offer he came unglued. He didn't want me out of his sight for a minute. We did everything together. Fortunately it was fun most of the time.

There were times when I resented and rebelled against his smothering affection. When I felt low, shopping usually cheered me up. Although Lee didn't raise the salary I reported to the IRS, he was always giving me cash, a thousand dollars or more every week. I used some of it to buy him surprise presents. His favorite surprise was getting a new dog. By the time Lee and I parted, we had accumulated a grand total of twenty-six.

At first we had a mixed pack of large and small breeds. But one horrible day they got into a fight and some of the big ones actually killed a couple of the smaller ones. Lee almost fainted. We'd never anticipated anything like that happening. After that we kept small dogs only, poodles, mixed breeds. Lee's favorites—seven or eight of them—slept with us every night. And Lee never complained when one of them had an accident, even though there were days when the house, and especially our bedroom, smelled like a kennel.

One of Lee's favorite projects, established before I appeared on the scene, was the foundation he'd created to give college scholarships to needy music students. The foundation, and St. Francis Hospital, where Lee had made his miraculous recovery from uremic poisoning, were Lee's only charities. He did one benefit show a year for St. Francis but the scholarships were a continual project.

Lee chose which colleges to endow and the colleges chose the recipients of the scholarships. Lee, who always liked to champion underdogs, didn't give his money to well-known music schools like Juilliard. Instead he chose small schools where he knew his contributions would reach students whose lives could be altered dramatically by the gift.

The foundation was an ambitious project and could have been a considerable drain on Lee's resources. But he never permitted the situation to get out of hand. In Lee's fortieth-anniversary souvenir pamphlet, he boasted of the foundation having given $50,000 to schools across the country. Since Lee *was* the foundation, and he personally earned millions of dollars a year, that wasn't much to brag about. I think he would have been appalled if someone had suggested that he could afford to be as generous as Paul Newman, who gives all profits from his food company to charity.

Although Lee didn't plan to equal Newman's phenomenal generosity, Lee was deeply interested in the foundation. He wanted it to be self-sustaining, so it could go on providing scholarships whether he continued to work or not. Early in our association he got a brainstorm. He'd create a nonprofit organization to open and run a Liberace museum, and the funds generated by the museum could support the scholarships. At the time, the only other entertainer to have his own museum was Roy Rogers. Lee's plan sounded audacious but, knowing the loyalty of his fans, I didn't doubt it would succeed.

To those faithful followers who saw him perform year after year, Lee had an appeal that transcended ordinary star power. His charismatic quality can better be compared to the television evangelists than to his own show-business peers. Lee was the Jim Bakker of the nightclub circuit, with his own devoted group of fans. They gave, gave, gave—and Lee spent, spent, spent.

He took full advantage of their devotion by setting up Liberace concession booths wherever he appeared. The booths sold his albums, autographed pictures, Liberace piano books, jewelry, pillboxes—anything Lee and Seymour Heller thought the public would buy. If no one else in the entourage was available to man those booths, Heller would preside over them himself.

Lee used to call the income produced by his concessions "funny money." The only funny thing about it was that fans so willingly shelled out so much cash for those trinkets and that Lee told me he never reported the income, although he boasted of banking up to $20,000 a week in "funny money."

If people would stand in line to buy Liberace souvenirs, he saw no reason why they wouldn't stand in line to tour a museum where his most treasured possessions would be on display. He'd had a small prototype museum in the house on Herold Way but the neighbors complained about its being a commercial enterprise and, in any case, Herold Way was too out of the way to attract a steady flow of tourists. Vegas, on the other hand, doesn't attract much else. Lee decided it would be the ideal place to create a monument to his own career.

A six-month gestation period passed from the idea's conception to the actual opening of the museum. During that time Lee and I devoted every free minute to turning his dream into a reality. Scotty Moore, Lee's real estate agent, found a suitable property on Tropicana Avenue: an old shopping center that held about fifteen small stores. The architecture was pseudo-Spanish, the size right, the location excellent.

Lee paid in the neighborhood of three million dollars for the property. That sounds like a fortune but, since Lee was donating the land and building to his own nonprofit organization, he'd given himself a terrific tax writeoff. Another half million went to renovating the space. In addition to the museum, it would also hold Liberace's antique store—to be replaced in a few years by Liberace's restaurant, the Tivoli Gardens—and a Liberace gift shop that sold the same things as the concession booths.

When the renovation was well under way, Lee and I went through all his houses systematically, picking items to put in the museum. First, of course, there were costumes he could no longer wear. Then there were paste replicas of his enormously valuable jewelry collection. Over the years the jewelry, like the pianos and the cars, had become Liberace trademarks. I can still hear him saying, when asked how he could play the piano with so many huge rings on his fingers, "Very well indeed!"

Many of Lee's cars, including the piano-key station wagon, the patriotically custom-painted red, white, and blue Rolls, the Auburn he used in the act, his first limousine, his '57 T-Bird, would also be on display in the museum. Many of the things Lee had been unable to part with, though they crowded even his vast homes, were slated for the museum. We stayed up three nights straight just going through the Vegas house, and the task had to be repeated in all the other homes. Rare antiques were slated for permanent exhibit as well as some of Lee's more unusual pianos. He had one that had reputedly belonged to Chopin and another that was supposed to have been played by Liszt, which Lee said gave him goose bumps to play. The value of each of the items was duly noted and added to the figure to be written off Lee's taxes.

Lee was in seventh heaven all the while. He'd managed to have his cake and eat it too. First, his ego got a maximum stroking by the creation of a museum devoted to him. Second, he was actually going to help a lot of gifted kids. Third, he'd finally found a place for all the stuff he'd been accumulating. Fourth, as the vans began taking major items from each of his properties, the gaping holes they left created a need to buy new things. Fifth—but far from last—Lee had the tax shelter to end all tax shelters.

He asked George and his wife, Dora, to move down from Sacramento to manage the museum. George seemed like the natural choice. Despite their past problems, he was family and

Lee, with his Polish-Italian roots, still believed in family even if he complained that they were an occasional pain in the neck. George had also been very closely associated with Lee's early career and many fans still asked Lee, "How's your brother George?" Now, when someone asked, Lee could tell them to visit George in the museum.

Managing the museum was a golden opportunity for George, who was getting old for life on the road. He accepted the offer and Lee bought him a condominium in Vegas. The Liberace family was getting closer, geographically if not emotionally. Although the brothers didn't socialize often, I had a chance to get to know George better. He was a gentle, kind, considerate, unassuming man—the kind of man Lee might have been if he hadn't been so driven.

The museum proved to be a smashing success from the day its doors opened. It generated an enormous income for those scholarships. At the end of the first year Lee told me it had earned a million dollars. Although I suspect he greatly exaggerated the actual figure, no one had expected the museum to do as well as it had. From Lee's standpoint, the unexpectedly large profit should rightly have been his to control, to spend as he saw fit. Of course he would have given a portion of the money to his foundation—but so much? Did he need to be that generous?

It began to eat away at him, the thought of all that money he'd allowed to slip out of his control. Even the tax shelter he'd created failed to cheer him. He made up his mind to dismantle the nonprofit organization so he could take advantage of the money-making machine he'd created. But this time Lee wasn't slated to have his way. He told me that disbanding the nonprofit organization proved impossible. Today, Lee's foundation appears to be a major beneficiary of a will that Lee signed just a few weeks prior to his death. In the future, dozens of students will complete their arts education because Lee miscalculated the depth and breadth of his fans' loving support.

14

When I first moved in with Lee, I was both ignorant and relatively innocent. I didn't understand his lifestyle, his need for secrecy. I'd grown up thinking being a homosexual was neither good nor bad, but simply a fact of life. By contrast, Lee was determined to keep his sexual preferences from his fans. It was only after living in the entertainment community, and learning something of the history of gay performers, that I began to understand Lee. To understand Lee's life, and therefore my own, the reader has to know what I learned.

First of all, the entertainment industry is like no other business in the world. People who work in movies or on television are often extraordinarily attractive, creative, and talented. They are also the most foul-mouthed group I know. Imagine a business where new projects are commonly referred to as a "piece of shit," and you'll get the idea.

In Hollywood's early days, before the Hays censorship office helped the community clean up its act, the town was known as a sinkhole, fueled as much by booze, sex, and drugs as by talent. The industry has struggled to overcome that reputation ever since, with varying degrees of success. Despite the best efforts of studios, agents, and most stars, memorable scandals have been easier to create than memorable films—and many of those scandals have involved stories of homosexuality. In a homophobic society like ours being gay is often traumatic, but being secretly gay while burdened with public celebrity can be sheer hell. It was a hell Lee knew all too well. And he was just one of a long line of celebrity "closet gays."

In 1922 the first of Hollywood's homosexual scandals, the murder of handsome, successful William Desmond Taylor, rocked the film industry. The noted director's corpse was discovered by his houseboy, Henry Peavey, when Peavey came to work early one morning. Taylor had been shot to death in his Alvarado Street bungalow. Peavey, a very discreet employee, chose to call Paramount Studios, where Taylor worked, before he notified the police. The executives at Paramount had good reason to be concerned. They knew that Taylor was gay, a fact they didn't want to have revealed in a murder trial. George Hopkins, a set director and Paramount employee who was an intimate of Taylor's, made a hurried trip to the Taylor bungalow, where he was met by people from the studio. Working in haste, they picked up photographs and letters that might have helped the police to identify the murderer, simply because the letters and photographs attested to Taylor's homosexuality. Apparently the studio thought an unsolved murder would cause less of a scandal than public revelations about the dead man's sexual preference.

Like Liberace, most of Taylor's closest associates (men such as Peavey and Hopkins) were homosexual, part of Taylor's network of friends who supplied him with a steady stream of young male bedmates. Like Liberace, Taylor also used titles such as houseboy or chauffeur for his companions. The loyal Peavey had been jailed once for soliciting boys intended for his master's bed. But when the studio applied political pressure on the newspapers and the police, these scandalous events were successfully hidden from the general public. Taylor's murder was destined to go unsolved for decades. (To my surprise, after being told this story, I learned that the mystery of Taylor's death was solved in a book called *A Cast of Killers*.)

If the happenings of the twenties sound bizarre, consider the actions of Liberace's people who helped Lee to conceal his homosexuality from his fans. While Lee lay dying of AIDS, his personal physician announced to the press and public that Lee's illness resulted from a watermelon diet and anemia. To this day his people cling to that story. When the end came the same loyal doctor wrote a death certificate listing, in layman's terms, heart failure as the cause of Lee's death.

Their protection continues to obscure the truth, even now. On May 12, 1987, as reported in the *Orange County Register*, the estate of Liberace filed a claim for unspecified damages against Riverside County, California, alleging that Liberace's reputation had been damaged when the county coroner gave a nationally televised press conference at which he revealed the presence of the AIDS virus in Lee's body. Apparently Joel Strote, Lee's attorney, is still trying to suppress information about the true cause of Lee's death. I can only assume Strote is misguided by loyalty.

The homophobic society that breeds extreme behavior on the part of gays and their friends has existed for a long time. Lee once spoke of Oscar Wilde, as clever a playwright as ever wrote in the English language. Wilde, who lived in the second half of the nineteenth century, had a flair for drawing attention to himself, a passion for flamboyant dress that bears comparison to Lee's. The public tolerated Wilde's eccentricities until he flaunted his affair with a male member of the aristocracy. Then Wilde was put on trial for breaking the law that prohibited homosexual relationships. Today, in America, many states still have such prejudiced and unfair laws on their books. After a stormy, highly publicized court case Wilde was sentenced to two years at hard labor. The Wilde trial took place in the same London where Lee defended his own reputation in a court of law. And, in Lee's opinion, the fifty years that had passed since Wilde's trial had done nothing to soften or temper public dislike of homosexuals.

I hope that someday one of Hollywood's super-macho studs, at the peak of his career, will have the courage to step forward and say, "I'm gay." If his career survives the controversy that is sure to follow, the world and the entertainment industry will be forever changed for the better. But until that *someday* comes men like Lee will pay a heavy price for a sexual preference they cannot control.

Rock Hudson, who conveyed a superb sense of masculine self-assurance, would have been the ideal candidate for such a heroic deed. But Hudson was determined, up until a few weeks before his death, to keep his homosexuality a secret. Like Lee, Hudson dated starlets in public while romancing a string of male companions in private. He even married, at the age of thirty-five, when it seemed one of the tabloids was on the brink of publishing a story about his homosexuality. As his life drew to a close he took a possible chance with the health of his friends rather than admit to having contracted AIDS.

The entertainment industry has always offered mixed blessing to homosexuals. On the one hand gay men and lesbians are drawn to the freedom of artistic expression they find onstage or in film. But those who achieve success feel forced to walk a tightrope of secrecy to prevent public revelations about their sexuality from ruining their careers.

Lee and I used to speculate about the percentage of homosexuals in the business. We estimated that 20 to 25 percent of stage, screen, television, and nightclub performers are either gay or bisexual. That figure can safely be doubled when the estimate includes the people who work behind the scenes. From the lowliest extra on up through the ranks of dancers, chorus boys, musicians, makeup artists, set designers and decorators, writers, directors, and producers, the entertainment industry is home to gays, lesbians, and bisexuals. And even those who claim to be 100 percent heterosexual have often experimented, just for kicks.

But the still powerful studios and their coconspirators, the radio and television networks, manage to protect the people they have under contract. Those homosexuals who are not under contract are often less fortunate. Lee sometimes wondered if all the speculation and rumors about his sexuality kept him from having the number of television specials that his obvious success and popularity should have commanded. In view of the morals clauses that used to be part of network and studio contracts, he may have been right. The entertainment industry is a two-faced business. It thrives on scandal and yet its members fear being penalized if their private lives explode into the tabloids. Lee knew all too well the risks he ran and the price he paid for his choice of bedmates.

No less an international star than Burt Reynolds saw his career take a nosedive because of completely unfounded rumors that he had AIDS. The only way Reynolds could quiet these stories was to simply outlive their credibility. But his career has yet to recover its former luster.

People who are greedy to hear and believe the very worst about public figures will get all the genuine bad news they can handle in the future. AIDS is, by any measure, a new plague. And no one—gay or heterosexual—is immune to its scourge. To date as of this writing, aside from Hudson and Liberace, two major clothing designers, one U.S. congressman, and a major Broadway choreographer/director have died from AIDS. The *Hollywood Reporter*'s obituary column is full of the names of behind-the-scenes workers who have died from the disease. I hate to hear people speculate on who might be the next victim.

Despite the dangers and risks, the modern entertainment industry has a history of employing gay leading men. Friends in the business have told me of Ramon Novarro, a darkly handsome Latin lover of the silent screen, who was a well-known member of the homosexual community. Like William Desmond Taylor, Novarro was murdered. Rumor has it that his killer was an angry one-night stand. When the actor's body was discovered, an art deco sculpture had been obscenely inserted in his rectum. In view of the ugly deaths of men such as Taylor and Novarro and the open persecution of gays (the gay bashing that is a weekly occurrence in Hollywood and other cities), it's not surprising that gay male stars go to great lengths to conceal their sexual identity.

Like Liberace, many of the past's superstars have been, are currently being exposed as gay or bisexual. It's ironic that Lee, who so feared having his sexuality discovered, enjoyed gossiping about the sexuality of other stars. Errol Flynn, one of the most macho swashbucklers in the history of film, a womanizer who faced a scandalous paternity suit in his lifetime, was described as a bisexual in a recent book about him. Tyrone Power, who often competed with Flynn for roles, competes with him now for revelations about a supposedly bisexual lifestyle. There is even talk that Clark Gable, one of the most masculine men in film history, may have had a homosexual affair early in his career.

The industry has also attracted a number of lesbians, some of whom went on to become famous household names. Mae West, one of filmland's most sensuous female stars under contract at Paramount in the 1930s, was plagued by rumors and gossip relating to her sexuality. At one time, there were stories that she was actually a man.

West, who built her career by flouting accepted standards, was one of Lee's few close celebrity friends. In public and in private she surrounded herself with good-looking men. What the public has never known is that most of those handsome males were well-known members of the gay community. Why West preferred the constant company of gay men has never been explained.

The sexual identity of a handsome young man she helped up the ladder of stardom is also a topic of current speculation. It was to Cary Grant, in one of his first screen appearances, that West uttered the memorable line, "Come up and see me sometime." Revelations in a recently published tabloid expose Grant as a supposed bisexual who had affairs with multimillionaire Howard Hughes as well as fellow actor and long-term roommate Randolph Scott.

Grant was a Liberace fan who came to Lee's shows once or twice a year and always came backstage to visit. On one of these occasions I saw Grant with a good-looking, obviously gay male companion. But there was nothing in their behavior to indicate that they were lovers. As for Grant, the secrets of his sexual identity were buried with him. If he was gay, he certainly had good reason to conceal it.

Stage actress and star Tallulah Bankhead was another Paramount star in the thirties. She was that rare, rogue personality who broke all the rules and seemed to get away with it. One lady reporter, who relentlessly pressed Bankhead for sexually incriminating statements, found to her dismay that the actress could claw when cornered.

After a particularly nasty interview session Bankhead insisted on escorting the frustrated reporter to the elevator. When the doors whooshed open, in the full hearing of an elevator crowded with onlookers, she said in her unforgettable husky tones,

"Thank you so much for coming over, daahling. But I *never* kiss on the first date." That biting wit served the actress well. But gossip about her sexual preference may well have cost her any hope of getting the coveted female role of the thirties—that of Scarlett O'Hara—for which Bankhead was quickly rejected.

Greta Garbo remains one of the greatest stars produced by MGM's efficient star machine—and one of the biggest enigmas. The personal discovery of Louis B. Mayer, the classically beautiful Garbo was the daughter of a Swedish laborer. Despite her heavily accented English, her career successfully spanned silent movies and talkies. Garbo left a brilliant career behind when she left Hollywood for good. In *Grand Hotel* she uttered her most famous line, "I want to be alone." Garbo, who never married, seemed to spend her life alone. But there were constant rumors about her romantic relationships and the Hollywood gay community always regarded her as one of their own.

A recently published book written by Joan Crawford's daughter disclosed the bisexual behavior of the screen goddess. The star is described in *Mommy Dearest*—written by her daughter Christina—as having a clandestine affair with one of their household maids. Fortunately, the story wasn't made public during Crawford's long reign as a leading lady.

A famous English actor suffered a similar fate in the 1950s when Hollywood gossips questioned his sexuality. Michael Wilding was a distinguished-looking, mild-mannered man who had been married to Elizabeth Taylor and seemed to inherit the kind of roles earlier played by Walter Pidgeon. But rumors about Wilding's alleged affair with another actor cooled studio ardor for his services. Coincidentally, Pidgeon is also regarded by the gay community as one of their own.

Perhaps the most successful homosexual in the history of Hollywood was a small, ambitious brunette whose short, straight bangs and horn-rimmed glasses became well-known trademarks. Edith Head was a costume designer with a genius for self-promotion that helped her win eight Oscars. Head's lesbianism was so well known that for years Hollywood insiders joked, "Head gives good gowns."

The list of names of homosexuals and bisexuals who have found a home in the entertainment industry could go on and on.

But those whose careers aren't the focus of public attention seldom suffer the trauma that plagues homosexual stars. George Hopkins, the set decorator who was given the task of getting rid of evidence in the William Desmond Taylor case, went on to work in the industry for many years, winning three Oscars along the way. Noted hairdressers and makeup artists were also able to enjoy long and lucrative employment, despite being gay, free of the fears that plagued the stars.

The 1950s are memorable for the number of gays who achieved stardom or became celebrities. Aside from Liberace and Rock Hudson, Sal Mineo and Montgomery Clift made their mark during that decade. But their brief careers ended tragically. Clift took his own life while Mineo was murdered in West Hollywood in a manner reminiscent of the Novarro killing.

Jim Nabors of "Gomer Pyle" fame is another performer who climbed the precarious path to success during the fifties. But his brief fling with stardom didn't survive the rumors of his marriage to Rock Hudson, rumors that had been started by a group of gay men who, as a joke, sent out invitations to the event. One of the phony invitations fell into the hands of a columnist and from there the story took wing. Hudson was already a superstar, so handsome that women everywhere adored him, while Nabors was a funny-looking guy whose comic talent didn't seem half so humorous in the light of his supposed sexual preference. After stories of the so-called wedding circulated nationwide, Nabors's ratings dropped and "Gomer Pyle" was canceled. But Hudson, protected by a powerful studio and his equally powerful appearance of unassailable masculinity, survived the mess.

According to Lee, throughout the fifties Henry Willson was a prime mover on the gay scene as well as one of the most successful agents in the business, a man with an uncanny knack for picking future stars. Willson was also famous for giving his protégés catchy names like Rock or Tab or Troy. Many of the young men he represented were gay, but Hollywood gossip suggests that those who were not suffered because of their association with Willson. Of all Willson's promising young clients, Hudson alone achieved lasting success.

Lee was terribly aware of the history of gay entertainers and of the danger he faced if his private life should be exposed to intense public scrutiny. Keeping the secret placed an almost intolerable burden on him and on our relationship. It explained his need for seclusion, his almost paranoid desire to hold the entire world at arm's length. I understood what motivated Lee's behavior, but understanding it didn't make it easier to live with. At fifty-eight and fifty-nine, Lee had done all the partying he wanted to do. He was more than content to stay home when he wasn't working. But staying home all the time doesn't cut it for an eighteen- or nineteen-year-old.

When I complained Lee called me a kvetch and said he intended to keep his private life private. The only time his reserve broke down was when he drank and then it was "Nellie Bar the Door," anything goes. Lee was the world's happiest, most amorous drunk. Since he almost always drank too much when we flew home at the end of a tour, I often found myself having to fend off his advances on the plane. We'd made a pact that I would treat him like a superstar in public but that was a little hard to do when he got high and started patting my leg and calling me "Boober" in front of some wide-eyed stewardess. It was embarrassing and humiliating. I'm not ashamed of being gay, but I hated being groped in public. At the same time, I couldn't help laughing. We must have been quite a sight.

15

When we first met I mistakenly assumed that Lee's enormous luxurious homes would be the sites of fabulous parties. He even boasted that the Cloisters' huge garages, with their finished walls and floors, could easily be converted to a ballroom. But after that first brunch where Black and I were his guests, Lee didn't entertain again for months, not until the Christmas dinner. Our socializing consisted of talking to salespeople in the various stores we frequented. When Lee wasn't working he hated getting dressed and often spent the entire day unshaven, lounging around the house in an old terry-cloth robe so worn it was full of holes. Since he demanded my constant companionship, I felt completely cut off from the rest of the world.

Lee preferred living like a hermit. We might as well have been stranded on another planet instead of living just blocks from the glittering, twenty-four-hour-a-day world that is Vegas. It didn't make sense. Lee knew everyone, all the celebrities, and everyone knew him. Other stars frequently came to see his show, yet he rarely returned the courtesy. Away from the stage the two of us existed in a vacuum. All that isolation drove me up a wall.

I'm gregarious by nature and the lack of social contact made me very unhappy. Lee and I operated by different rules. He felt compelled to keep secrets, to isolate himself from society; I'd spent my short lifetime reaching out to other people, looking for friends to replace the family I didn't have. No matter how much I cared for and about Lee, I couldn't accept the solitude of his lifestyle.

Since Lee wouldn't let me go out without him I began asking, then nagging him to go out with me. At first Lee felt hurt. "Any other boy in the world would be thrilled to be in your position," he said. "No matter how much I give you, you're never satisfied." At first, Lee responded to my desire for some kind of social life by buying more presents for me in the mistaken belief that happiness, mine or anyone else's, could be bought and paid for.

Lee couldn't have been more wrong. I didn't want another fur coat or another car; I just wanted to go out at night, talk to people, and have some fun. It took a while but Lee finally relented and agreed to go see an occasional show when he wasn't working. On one of our early outings we went to see Jim Nabors and Dom De Luise, who were appearing at the Riviera. During the show De Luise had the maître d' deliver a note to our table. It was an invitation to join him for dinner after the performance. Lee barely knew De Luise so the invitation came as a surprise, but I urged Lee to accept.

When the show ended we drove to De Luise's rented house. Even from the outside, the noise level told me a party was in full swing.

De Luise was in rare form that night, a funny, genial host who kept plying us with drinks. When we finally went to the dinner table Lee was seated at one end, next to a very good-looking guy, and De Luise asked me to sit next to him. That proved to be one of the most uncomfortable meals I've ever had. I kept on watching Lee at the other end of the table, wondering if he was attracted to his handsome companion and feeling a little jealous.

Larry Gatlin appeared in Las Vegas once or twice a year and Lee and I met him a number of times. One night, when one of my female cousins happened to be in town for a visit, Gatlin called and asked me if I'd like to come up to a party in his hotel suite. Lee wasn't around and, thinking I'd really impress my cousin, I accepted at once. Fifteen minutes later we stood outside of the suite as I knocked on the door.

"Who's there?" Gatlin called out.

"It's me, Scott," I replied. The door flew open and there stood Gatlin. Over his shoulder I could see a room full of men and women, half clothed and partying like crazy. I think I said something stupid like, "Thanks but no thanks," before pulling my cousin away from the incredible scene. I must say, she was *impressed*! To this day I have no idea why Gatlin called me that particular night unless it was because he assumed that my being gay ensured my participation in such a party.

Years later, I felt sorry after I was told that Gatlin had been going through a difficult period in his life; that drugs and liquor had been in control of his behavior. I soon learned that it's a common show-business problem. Sudden stardom can be hard to handle. Once people can afford anything they want, they tend to think they can *do* anything they want. Their confusion is aggravated by the fact that fans tend to put them up on pedestals. A few celebrities begin to believe that they can do no wrong. And so they start experimenting with sex, booze, drugs— whatever turns them on.

Fortunately, most stars manage to keep their feet firmly planted on the ground. One of the nicest, and a regular on the Vegas scene, is the flamboyant performer Charo. Despite her image as a sexy Latin bombshell, Charo is a real earth mother. Her accent is real, her figure mind-blowing; the rest of her off-the-wall image is carefully cultivated. In private, Charo loves animals, children, cooking, taking care of her family. The first time she came to the house she got down on the floor while our dogs tumbled around her, and there she remained for the rest of her visit.

Charo, who is happily married to a man as nice as she, became a regular guest in our home and never failed to attend my birthday parties. Her first husband, Xavier Cugat, also visited with us when he was in town. Lee and Cugat were close in age and enjoyed reminiscing about their early struggles. Unfortunately, their talks about a past I wasn't old enough to remember always reminded me of the age difference separating Lee and me.

Although it took a considerable shove to get Lee out of the house and into a social setting, he seemed to have a good time once a party was under way. But he always worked at being Liberace when we were out. He never relaxed, not even at informal gatherings with other celebrities. I think that's why I liked Charo so much; she was a very genuine person.

Debbie Reynolds is another down-to-earth, warm, funny lady. She often worked the same hotel as Lee and we came to know her quite well. Although Debbie was several years my senior, she had a vitality and sense of the ridiculous that made her seem more like my peer. Reynolds had used Seymour Heller as her agent in the past and I could feel the ice in the air whenever the two of them were in the same room. According to Lee, she'd had a disagreement with Heller, and the one thing she didn't like about working in the same hotel with Lee was the fact that it meant seeing so much of Heller.

One night after the show she flew into Lee's dressing room in a rage over a recent encounter with Heller, insisting that Lee tell Heller to stay away from her. Debbie's open emotion was refreshing compared to the behind-the-scenes maneuvering Lee employed when he was upset or angry with one of his people.

I wasn't particularly fond of Heller myself, so I sympathized with her. I didn't blame her for being upset. Poor Lee felt torn between the two of them. Since Heller was present at almost all of Lee's performances, there seemed to be no way to keep Debbie from running into him. Lee, who avoided confrontations, had no intention of discussing Debbie's problems with Heller. But he liked Debbie and didn't want to lose her friendship. So he decided to play peacemaker and invited Debbie to come home with us to talk things over.

The Shirley Street house was lit like a Christmas tree when we arrived and looking its glittering best. As Debbie walked through the mammoth front doors she threw her arms wide, turned to us and said, "I used to live like this before my husbands took all my money."

From what she told us of her unhappy marriages, she had every reason to be bitter. But Debbie is the kind of person who will always triumph over adversity by laughing at it. That night, after her initial anger cooled, she kicked off her shoes, sat on the kitchen floor, and drank wine with us until sunrise. It turned out to be one of those rare evenings when Lee forgot about being Liberace the legend and allowed himself to be Lee the man.

Tony Orlando was another of my favorite Vegas entertainers. Tony was battling drug addiction in those days, a problem he has since conquered. He also suffered from manic-depression, a disease I knew firsthand from my experiences with my mother. Nevertheless, we spent most of our time laughing. Everything seemed funny when we were together. After seeing Tony's act a couple of times I told him he looked very pale onstage. Since his mental and physical problems were well known, the last thing he wanted to do was look sick onstage. It made a terrible impression on his audiences. Tony asked me to come over to his house one night to show him how I did my stage makeup. We laughed through the entire process, but Tony reluctantly agreed that the pancake base and blusher I used on him improved his appearance. When I began putting on eyeliner he got hysterical and made me stop.

"That's where I draw *the line*," he said. Tony made no bones about being heterosexual but that didn't stop us from being friends. Lee was jealous at first, as he would have been jealous of anyone I was close to. But he came to enjoy having Tony and his wife, Elaine, visit the house. They were our guests one Christmas, along with their son. Having a little kid around made that a special holiday. Show business is full of nice people like Tony, Debbie, and Charo and, once Lee got used to the idea, he began to enjoy mingling with them on a social basis.

One night when we were working the Sahara Tahoe and living at the Tahoe house, we had two of our most memorable dinner guests. Ray Arnett, who'd been a Broadway hoofer in his youth, had a wide show-business acquaintanceship. Shirley MacLaine had worked with Ray and, when she brought her act to Tahoe, Ray suggested that Lee invite her to dinner. Bella Abzug, who was visiting Shirley, came too. There were six of us at the table that night: Lee, Bella, Ray, me, Shirley, and her current lover.

Since Shirley chose not to name her lover in her book *Dancing in the Light*, I'll just say he was a well-known director, born and raised in Russia but successful in the States too. As happened so often before, people we barely knew—like Shirley and her lover—seemed to have no qualms about being up front about their relationship with us. The two of them were obviously crazy about each other. In fact, they could hardly keep their hands off one another.

At first Shirley and Ray dominated the conversation, reminiscing about their early days on Broadway. But then, as it was bound to with Bella at the table, the talk turned to politics. Bella was an outspoken activist, an articulate liberal devoted to causes like women's liberation. She and Shirley expressed their views enthusiastically, talking on and on while Lee got quieter and quieter—until his eyes began to glaze. I remember that Shirley and Bella were quite agitated about a recent incident involving police brutality, but by then I was so afraid that Lee might actually fall asleep at the table that I don't recall where or when the police brutality was supposed to have taken place.

Politics, world affairs, local problems, meant nothing to Lee. At the time there was a musicians' strike at the Sahara Tahoe that he had completely ignored. I don't think Lee would have noticed it unless a picketing musician had thrown himself under our car. Lee was amazed when Bella refused to be his guest at our show because she didn't want to cross a picket line. Bella and her concerns were totally alien to him, a part of the wider world that Lee chose to ignore. But later he enjoyed telling other celebrities about having his "good friend," the fabulous Shirley MacLaine, as his dinner guest.

Loretta Lynn, the legendary star of country music, was the exact opposite of outspoken MacLaine and Abzug. Lynn was quiet, soft-spoken. In person she seemed like a shadow of the vibrant performer she became onstage. I first met Lynn in Gary, Indiana, while we were doing a talk show, and we hit it off immediately. From then on Loretta and I made a point of getting together whenever we happened to be in the same city. I liked her a lot, but she concealed a great deal of unhappiness beneath her public façade.

Shortly after the release of the hit film *Coal Miner's Daughter*, based on Loretta's life, she returned to Las Vegas, where she was to appear at the Riviera. The night I planned to see her show she came down with "Vegas throat" (caused by working in the smoke-filled showrooms) and had to cancel her appearance. But she invited me up to her suite for a visit. Her secretary let me in and showed me to the bedroom, where Loretta lay propped up on a pile of pillows. We talked for a while and then I brought up the film, for which Sissy Spacek was to win an Academy Award.

"Don't believe everything you see in that picture," Loretta told me.

When I asked her what she meant she put a finger over her mouth, hushing me. "I don't want anyone to hear what we're saying," she whispered, although the only other person in the suite was her secretary. "You see," she added, "I can't trust anyone. There are spies everywhere." Loretta looked and sounded like a frightened women as she talked about her life, her *real* life rather than the fable dished up on the screen. According to Loretta, she had an unhappy marriage and was actually afraid of her husband. She sounded very sad as she ended our conversation by saying, "I'm an old-fashioned country girl and I believe a woman should stay with her man—until she dies."

At one time or other every major star seemed to show up in Vegas. Lee introduced me to another living legend, Lena Horne, when she appeared there. If ever Lee looked up to a woman, it was Lena. "She's been through so much adversity and prejudice—and triumphed over it all," he said, "that every time I see her up on stage wowing an audience, I get goose bumps!"

Before we went to see her perform he bought her a magnificent Japanese kimono as a welcoming gift. Then he was so anxious to see her that he decided to visit her dressing room before the first show. That's considered a taboo in Vegas; most stars don't want to be forced into sociability when they're getting ready to go onstage.

Not Lena. When Lee knocked on her dressing-room door she opened it herself. I barely recognized her without makeup. "What the hell are you two guys doing here?" she asked, smiling warmly as she invited us into the room. She seemed serenely unconcerned about her appearance, adding, "You all come in here and keep me company and you can see how gorgeous I'm going to make myself."

I couldn't have been more surprised. The stars I knew, including Lee, had too much ego to let anyone watch them apply their stage makeup. Lena made a terrific impression on me. She was a real sweetheart. Lee's gift delighted her. "I just love things like this," she said, promising to wear the kimono during her performance that night.

Lena began to get ready for the show, chatting easily with Lee and me the entire time. I remember thinking how lucky I was to have met her. And I owed it all to Lee. He'd given me everything except friends my own age—a gap that would soon be filled by Andrea McArdle and Michael Jackson.

16

I always thought of Gladys Luckie as more than a housekeeper. She became a friend, a good one. On the days when Lee and I were home, I used to enjoy watching television with her in her room. Her comments on the programs were down-to-earth and often perceptive. It was in Gladys's room, one evening in 1979, that I first saw Andrea McArdle on a variety show. Gladys and I were immediately impressed by the young Broadway star. The minute I heard McArdle sing I knew she'd be right for Lee's act. Fortunately, he was nearby and I managed to get him to Gladys's room while McArdle was still on the screen. "Lee, with that big voice, she'd be perfect for Vegas," I said enthusiastically.

He was putting together a new act and that meant finding new talent. I was eager to help. A few weeks earlier I'd watched the Radio City Music Hall Rockettes and suggested they might be a terrific addition to the new act. There'd been talk about disbanding the Rockettes and their many outraged fans had risen up in their defense. The Rockettes, famous for their high-kicking precision dance numbers, were an American institution, like apple pie and baseball. Lee had instantly agreed with the idea of making them a part of his Vegas show. By employing the

Rockettes he'd have a chance to help preserve the act and, at the same time, benefit from all the publicity generated by their proposed disbanding. Lee couldn't resist the combination.

"Terrific idea, Scott," he complimented me. "We'll bring New York to Las Vegas." It was the kind of "high concept" he favored.

After he heard McArdle sing, his response was equally enthusiastic. "I think we should audition her as soon as possible," he said. Seymour Heller was given the job of making all the arrangements.

Lee worked with young people whenever he could, in part because audiences were always sympathetic and predisposed to like young performers. In the early days he'd done his chopsticks routine with children from the audience. After the act got too big and elaborate to keep that up, Lee started to feature young performers instead. McArdle would be part of a long line that included such acts as the Little Angels of Korea, the Young Americans, the teenage, banjo-playing Scottie Plumber, and the amazing, under-ten-year-old acrobat David Lee. They were a formidably talented group of young people and very popular with the Vegas audiences. In the future he would pluck his next protégé from their midst.

McArdle flew to Vegas for her audition and she was even more impressive onstage—in person—than she'd been on television. She'd learned her craft on Broadway, where she was an enormous hit in the long-running *Annie* before growing too old for the part. Those months in a hit show had given her tremendous confidence, a sure knowledge of stagecraft, the ability to project. Her big voice easily filled the cavernous Hilton showroom and barely needed amplification.

She seemed completely at ease both onstage and in the adult world of Vegas. Lee took to her immediately; but, at first, I had reservations about Miss McArdle. She was too self-assured to suit me. Confident, almost arrogant, she came on like a superstar instead of the sixteen-year-old girl she was. In the case of many performers, that cocky attitude covers the real fear that success and fame are all too fleeting, that next year someone else will be the public's darling. Many big stars suffer painful feelings of inferiority and prolonged bouts of self-doubt. McArdle was not among that group. She was good and she knew it. But I soon discovered that a very sweet girl hid behind the confident performer, a girl who was as normal a sixteen-year-old as anyone could have been under the circumstances.

Andrea McArdle appeared with Liberace, in both our Vegas and Tahoe shows, for the next year and a half. No longer a child and not yet a woman, she was at an awkward age when it came to being cast in movies or stage plays—but she was the perfect foil for Lee's act. Over the months Andrea and I became good friends. Lee was very fond of her and got along well with her mother, who proved to be a watchful guardian and chaperone. They spent quite a bit of time at our homes in both Vegas and Tahoe.

Andrea and I were thrown together constantly. I guess it was inevitable that we'd get crushes on each other. But Lee and Mrs. McArdle seemed oblivious of our growing attraction. I guess Andrea's mother thought she was safe with me because I was involved with Lee. As for Lee, he was so thoroughly homosexual that it simply never occurred to him that I might be attracted to a girl, not even one as lively, talented, and dynamic as Andrea.

Occasionally, we managed to escape our elders' watchful eyes and have a wonderful time together. One crazy, fun-filled day Andrea and I, along with a few of the Young Americans (a singing group composed of talented youngsters), Kristy McNichol, and Lee's niece, Ina Liberace, decided to go skiing in the nearby mountains. At the time, Kristy was starring in "Family," a successful television series. She and Ina, the daughter of Liberace's deceased brother Rudolph, were good friends.

I was chosen as the chauffeur for our skiing expedition. Everyone piled into my van early in the morning, laughing and carrying on like kids playing hooky. Andrea sat next to me; Kristy, Ina, and the Young Americans filled up the rest of the seats. We talked and listened to music, our kind of music—rock 'n' roll—all the way up the mountain. It was a rare chance for me to feel and act as young as I really was. When we reached our destination and tumbled from the van a wild snowball fight broke out.

As it turned out, everyone could ski but me. I watched, thoroughly impressed, as Kristy, Andrea, and the rest schussed down the slopes, while I could barely stand upright on the flats. But it didn't matter how many times I fell or how much my friends laughed at me. I felt free for the first time in years. That one carefree day made me realize that no matter how much Lee meant to me, I was constantly on guard around him, measuring every word, every gesture, for its potential effect on him. I lived and worked not in an adult world, but in a completely middle-aged one—with a man who could swiftly change from indulgent parent to ardent lover to outraged tyrant.

In the mountains, on that one day, I was able to forget everything except enjoying myself. But the real world intruded soon enough. My van broke down on the way home and I had to call Lee's driver to pick us up in the limousine. The group's laughter was a great deal more subdued as we returned to Vegas and our adult responsibilities.

Stardom can be very hard on youngsters. Andrea, who'd cut her eyeteeth in the theater, handled it very well. The next performer I met seemed oppressed and burdened by a career that had begun during his childhood and grown to mammoth proportions. By the time Michael Jackson called the house one day in 1979, I'd grown used to stars appearing on our doorstep. But no young adult could be blasé about talking to Michael Jackson.

Strangely enough, Michael Jackson and I had attended the same elementary school for a brief time. I attended Gardner Elementary during a period in my life when I was being shuffled from one foster home to another so fast that I don't recall the name of the family I lived with. But I do remember Michael, who was already famous, in the class just ahead of mine. I'd been his fan ever since.

When Michael telephoned he told Lee how much he'd always admired his work. Lee was very flattered and invited Michael out to the house for lunch. He told Gladys to fix something special and she decided Kentucky fried chicken would be an appropriate dish to serve rock 'n' roll's superstar. Michael wasn't in the house more than a few minutes when he said, "Oh, by the way, I guess I should have warned you that I'm a vegetarian."

I wish I'd had a camera because the look on Lee's face was priceless as the delicious aroma of fried chicken wafted throughout the house. He jumped up and fled to the kitchen, leaving me to entertain a somewhat startled Michael. When Lee returned a few minutes later he had regained control, both over the menu and himself. Then, playing the good host, he offered Michael a drink.

"Do you have any fruit juice?" Michael asked. "I never touch liquor."

Lee's eyebrows rose. A rock 'n' roll star who didn't eat meat or drink liquor? At that point I don't think he could have been more surprised if Michael had announced that he was a practicing celibate—which we later learned he was, because his religion forbade premarital sex. Lee, who gloried in all the pleasures of the flesh—eating, drinking, and lots of sex—thought Michael was a very weird guy. But from then on Lee enjoyed referring to Michael, who was one of the biggest superstars in the world, as "my very dear friend." In reality, it was Michael and I who became dear friends.

At the time of his first visit, Michael was redoing his home in Encino, so Lee gave him the grand tour of the Shirley Street house. At last the two entertainers had found an interest in common: decorating. Michael fell in love with some bronzes we had and wanted to know where he could get them. Like many of Lee's most treasured possessions, Lee loved those bronzes as much for the bargain price he'd paid for them as for their beauty. They'd come from a place in Los Angeles on Robertson Boulevard, a shop where Lee and I were well known and got a substantial discount.

"You'll get them cheaper if I send Scott with you to buy them," he told Michael. I was always annoyed when Lee, who made millions of dollars a year, went to great lengths to save a few hundred. But I never learned if saving a buck was important to Michael too. That afternoon, Lee was so determined to do Michael a favor that he arranged to have me drive into L.A., pick up Michael, and buy the bronzes with a check written by Liberace so that Michael would get the biggest possible break on the price. It seemed like a tremendously elaborate scheme to save a few hundred dollars, since Michael undoubtedly considered that kind of money to be petty change. But I didn't object because it meant I would have a chance to get to know Michael better.

It wasn't easy. He turned out to be the shyest person I'd ever met. I had a hard time reconciling the soft-spoken, almost withdrawn young man wearing his habitual faded blue jeans, baseball cap, and two-dollar T-shirt with the gyrating, sequin-gloved performer the world knew. Offstage, Michael was often forced to hide within a protective cocoon created by his security people. His undistinguished dress and dark glasses were a poor disguise that failed to fool the avid Jackson fans who pursued him everywhere. He never went anywhere without Bill Bray, his head of security, by his side. But it would have taken a full-time army to give Michael the kind of protection he needed. He bore the burden of his fame quietly, but anyone could see that it was almost intolerable.

Lee and I saw Michael and his sister Janet off and on over the next few months. When they were in Vegas they came over to our house to swim because they couldn't relax around a pool in public, not even at a posh Vegas hotel, without being mobbed. But it was in London, where Lee was making another appearance at the Palladium, that I came to know Michael well.

Before every show, Lee had me "walk the house" to get an idea of the size and mood of the audience. One afternoon, as I walked the Palladium's aisles before a matinee, I saw a single darker face in the midst of all those pale, English complexions. The owner of the face jumped up from his front-row center seat and, calling my name, waved at me frantically. It was Michael!

Neither Lee nor I had had any idea that he was in town, let alone that he would be in the audience that day. Michael, who had come to England to do an album with Paul McCartney, was feeling lonely and anxious to see a familiar face from home. For the next few weeks we saw each other every day. We talked about music, show business, his passion for cars—which I shared—as well as his love for animals. Just a year apart in age, we seemed to have a great deal in common.

To my surprise, Lee didn't object to the many hours I spent away from him in Michael's company. I think even he was in awe of Michael's giant fame. I still spent my evenings with Lee, but during the daylight hours, Michael and I roamed through London. I went to the recording studio to watch him work and, when he was finished, we went to all the usual tourist places.

At Buckingham Palace we decided to try to shatter the impressively uniformed guard's perfect composure. Those guards are supposed to stand in front of the gates, hour after hour, without giving any indication that they are aware of the steady stream of tourists who come to stare at them and take their pictures. Considering his fame, Michael didn't think he'd have any trouble getting their attention. When they failed to respond to his overtures he approached one of the guards and put a pound note on the end of his bayonet. The guard didn't even blink. So Michael put another pound note on the bayonet and stepped back to see if he would get any reaction. Again, the guard didn't blink. Then, with increasingly frenzied glee, Michael put more and more pound notes on the bayonet until it was completely covered with money. I was laughing so hard by then that I almost fell down. Several hundred pounds later I managed to tell the guard that all Michael wanted was to have his picture taken with him. Although it is against all the regulations the guard finally obliged, stripping his bayonet of the hundreds of pounds he'd collected at the same time.

The rest of the day was equally crazy. Thinking he'd be safe from being mobbed in laid-back London, Michael had gone out with just one bodyguard, Bill Bray. We'd toured Buckingham Palace and gone to the Tower of London to see the crown jewels without having any trouble. But our luck came to an end when we got to Piccadilly Circus, where we planned to do a little shopping. Michael was recognized and a few fans began to follow us.

At first it wasn't too bad. They jostled and pressed close, but Bray and I managed to keep our bodies between Michael and the young people who seemed to want nothing more in this world than to touch him. But then the teenagers were joined by a noisy, aggressive group of punk rockers, and all hell broke loose. We were desperately trying to flag down a cab as the crowd grew larger and more unruly. By then all three of us were running and it was obvious Michael would be in real danger if we didn't get him away quickly.

It was a terrifying experience. The fans, who'd seemed merely curious minutes before, were now pursuing us frantically, breathing down our necks and shouting at us. Bray finally got a cab and we jumped in and pulled away, with desperate teenagers still clinging to the door handles. Three cab changes later, we'd finally shaken the last of our determined pursuers.

After that ordeal I better understood Michael's fear of people. His fame cut him off from the world as surely as if he'd been marooned on a desert island. I'd been somewhat envious of his position, but the events in Piccadilly Circus convinced me that I wouldn't change places with Michael for anything in the world. For me, it had been a once-in-a-lifetime experience. But he faced danger from that kind of manic adoration every time he went out. Our final experience in London proved to be equally unpleasant and served to ring down the curtain on our friendship.

Lee, Michael, and I had been invited to dine at Lord Montague's palatial mansion on the outskirts of London. Neither Michael nor I knew the nobleman but Lee had met him several times and we had all heard stories about him and his opulent lifestyle. As we drove out of London all three of us were excited over the prospect of seeing Lord Montague's internationally famous collection of cars, which now boasted the addition of the great Harrah collection.

His home proved to be an incredible display of inherited wealth and privilege, far surpassing even the largest mansions in the United States. Lee practically drooled over the antiques, all of them authentic pieces that had been in the Montague family for generations, rather than bargains carefully purchased at flea markets the way so many of Lee's had been. Lee's taste may not have been flawless, but he knew the real thing when he saw it.

Six of us sat down to eat in the main dining hall that night at a table that would have comfortably seated forty. What the room lacked in intimacy, it more than made up for in grandeur. I was relieved when the main course turned out to be fish. Thank God, I thought to myself, Michael will be able to eat.

That night Lord Montague's companion was a young woman—the blonde flashy, trashy type that manages to insinuate herself into high places because of her looks rather than breeding or brains. We were all seated at one end of the table, our voices echoing in the huge room, when the young woman gave Michael and me a long, appraising look.

"Tell me," she said in an accent that sounded more like Piccadilly than Mayfair, "do you and Michael get it on? You're always together."

Lee and Montague pretended not to hear her. They continued talking about cars, but I could feel myself turning beet red from embarrassment and rage. Next to me, Michael shifted uncomfortably in his chair. Somehow, I knew our friendship would be ruined from then on. Rumors about Michael's publicly acknowledged virginity and apparent lack of masculinity were already circulating. He couldn't take a chance on being branded as gay because of his association with gay men, no matter how innocent that association might be.

I saw him a few more times after we returned to the States, but the carefree quality of our friendship had been irreparably damaged by that one thoughtless remark.

17

Lee said that age is just a state of mind. "You're as old as you feel," he'd boast. And he felt very good as he began his sixth decade. When he was involved in one of his pet projects, decorating a new house, buying a car, planning a new act, playing with a new puppy, his enthusiasm and energy were absolutely contagious. He had a childlike quality that his advancing years didn't diminish.

Less charming was his ability to shut out everything that displeased him. He mercilessly erased unpleasant realities from the slate of his life. If they *had* to be dealt with, he delegated that responsibility to Seymour Heller. One of the unpleasant realities Lee chose to ignore was the fact that he was growing older. "You make me feel young," he'd say, as if he could pay me no higher compliment. Feeling young had a very high priority in his life. Looking young was equally important.

One night, after taping the "Tonight" show, Lee unexpectedly found himself face to face with the reality of how much he'd aged. He hadn't done television or movie work in a while, hadn't subjected himself to the camera's harsh scrutiny. That night we were in the Carson show green room, watching the tape of Lee's interview. Lee had done his own makeup prior to the taping, doing it exactly the way he'd been doing it for years. But the lighting on the Carson show was not flattering. Lee looked lousy on screen, old and tired—every sag, every age line exposed by the camera's inquiring eye. I could see that it really bothered him even before he turned to me, whispering, "I look like hell. Why hasn't anyone told me how *old* I look?"

I couldn't answer. Lee was Lee, so close and familiar to me that I'd long since stopped seeing him objectively.

From then on he became obsessed with his appearance and the need to repair the age lines and bags under his eyes. If Lee could have arranged for a face-lift the next day, I'm sure he would have. I'd grown so used to seeing him morning, noon, and night, in stage makeup or scrubbed clean after a shower, that I'd paid no attention to the deepening grooves on either side of his mouth or the fact that his eyelids sagged. Sure, he was jowly, but Lee had ballooned up to 250 pounds during the years we'd been together. I weighed 240 myself—the result of Lee's and Gladys's good cooking and very little exercise. It had happened so gradually that I hadn't paid attention to the way either of us looked.

After the Carson show, Lee couldn't think about anything else. "I need a complete face-lift," he moaned, after seeing himself on tape.

Lee had already been through at least one face-lift. But he chose not to use the doctor who had operated on him in the past. He couldn't seek out a new plastic surgeon the way anyone else would, by talking to a number of physicians and choosing the best doctors from a list of candidates. He didn't want anyone to know that he was about to go under the knife. It had to be kept secret so that his public image of vitality and agelessness, so important to what he called "the legend of Liberace," would remain untarnished.

I didn't agree with the need for secrecy, but I knew Lee too well to argue with him. One of my best friends, a man who made all of Lee's wigs, had recently had a successful face-lift and I told Lee about it. He knew the man well and invited him to visit us in Vegas so he could see the results of the plastic surgery for himself. When my friend arrived at the house, Lee and I were impressed. The man had seemingly shed a decade or more in the months since we'd last seen him. Lee decided he need search no further for a doctor. The man who'd operated so masterly on our friend would be asked to do the surgery on Lee as well.

Jack Startz was a Beverly Hills plastic surgeon with an impressive address. Lee wasted no time calling and asking Startz to fly out to Las Vegas to discuss what Lee wanted done. My first impression of Startz wasn't very good. He was a poor advertisement for his profession. His face had so many silicone implants that he looked more like a Kewpie doll than a living, breathing human. He also seemed very fond of booze. Lee had offered him a drink and the doctor had taken several in quick succession. Tragically, in view of what happened as a result of my association with Startz, I failed to see that as a potential sign of danger. We were all drinking that afternoon and the fact that Startz had more than anyone else didn't seem worth worrying about. I would later learn that the doctor was addicted to both alcohol and drugs but, by then, it would be too late.

Lee told Startz that he wanted to be rid of his drooping eyelids, the heavy lines on either side of his mouth, the spider web of wrinkles that were slowly turning his face into a road map. Startz checked him over and then recommended a complete facelift, with silicone implants to prevent the return of the lines around Lee's mouth. He also recommended that the face-lift be followed in a few days by a deep skin peel. The doctor assured Lee that the results would be fabulous. "You'll look younger than Scott here."

Lee was thrilled by the prospect. Startz had promised that the operation would remove all the lines, sags, and wrinkles that spoiled his appearance. In addition, he said the deep skin peel would give Lee the skin of a thirty-year-old. It sounded like a dream come true. Startz did quite a selling job. He'd found Lee's weakness—his fear of aging—and played on it. Both of us were impressed by the man's self-assurance, his firm conviction that he could give Lee whatever he wanted.

When they finished discussing the surgery, Lee suddenly said, "I want to talk to you about doing some surgery on Scott."

It really took me by surprise. No way, at the age of twenty, did I need a face-lift. Nor had Lee ever voiced any unhappiness with my appearance, other than to suggest I try to lose a little weight—a suggestion I intended to take very seriously. I'd always been Lee's "blond Adonis"—his words, not mine. So the mention of plastic surgery for me came as a complete surprise.

Startz turned and began to study my face. "What would you like me to do with Scott?" he asked.

Lee jumped up and ran into another room, returning with a large oil portrait of himself. "I want you to make Scott look like this," he said, propping the painting up in front of the doctor. I was so stunned that I didn't say a word. Meanwhile, Startz looked at the painting and then back at me, studying my face and then the painting with intense concentration. It was a full-face portrait of Lee and one of his favorite paintings of himself, clearly showing his prominent cheekbones, slightly arched nose, and pointy chin in the most flattering way. If anything, it also emphasized the differences between my face and his. Even the most casual observer could see that Lee had a heart-shaped face while mine was round. We had completely different bone structure.

"Yes," Startz said into the room's silence, "I think I can do what you want. He'll need to have a nose job, and I'll have to restructure his cheekbones and chin with silicone, but it's possible. I can make Scott look a lot like you, if that's what you want."

The two of them were discussing me as if I wasn't in the room, but it didn't occur to me to object. I'd never been crazy about the way I looked and felt flattered, touched, by Lee's desire to have me look like him. I didn't think he was handsome in the conventional sense, but he had an interesting face, whereas I always thought mine looked as if it had been made from Play-Doh. If Dr. Startz could give me a clearly defined bone structure like Lee's, I wasn't going to object. In any case, I knew it would do no good. Once Lee made up his mind to do something it would take an act of Congress to prevent him from doing it. If he wanted me to have a new face I could either go along with it or get out of his life. The choice was that simple. No one defied Lee—not ever!

Startz advised Lee that he would need to plan on spending two months at home after his face-lift. But he also promised that Lee would return to work looking like a new, much younger man. They agreed to schedule the surgery in six months when Lee had a large block of time free. The whole thing had to be planned like a covert military operation because of Lee's desire to keep the entire procedure a secret from his fans.

Lee and I never discussed the surgery he wanted me to have, either before or after the doctor's visit. I knew how pointless any discussion would have been, even if I had any real objections. The truth is it never occurred to me to oppose Lee. My future was completely in his hands, as it had been from the day I accepted his offer of employment. Lee was much more than my lover, from the beginning. If he wanted me to spend the rest of my life with a new face, one that looked like his, that's exactly what I would do.

The six months between our first meeting with Startz and the scheduled surgery passed quickly. Lee was busy, working very hard, and we were happy together. Occasionally I'd be swept by waves of restlessness, concern about where my life was headed. I'd remember my dreams of being a vet and working with animals, look at the life I had instead—however rich and luxurious—and wind up feeling disgusted with myself. My youthful dreams and plans hadn't included being a gigolo for men. When I tried to discuss my doubts and concerns about my future and where I was headed with Lee, he'd act withdrawn and hostile.

"Don't be a goddamn kvetch," he'd say. "There are thousands of boys who'd love to be in your position!"

Of course, he was right. Sections of Vegas and L.A. teemed with hungry-looking, runaway kids—guys who would do anything to make a connection with someone like Lee. The entertainment industry was full of struggling young performers who would give their souls to be in my place. Lee's eyes were constantly straying toward such men and he often flirted with them outrageously. I felt threatened and insecure every time he behaved that way and we would wind up having a fight about it. Then Lee would sulk. It wasn't easy to live with him, day in and day out, but I could no longer imagine my life without him.

My family and friends all told me how lucky I was. One former foster mother even said she'd never speak to me again if I screwed things up by alienating Lee in any way. There are far worse things, she told me, than being Liberace's shadow. The Scott Thorson I liked, who had initiative—the kid who'd found his own foster home with the Brummets so he'd have a home for his own animals, that kid was getting lost as I followed wherever Lee led. Life in the fast lane had changed me, and not necessarily for the better.

I'd become dependent, unable to make a major decision on my own, and admittedly spoiled. I'd met Lee at a time when other young men my age were getting out on their own. But Lee didn't want me to take responsibility for myself. He wanted unquestioning loyalty and slavish devotion, and he was willing to pay for it. All I had to do was admire something once and it was mine. I had a closet full of clothes and furs, a jewel case loaded with rings and necklaces, a Rolls-Royce, a Camaro, a van, a Cadillac, an Auburn, my three dogs, a couple of horses, and my own house; and, in addition, my salary had been increased. I lived in the average man's idea of paradise. But, in the end, I'd pay a high price for the years I spent loving Lee.

On the day before Lee's surgery I drove him into Los Angeles and we stayed at the penthouse overnight. The plan was for him to have his operations first because he wanted me to help with his postoperative care. Once he was on the road to full recovery it would be my turn. The actual operations would be done in Dr. Startz's own operating room, adjacent to his offices on San Vicente Boulevard. Lee wanted his wig to remain on during the procedure and had relented only when Startz said he'd have to resign from the case if Lee forced him to operate under those circumstances. Strangely enough, Lee seemed more apprehensive about the fact that the doctor and his assistants would see his bald head than he was about going under the knife.

Although I wasn't crazy about the idea, Lee insisted I be by his side during the entire procedure. Thank God, the doctor had vetoed that idea too. No way did I want to see Lee cut up, his skin sliced and stitched. However, I was permitted to stay with him while he was prepped and sedated. I even accompanied him into the operating room. Not until he was completely unconscious did I leave his side.

In those days, Lee didn't like me to have large blocks of free time. He wanted to know where I was and who I was with every minute. Since he'd been told he'd be unconscious for hours he'd arranged to have Seymour Heller keep me company. According to Lee's previous instructions, I drove to Seymour Heller's house

141

to wait out the operation. My relationship with Heller had improved from the early days when he'd been obviously antagonistic toward me. Heller had grudgingly accepted my place in Lee's life and now treated me with a forced friendliness that was endurable if not enjoyable. All Lee's people had started treating me that way after he'd insisted on it.

I picked Heller up and we went to a delicatessen to eat before returning to Startz's offices. Lee's operation took seven hours, the longest seven hours of my life. By the time the doctor came into the waiting room to tell us that everything had gone well, I was convinced Lee had died. Although Startz explained that he'd just finished stitching Lee and hadn't yet bandaged him, I demanded to see him.

The doctor agreed and escorted me to the room where Lee lay on the operating table, his bruised face covered with blood and tiny black sutures, looking like an accident victim. "Oh, my God," I said, turning to Startz, "are you sure he's all right?"

"Positive," Startz replied. "Why don't you talk to him."

I walked up to Lee and bent over him. "Booberloober," I said, using my most loving nickname for him, "are you okay?"

"Yeah, Boober, I'm fine," he responded, sounding relatively normal despite the way he looked.

My stomach churned and I could feel that deli sandwich threatening to come up as I squeezed Lee's hand, trying to smile reassuringly. Hell; if this was what plastic surgery did to you, I didn't want any part of it. Lee looked like he'd been hit by a truck. Once I'd made certain he was still alive, nothing in the world could have persuaded me to stay in that room. I totally freaked out. Lee looked like a piece of bloody meat. I just couldn't imagine that anything good would result from that surgery.

Startz had rented a fully furnished apartment for us under an assumed name, part of the covert operation. A couple of hours later Lee had been bandaged and was ready to leave. The doctor had canceled all his other appointments in order to be with us during Lee's postoperation recovery period. As I pushed Lee's wheelchair across the busy street, I couldn't help thinking that Lee needn't have been so worried about secrecy. He looked like he'd dressed up to play the invisible man, with his entire face swathed in bandages and just tiny slits to permit him to see, breathe, and eat. At that moment he looked more like a mummy in a cheap horror film than a world-renowned entertainer. Five days after the face-lift we wheeled Lee back across the street to Startz's office for the deep skin peel.

Once again, Lee emerged swathed in mummylike bandages. After spending a final night in the apartment we drove to Palm Springs, still accompanied by the doctor. Lee was in great pain but, even worse, those bandages made him feel horribly claustrophobic. In fact, they almost drove him out of his mind. Startz had the solution to the problem. He kept on shooting Lee full of Demerol. Meanwhile, he revealed his plan for my transformation.

First, he wanted me to slim down and put me on what he euphemistically called the California Diet. The diet consisted of a prescribed course of oral medication that would completely kill my desire to eat. Startz guaranteed a loss of at least fifteen pounds in the four weeks preceding my own surgery. I didn't know it at the time, but the medications he gave me included pharmaceutical cocaine, amphetamines, and Quaalude. Before then my drug intake had been limited to the nicotine in cigarettes, the alcohol in liquor, and an occasional aspirin. Unlike many kids of my generation, I'd never turned on to drugs. I'd tried marijuana and hadn't enjoyed it, and I'd tried Lee's amyl nitrite and hadn't liked that any better.

But I had no hesitation about taking the pills that Startz prescribed, never realizing that a medical doctor would be handing out highly addictive drugs as if they were no more than placebos. My first day on the California Diet, I was in a total fog, off in a little world of my own. I had a mild case of the shakes and a massive case of unreality. It seemed like a powerful effect from what I'd been told were just diet pills. As promised, I had no appetite at all. Startz spent the next few weeks drinking heavily, feeding me pills, and shooting Lee full of Demerol. The only sane person in the house, aside from the help, was Angie. She had volunteered to come and stay throughout Lee's recuperation.

During the years, a few alterations had occurred in the way Lee treated his family. When I discovered that he preferred to put them up at hotels rather than let them stay with him during their visits to Vegas or Palm Springs, I'd become very upset. "For God's sake, Lee," I had argued, "they're your *family*. How can you ask them to stay in a hotel when we have so much room?"

I don't know if I changed Lee's way of thinking or if he was simply growing older and mellower, but he now permitted members of his family to stay in his homes. The tensions that kept the family divided for so many years had slowly dissipated. I was genuinely fond of Angie, George, and Mama Liberace, and delighted to see the Liberaces draw closer together. It made me very happy to think that I'd played some small part in making that happen. So Angie was with us during Lee's recovery. She would play an even greater role in his life in the years to come.

A few days after we arrived at the Cloisters Lee's dressings were removed. He looked awful. His face was badly swollen, the skin mottled with black-and-blue marks and covered with scabs from the peel. Lee refused to have anyone see him in that condition. His closest associates, Heller and Arnett, were barred from the house. For the next few weeks, while Lee healed, he and I and Angie and Startz were holed up in the Cloisters. Seeing how bad Lee looked sure gave me second thoughts about my own impending operation. But, in view of the fact that Lee had his heart set on having me transformed into a Liberace look-alike, it was too late to back out.

The Hollywood Diet was working. Although I couldn't eat at all, Startz encouraged me to drink with him. We partied all day. I was in a complete fog from the time I took my first pill in the morning until I fell into bed at night. The old Scott Thorson was beginning to emerge from the blubber I'd acquired over the last few years. I could see the growing approval in Lee's eyes every time he looked at me, and that encouraged me to continue with the regimen. Ultimately, I dropped more than the promised fifteen pounds in the weeks between his surgery and mine. My goal was to lose sixty.

Meanwhile, Lee felt and looked better every day. First, the swelling and discoloration receded. Then one day he came out of the shower and all his scabs had washed away. His skin looked pink, shiny, new and unlined. Lee could easily be taken for a man in his late forties rather than a sixty-year-old. As far as he was concerned, Startz had worked a miracle. For the first time in years Lee looked as good as he felt. He wasted no time ordering several new wigs, with dark hair instead of gray, to match his youthful appearance. He began seeing people again and everyone complimented him on the way he looked.

One unfortunate problem resulted from his operation. Lee's eyes had changed, in appearance and function. He couldn't close his lids completely. They remained slitted open even when he struggled to keep them shut. At night, when he slept, his eyes would open slowly and that's the way they would stay. Even worse, they had always been one of his nicest features but now they had a slightly sinister appearance. Lee feared that Startz had cut out too much skin while attempting to remove all the sags and bags around Lee's eyes. But Startz assured Lee the problem was temporary. He prescribed drops to keep Lee's eyes from drying out at night and told him time would take care of the rest.

The drops made Lee more comfortable, and he stopped worrying. But it was odd to wake up at night and see him in bed beside me sleeping soundly, his eyes half open—odd and a little frightening. My face would soon be entrusted to the man who had done that to Lee. I'd get up in the morning determined to tell Lee that I'd changed my mind, that I didn't want to have an operation, but then I'd take that first pill and nothing seemed important afterward. I was cocooned in a dream world, all cares erased by the drugs—suspended in an exotic, pleasurable dreamland. While using drugs I didn't think of myself as a prisoner in paradise or as Lee's shadow. In fact, I didn't think at all.

When it was my turn to be driven to the doctor's office in Beverly Hills I went happily, like the proverbial lamb to the slaughter.

18

My surgery took place about a month after Lee's. The day before, we drove back to Beverly Hills and checked into a luxurious suite at L'Hermitage, a posh hotel that caters to the superrich. That night we went out for a fabulous dinner, Lee's first public appearance after his operation, to celebrate the way he now looked. He was equally excited about the prospect of my becoming a Liberace look-alike.

"Ooh, Scott," he said, bubbling with enthusiasm, "I can't wait to see what Startz is going to do with you."

The next morning he accompanied me to the doctor's now familiar San Vicente office. My surgery was slated to be a two-step procedure. First, Startz would work on my cheekbones and chin, using silicone implants to reshape my round face into a reasonable facsimile of Lee's heart-shaped one. Five days later I'd have the more traumatic procedure, a nose job to narrow and lengthen my nose. At the last minute, in a brief rebellious moment, I asserted myself enough to ask Startz to give me a dimple in my chin—even though Lee didn't have one. After all, it was my face!

The first surgery didn't take more than an hour and a half. Lee stayed with me until the anesthetic took effect. When I woke up a few hours later my face, with its silicone implants, looked and felt like it belonged to someone else. Late that afternoon I returned to the hotel, where my steady intake of drugs, all prescribed by Startz, ensured I would feel no pain before the second surgery. The drugs were so powerful that I floated through the next few days, as compliant as an aging lapdog. Then back we went to Startz's office for my nose job.

When it was over I had difficulty breathing and felt horrible in general. The doctor assured me that this was perfectly normal and gave me some new pills to alleviate my anxiety. The first time I saw myself in a mirror, all swollen and black-and-blue with horribly bloodshot eyes, I felt certain I'd made the mistake of my life. We stayed in the hotel for another week and Startz casually doled out pain pills and his own special brand of diet pills every day, as if they were nothing more than aspirin instead of a dangerous combination of highly addictive drugs. Several years would pass before I learned from some of his other patients that Startz was responsible for addicting many of his own clients. Before, during, and after my surgery, I took my medications without asking a single question about what they were and why he'd prescribed them. I floated in and out of reality until it was time to leave for an engagement at John Ascuaga's Nugget in Sparks, Nevada.

All Lee's acquaintances had been told that he had been on vacation. Lee was elated at the prospect of appearing onstage for the first time in two months with his new youthful look. He couldn't wait to get John Ascuaga's reaction.

His old friend didn't disappoint him. "You look terrific!" Ascuaga told Lee. "The rest must have been just what you needed."

The Nugget's stage couldn't accommodate the Rolls or the other elaborate props that were part of Lee's Vegas act. Basically, it was just Lee, the piano, the candelabra, and a series of costume changes. Although the Nugget's audiences didn't know anything about Lee's surgery, they reacted enthusiastically to his buoyant, vigorous performances. I didn't have to appear with him, a good thing considering how lousy I looked. While I continued recuperating, Lee was at the top of his form off- and onstage: exuberant, full of energy and enthusiasm. His new look had given him a new lease on life. Birthdays didn't count;

looking young was the same as being young! He couldn't have been happier.

By the time the Sparks booking drew to a close, the swelling and discoloration that marred my face had faded. A totally new Scott Thorson was emerging from the postoperative trauma. As Startz had promised, I looked like a younger, Nordic version of Liberace, with high cheekbones, a narrower nose, and a pointed chin. Often, when I caught a glimpse of myself in a mirror, I'd find myself wondering who that stranger was. I literally didn't recognize myself. I remember taking time to stop and stare in fascination at the Liberace look-alike I'd become. Anyone who has ever colored their hair, worn new glasses, or transformed their appearance in any way will know what I mean when I say it takes time to get used to the change.

Lee loved my metamorphosis. He'd look at me and say, "A beauty—a star is born."

When I looked well enough to work in the concession booths at the end of his shows it wasn't unusual to have women come up to me and ask if I was Lee's son. Not exactly, I thought to myself. But those remarks did get us to thinking. Lee was thrilled every time someone suggested a blood kinship between us. Over the years, I'd changed from being his lover or companion to become a perfect reflection of Lee himself— flamboyant, a little crazy. Lee had often talked about how much he would have liked to have a son. Even before my surgery it wasn't unusual for him to say that in many ways I'd become a son to him. We felt psychically connected to each other in ways that had nothing to do with sex.

When we established our relationship Lee had talked about adopting me, but we'd never taken the trouble to find out what it would take legally. Now the constant comments about how much I looked like Lee made him seriously consider the idea.

"You know, Scott," he said, "no one's ever been closer to me than you. I want to make sure that you're cared for forever, no matter what happens to me."

In the past Lee had discussed giving me one of his homes, making sure that I'd always have sufficient funds to take care of myself and all the dogs in case anything happened to him, and, ultimately, we signed a document guaranteeing it. He'd also named me a beneficiary in his will. But those were just pieces of paper tucked away in a file; they didn't reflect the deep emotional bond between us. Adoption would. We both recognized that other people, even those in Lee's organization, wouldn't understand our motives for wanting to formalize our status. I warned Lee that Heller and Strote would probably tell him he was making a terrible mistake, that I was after his money. It was their standard complaint when it came to me.

But they would have been wrong, dead wrong. Sure, I enjoyed Lee's money. Anyone would. Everyone associated with him benefitted from his earnings in one way or another. The more Lee made, the more Heller and Strote and Troulman and Cunningham all made. They were all tied to Lee financially. He used it to control them just as he used it to control me. But his wealth was not the prime motivation in my wanting to be adopted. All through my childhood, I'd been tormented by the feeling that I didn't belong to anyone—except maybe state welfare agencies. I wanted to be loved, to be cared for, and to give all those things in return. To belong. Adoption would have accomplished all of that and more, fulfilling both Lee's needs and mine.

Lee had a deep desire to pass his name on to someone else, while I wanted us to be legally bound so that Lee would always be part of my life. More than my lover, he was my mentor—the rock on which I'd built my entire existence. I was wet behind the ears when we met, untutored and unsophisticated, and I'd grown up under his guidance. My view of the world had been shaped by his interests, my opinions formed by things he'd told me. I shared his love of animals, of cooking, of decorating. Mentally— and physically, following the plastic surgery—I was Lee's creature. He'd been my Pygmalion. Although it sounds crazy now, I'd begun to think of myself as an extension of Liberace, a part of him rather than a full-fledged individual. Even now, looking back, I sometimes feel that my life began the day Lee and I met and ended the day we parted. Adoption sounded like the logical culmination of everything we'd been to each other.

We agreed not to tell anyone what we were contemplating. None of them, from Heller to Strote to Cunningham, had ever shown a genuine liking for me. As long as Lee loved me they had no choice but to treat me well, but that's as far as it went. I didn't think they had my interests in mind. When it came to my possible adoption, Lee didn't think so, either.

We decided to consult John Mowbray, a Las Vegas attorney, about the paperwork. Lee invited Mowbray out to the house, explaining that he wanted to keep the adoption proceedings quiet until it would have to be a matter of public record. Mowbray discussed the legal ramifications and said he'd be back in touch after drawing up the preliminary papers. I was on cloud nine after he left. Once Lee formally adopted me I'd finally belong to someone. In all the years of living in foster homes no one had ever loved me the way Lee loved me, no one had offered to make me a part of their family. I wanted to belong to Lee in the eyes of the whole world and know that he belonged to me.

About the time that Lee and I were looking into adoption I asked Joel Strote, Lee's attorney and mine, to draw up my will naming Lee as my beneficiary. Lee seemed more like family to me than my half brothers and sisters or my mother and father. I wanted to be sure that in the event of my death all the things I owned as a result of Lee's extraordinary generosity—my house, my cars, my furniture, my dogs, the things I'd bought with my salary—would be his. Although the will, the proposed adoption, the promises of lifetime support would all loom large in the future when Lee and I broke up, back in 1980 they seemed like nothing more than small pieces of the wonderful future we would share.

Lee seemed to love the new me even more than he had the old. By the time I recovered from my surgery I'd dropped over twenty pounds, a satisfying weight loss for so short a time. But I had gained more than sixty in the years Lee and I had been together. His favorite foods—pasta, fried chicken, meat loaf, gravies and sauces and breads—had turned me into a tank. Lee wanted me to really slim down and I was only too happy to try. So I stayed on the Hollywood Diet. It proved to be the mistake of a lifetime. Slowly but surely, I became addicted to the drugs Startz prescribed. They helped me lose weight, alleviated my postoperative pain, but, more important, they made me feel relaxed and confident.

Startz renewed my prescriptions on request. Addicted to drugs himself, he seemed to have no compunctions about prescribing addictive drugs for his patients. Who knows? Maybe misery loves company. There's certainly no more miserable human being than a doctor like Startz. I blame him for an addiction that would eventually make my life a hell on earth. It is absolutely no consolation that Startz was in that hell with me, and that he ultimately blew his own brains out.

By the time I'd been on the California Diet for six months and lost fifty pounds I was hooked on pharmaceutical cocaine. At that time Lee began to voice some concern about my health. "You're getting too thin," he said, adding that some of his people were saying I was anorexic and emotionally unstable. "I want you off that diet," he insisted.

How I wish it had been that easy. I was beginning to realize how dangerous Startz's drugs were and I wanted to stop taking them. God knows, I tried hard. I could go days, sometimes weeks, without taking anything. But every time I felt unhappy or unsettled, every time Lee and I had a disagreement, every time some of his people made me aware of how much they disliked me, I'd soothe myself, help myself over the rough spots by taking drugs. And Startz didn't hesitate to go right on supplying them. Since I seldom had the cash to pay for them, I'd buy jewelry on a credit card that Lee and I shared and then turn the jewelry over to the doctor in return for prescription bottles full of pills. Lee, who had an almost uncontrollable passion for jewelry himself, never questioned those purchases the way he would have questioned me if I needed large amounts of cash.

Taking pharmaceutical cocaine had one other obvious advantage. It was perfectly legal. I could take it with me when we toured and not have to worry. Startz kept me supplied for six months after I formally went off the diet. During that time I made every effort to control my cocaine usage and to gain back a little weight. And, to a great extent, I succeeded. By the time that Startz, fearing discovery, cut me off completely, my small drug need could easily be supplied by casual friends.

In those days cocaine was the drug of choice in the entertainment industry. I could purchase it from the stagehands or even have some given to me, gratis, at parties where it was used openly. By now most people are familiar with the stars who have admitted to a drug problem. Boy George, Stacy Keach, Richard

Pryor, Larry Gatlin, Tony Orlando, Richard Dreyfuss, Liza Minnelli, have all been courageous enough to talk about their addiction. But they are just the tip of the iceberg. Coke was everywhere early in the eighties. Even today, after all the negative publicity, anyone who wants cocaine can find it; and it is cheaper than ever.

For two years following my first meeting with Startz I kept my cocaine habit on a manageable level. Most of the time, I could take it or leave it. Then my drug usage came to the attention of a man I shall call Mr. Y, someone I met through Lee. Y was an easterner from the Boston area. He and Lee went way back; they'd tricked around when Lee was scrounging a living playing small East Coast clubs. Mr. Y was one of the more unsavory characters in Lee's life. He ran a gay nightclub in Hollywood and openly boasted of his underworld connections. At one time, after a much publicized gangland-style killing, Y even hid out in one of Lee's properties. One of Mr. Y's close friends—I'll call him Joe because it wouldn't be smart to use his name either—was accused of equally serious crimes. In a totally ironic twist of fate, today Joe has become a sort of mentor to me, and has more than made up for things that happened in the past. But that's a whole other book.

Back in the early eighties, Mr. Y and Joe must have thought of me as the perfect mark, a guy with a drug problem and, through Lee, the means to support it. For the next year Y, while pretending to be my friend, served as my supplier. He and Joe systematically stripped me of my savings and some of my cars, and Y introduced me to freebasing, the most dangerous form of cocaine addiction. But I'm getting ahead of my story.

19

Lee went to Europe every few years after his first appearance at the Palladium in 1956. He boasted of his enormous popularity abroad, talked of people in England standing in line to buy tickets to see his show. Despite the British critics' ongoing antipathy toward him, he told me that the Queen Mother could be listed among his most ardent fans. But I didn't pay too much attention to his bragging. Lee often exaggerated, stretching the truth to make himself look good. It was a harmless fault, one I ignored.

I can still see him holding up his beringed hands and telling an audience that one of the rings had been a gift from Barron Hilton and one of the others a present from Queen Elizabeth. In fact, no one bought Lee jewelry. It was all custom-made for him by Bob Lindner, a Vegas jeweler who gave Lee a real deal. In exchange for the right to call himself Lee's exclusive jeweler, Lindner cut prices drastically on everything Lee ordered.

So much of what Lee said and did was carefully calculated to build up his image that I think even he had trouble separating truth from fiction at times. But when we toured Europe, I learned that Lee had given an accurate description of his popularity abroad. A huge crowd waited for his arrival at Heathrow Airport outside London the day we flew in on the first leg of our journey. I can't imagine any movie or rock star getting a more tumultuous welcome. Huge banners that read WELCOME LIBERACE decorated the double-decker buses that had brought hundreds of his fans to the airport. The British bobbies were out in force to control the excited crowd.

A phalanx of security people met us as we deplaned, rushed us through customs and out into the airport itself. Then all hell broke loose. An immense crowd of aggressive fans streamed forward, eager to see Liberace or, better still, to touch him. I'd talked to stars who'd had their hair pulled, their clothing ripped off their backs, when crowds reacted like that. The security force formed a flying wedge around Lee's body and, in so doing, pushed me aside. Suddenly dozens of people filled the growing space between Lee and me.

I could see him moving toward the airport exit, his entourage churning their way through a human sea. Seymour Heller and his wife Billy, Ray Arnett, and the three traveling members of Lee's band were somewhere in the mob, but I didn't see a single familiar face around me. I'd almost resigned myself to a long, lonely trip into London when the crowd of security people around Lee ground to a sudden stop.

"Where's Scott?" I could hear Lee shouting over the sounds of the crowd, and then more frantically, "I'm not going anywhere until I find Scott!"

Although I could see people urging Lee to leave that madhouse as quickly as possible, I knew he'd be immovable until I joined him.

"Over here, Lee," I shouted, jumping up above the heads of the crowd so I'd be seen. A couple of policemen came to my rescue at once. When I caught up with Lee he reached for my hand and held it tight. And later, when the tour promoters wanted me to ride in another car so they could ride with Lee, he said, "You fellows can take a cab. Scott goes with me!"

In many ways that European tour was the highlight of our life together. We'd never been closer or happier. Lee was thrilled with my new face, and I was relaxed enough personally to have no need for cocaine. During Lee's three-week appearance at the Palladium he'd made arrangements to stay at the home of an old friend, the great British female impersonator Danny La Rue. Meanwhile, Danny was appearing in Hollywood and staying at Lee's penthouse. The arrangement was ideal. We'd have the privacy of a large and comfortable house, complete with a butler and a chauffeured limousine while La Rue enjoyed the luxury and convenience of the penthouse. Danny's home at Henley-on-Thames was everything we could have wished for, beautifully decorated and well staffed by Danny's own brother and sister.

Opening night at the Palladium we did a command performance in front of the Queen Mother. Afterward we were to be presented to her. As we dressed for the show I kept on thinking what a long way I'd come from the foster kid nobody wanted. Lee had met British royalty in the past and knew the protocol, but I had to be coached on the proper etiquette of going through a receiving line and meeting royalty. Above all, I was told not to attempt to shake the Queen Mother's hand. If she wanted to shake mine she would reach for it.

I was very nervous about meeting a queen but Lee loved the pomp and circumstance the occasion demanded. He hadn't exaggerated one iota about how much the Queen Mother liked his performances. She applauded enthusiastically throughout the show and was positively beaming afterward as we came through the receiving line. Greeting Lee like an old friend, she told him how nice it was to see him again. He beamed back, giving her the full-voltage Liberace grin. While they had a brief chat I kept on reminding myself to keep my hands at my side when it was my turn to meet her. Then, there she was standing in front of me, a little chubby woman who looked more like your average grandmother than a member of the royal family. Like any reasonably well-mannered American male, I automatically stuck my hand out to shake hers. As soon as I did it I realized I'd made a mistake. Thorson, you dumb ass, I thought—this lady is not going to be pleased.

But the Queen Mother looked at me and began to smile, not the pasted-on smile people have going through a receiving line but a genuine grin. "That's really quite all right, young man," she said, reaching for my hand and shaking it heartily.

I guess you call that noblesse oblige.

Later, after the royal party had gone, we were shown up to the royal box. Luxurious and private, with gilt furniture and heavy velvet portieres, the whole place looked like something out of a fairy tale. This is where the queen and king sit, I thought, trying out their chairs. The one modern touch was a private bathroom, which Lee and I christened. "From now on," Lee said, "you can tell people you really did sit on a throne!"

As Lee expected, the British critics were less than enthusiastic about his reappearance in their midst. His weight was at an all-time high, and that, coupled with the silicone implants that smoothed out the lines around his mouth, made him look like a round-faced, over-age cherub. The press called him a "blimp." But Lee had no trouble ignoring them because he was playing to full houses. Night after night Seymour Heller walked the house to count the size of the crowd and then came in to our dressing room to tell Lee, as Heller always did when attendance was high, *"We're* doing great."

Conversely, in the past, when Lee played to less than full houses, Heller would walk into the dressing room, gloom written all over his face, and say, "Lee, *you're* doing terrible!" Heller's selective use of pronouns had become a standing joke between Lee and me. Fortunately, Heller had no reason to do anything other than smile during that entire European trip. *We* were doing great!

From London we flew to Berlin, where Lee played to a mixed German and American audience. Again, I was surprised at the size of the crowd that waited to welcome Lee. The German audiences didn't seem to mind that Lee did his show in English. He performed without the benefit of props, using just the piano, the candelabra, and a wild assortment of costumes to entertain them. His patter was all in English except for a few lines in badly accented German that he struggled through. Strangely enough, every time he said anything in German the audience gave him an ovation. But his music proved to be a universal language. His rollicking, bouncing rendition of American classics reached straight to the heart of those Germans.

The trip certainly proved one thing to me. Lee was a star with international appeal. I'd been thinking of him as a strictly American phenomenon, but they loved him all over the world.

While we were in Berlin we took the obligatory trip to see the wall, stopping at checkpoint Charlie. Lee wasn't at all political; however, this place really seemed to get to him. Freedom lay on one side—the right to be whatever you dreamed you could be—while a life of severely limited possibilities was on the other. Lee, who had dreamed big and seen those dreams come true, shuddered as he looked through that opening in the wall.

After leaving Berlin we played tourist for a while, going to Munich to sample the beer and then out into the countryside to look at castles. Lee really turned on to Neuschwanstein, the fairytale castle of mad King Ludwig II. That castle, with its fantastic turreted architecture, was the classic example of Lee's favorite saying, "Too much of a good thing is *wonderful.*" He claimed to feel a deep psychic connection with Ludwig, just as he claimed to feel a deep psychic connection to Liszt. Lee had an interest in the occult, in the possibility that he'd lived past lives, that the trip stimulated. Old things, houses, antiques, castles, turned him on. But there was another aspect of German life that turned him on even more.

We'd been told that Hamburg had the most outrageous nightlife—porno palaces—and Lee was determined to see them for himself. Hamburg more than lived up to his expectations. One night Lee and I, accompanied by Ray Arnett and Seymour and Billy Heller, went to a nightclub where the entertainment consisted of a variety of sex acts performed onstage. As a visiting celebrity, Lee was given a large, front-row table. He sat, riveted by the action, as a series of acts—homosexual and heterosexual—unfolded in front of us. It was the one sour note of the entire trip, the only time when Lee and I weren't on the same wavelength. I was embarrassed, especially with Billy Heller and other ladies sitting nearby. But Lee seemed oblivious of everything except the entwined bodies. He watched with an eagerness that was as unpleasant to me as the performances themselves.

By then Lee's fascination with pornography had become a major issue between us. I became furious when the maître d' approached to suggest that Lee could enjoy the sexual favors of any of the performers who interested him, in the privacy of the small rooms that ringed the club. Lee refused, but I suspect he would have accepted at once if he'd been on his own. Sex fascinated him, the kinkier the better. When we left for Paris a day or two later I was happy to leave "Hamburg after dark" far behind.

Although Paris is justifiably proud of its nightlife there would be no repeats of what we had seen in Germany. Lee was relatively unknown in France and had no performances scheduled. He took a suite at the Paris Hilton and spent the next few days playing tourist instead of piano. We went to places like the Louvre, the Eiffel Tower, and Versailles, where the Hall of Mirrors reminded Lee of his own hall of mirrors in the glittering Vegas house. Again, he talked of feeling connected to the past and the man who had built Versailles.

Lee loved the French restaurants but detested the rude French waiters who didn't seem to realize he was a star. Although he claimed to enjoy going out in public without being approached for his autograph, it was soon apparent that Lee could go only so long without public recognition. After a few days in France his anonymity began to annoy him. He'd smile expectantly at passing strangers, trying to elicit a response, and then frown angrily when he failed to get one. Lee was one of the few stars I ever met who liked being hassled by autograph seekers. I think it reassured him.

Next, we went to Monte Carlo, where there are always lots of Americans and Lee was treated like visiting royalty. He taped an appearance on a variety show hosted by Patrick Wayne, John Wayne's son. The made-for-television series was supposed to showcase international stars but we later learned that it failed in the ratings. Kris Kristofferson and Anne Murray appeared with Lee but we saw very little of them socially. Lee and I spent our time on gambling in the casino and getting a little sun.

From there it was on to Holland and more performances in front of large and enthusiastic crowds. After one of the shows the fans actually tried to break down the dressing-room doors to get at Lee. Our last stop was Oslo, Norway, and Lee was as popular there as he had been in London. When we returned home after eight weeks of traveling, I had a new understanding of the size and scope of Lee's fame, and a new respect for his talent. He'd reached across the barriers of language and culture to make people smile and give them pleasure.

That year we also went to Mexico, where El Presidente actually went to the trouble of meeting us at the airport. The welcoming ceremony began with a walk down a red carpet past an honor guard. Lee had earned Mexico's gratitude by featuring the Ballet Folklórico in his act and as a consequence he was treated more like a visiting head of state than a nightclub performer. We stayed at the Mexican White House, an incredible palace with the world's best-trained servants.

Few screen stars ever achieve Lee's international acclaim. At the beginning of the 1980s he stood at the pinnacle of his profession. He'd become the highest paid, best-known entertainer in the world—truly the greatest showman on earth. An outsider might have concluded that he'd long since fulfilled all his dreams. In fact, Lee still had two unfulfilled ambitions.

He wanted to play Radio City Music Hall. His desire had been born in his youth and fueled by the year and a half of performances when the Rockettes had been part of his own act. In 1979, when I first suggested using them, we'd flown to New York to discuss the idea with the Rockettes' management at the Music Hall. During the negotiations we were given a tour of the stage, one of the biggest and most elaborate in Lee's experience. It fired his imagination.

There were elevators to lift or lower props or pieces of the set from stage level, the most fantastic lighting, a pit that held a full orchestra. Lee's face glowed with barely contained excitement as it did whenever he got a new and exciting idea for his act. It was there that he and Michael Travis got the idea of having Lee make an entrance wearing an enormous cape that could later serve as the stage's back curtain—the costume he would eventually plan to wear in 1987. Lee could picture himself doing the show of his lifetime in that historic theater in the future.

"It would be totally outrageous," he said, giving the place the highest praise he could imagine. Lee met with Radio City Music Hall's management, talking at length to choreographer Violet Holmes about his ideas. But, back in 1979, with the European tour and the Mexican trips in the offing, plus his usual calendar of American bookings, Lee had to set aside the idea of working the Music Hall.

Most of his people breathed a sigh of relief. Lee's act was dynamite in front of the relatively unsophisticated audiences he encountered in places like Vegas or Sparks or Hershey, but not even his most ardent admirer believed he had what it took to conquer New York. No one seemed more anxious to see Lee abandon the dream of a Radio City appearance than Seymour Heller, who remained convinced that cosmopolitan Broadway theatergoers wouldn't appreciate Lee. Even Ray Arnett, ordinarily one of Lee's staunchest supporters, thought Lee would be running a risk if he chose to go through with his plan. Their objections seemed unfounded in view of the fact that Lee had played to standing-room audiences at Carnegie Hall early in his career, and had set an attendance record of sixteen thousand back in 1954 when he appeared at Madison Square Garden.

Lee's second unfulfilled ambition was to be an actor—a movie star. That desire had been reinforced by the years he'd lived in Hollywood, years when he failed to get the film industry to take him seriously. Deep down inside, he felt he'd be a standout playing character roles. Lee made his screen debut in the 1950s, playing a honky-tonk pianist in *South Seas Sinner* starring Shelley Winters. Then, in 1955, in the midst of the "white heat" period, he'd played the romantic lead in *Sincerely Yours,* a film created solely to showcase his talents. In 1965 in *The Loved One* he played a coffin salesman with oily charm. Lee was wonderful in the part and hoped it would lead to others. His pride was injured when he continued to be ignored by producers and directors. He hated feeling like a failure in films.

When his movies played on late-night television we would perform a silly ritual. The moment the credits appeared I'd say, "Dim the lights, low-key lighting please."

Lee would grin happily as his image appeared on screen. He'd make an expansive gesture and say, "Oh, look—a star!"

That, he confessed, was what he really wanted to be, a movie star. He enjoyed great triumphs as a live entertainer, earning a series of prestigious awards including six gold albums and two Emmys, as well as mention in the *Guinness Book of Records* for being the world's highest paid pianist. But Hollywood had denied him the recognition he craved. Lee still hoped to appear at the Academy Awards someday, as a presenter or performer if not as a nominee.

Now that Lee is gone I have one last dream for him myself. Today I live in West Hollywood, just blocks from Lee's former house on Herold Way. Hollywood Boulevard and the Walk of Fame are an easy stroll from my front door. Not a week goes by without some performer being immortalized by placement of a star bearing his or her name on the Walk of Fame. Many of the recipients are famous for their music or their stage work rather than their films and many of them are less than household names. In view of Lee's long reign as the leading showman of his day, of the fact that millions of fans throughout the world recognized his unique talent, it would be appropriate to have him recognized by Hollywood too. Surely on all those blocks of Hollywood Boulevard there is a place for a star bearing the name Liberace.

20

Lee's relationship with his family, and particularly his mother, played counterpoint to the life he and I shared. Frances was always there, a source of worry, occasional aggravation, and financial drain for Lee. With his staunch belief in duty to his mother, he couldn't ignore her—no matter how much he might have wanted to from time to time. During our early years he had her safely tucked away in Palm Springs and we saw her only during our stays at the Cloisters.

I never understood his reluctance to spend time with his mother. In my opinion she was a beautiful old lady with twinkling blue eyes that lit up whenever she saw her son; I would have been proud to call her grandmother. Frances Liberace seemed to come alive in Lee's presence and, according to her nurse's reports, really faded away when he wasn't around. Although Lee didn't give Frances as much time as she would have liked, she never lacked for any material comfort, including a luxurious home, furs and jewels, and round-the-clock care as her health began to fail. Lee took great pains to ensure that his mother had the best of everything.

But his mother didn't see it that way. In her book the best of everything was Lee himself; she wanted to live near him, to see him daily instead of occasionally. Even in her late eighties Frances was still a sharp, determined woman who knew how to get what she wanted: in this case, to spend her final years with her favorite child.

Sometime in late 1979 Lee began to get reports that his mother did not have long to live. During our visit Frances made it apparent that she felt lonely, forgotten, ignored by the only person she really cared about. "All I need," she told Lee emphatically, "is to be *near* you and I know I'll feel better."

In her sweet way, Frances Liberace managed to maneuver her son between a rock and a hard place. "What can I do?" he asked me. "Tell my mother that I don't want her living anyplace near me?" She'd raised him to respect his elders, to honor their wishes. The habit was deeply ingrained. Although Lee was sixty, his mother was still capable of getting him to do what she wanted. She knew exactly how to manipulate him. In her own quiet way Frances made Lee feel he'd condemned her to a slow decline by leaving her in Palm Springs.

He felt he'd had no choice but to move her to Vegas, the city that served as his home base. I sat in on all the discussions and arrangements, wishing that I could handle Lee as skillfully as his mother did. She played him even better than he played the piano. It didn't take her long to get what she wanted. I'm not denying that Frances was frail; but she used her frailty. When our visit ended I knew I'd witnessed a masterly performance. Apparently Lee had inherited his acting skills and his ability to manipulate people from his mother. They both loved to play Camille.

Before we left Palm Springs, Lee arranged to move his mother to the White House, the home he still owned in Vegas. In the past he'd rented it to people such as Diana Ross or heavyweight champion Larry Holmes. For the next few months it would be occupied by Frances and her nurses. The house was always kept immaculate and ready for immediate occupancy. Best of all from Frances's viewpoint, it was only five minutes away from Lee's own home.

Frances made a trip to Vegas in a limousine, accompanied by her own nurses and a doctor. Predictably, after a couple of weeks in Vegas Frances declared that she felt much better. Being near her beloved son was the tonic she needed to make the rest of her life worth living. It was obvious to me that he was her whole world, that seeing him daily really did make her feel better. We began a routine of stopping by her home for fifteen minutes every evening on our way to do the show. Frances would light up like a neon sign the minute Lee walked in. She'd loved Lee so much; it was sad that he couldn't love her back with the same intensity.

Lee had a habit of fluttering his fingers against any available surface, as if he was playing the piano, when he got nervous. He'd no sooner sit down with his mother than his fingers would start fluttering, and they'd be in constant motion throughout the visit. Their conversations went by rote. "How're you doing, Ma?" Lee would ask. "Are you feeling good? Are the nurses treating you well? Do you need anything?" Day after day, he always asked her the same questions and, when he'd finished and she'd answered, they didn't seem to have anything more to say to each other. It was kind of pathetic. They were mother and son, in the final years of their lives together, but they didn't know how to communicate.

Strangely enough, Frances seemed utterly unconcerned by my presence in her son's life. She knew we lived together, went everywhere together; she may even have suspected that we shared a bed. But, like Lee, she had an extraordinary ability to close her mind to anything that might have been unpleasant. She always greeted me warmly, with the same welcoming embrace she gave her son. It was impossible not to return her affection. If Frances liked you, she could be the warmest, sweetest person.

Frances never made a secret of her feelings. She complained bitterly about her nurses, who never seemed to able to please her no matter how hard they tried. If she didn't like someone she had a habit of hissing at them through closed lips while throwing up her arms in an almost defensive gesture. Much to my embarrassment, Joel Strote, who had known her for years, used to walk up to her to give her a hug, only to be greeted with that funny hiss and her up-thrown arms.

Gladys was one of Frances's favorite people. But even Gladys felt the sting of the old lady's tongue. One night when Frances had joined us at the Shirley Street house for dinner, Gladys made one of Lee's favorite meat loaves. When Frances saw what her son was being served, she turned to Gladys in outraged fury, saying, "I can't believe my son is going to have to eat meat loaf when the Blacks in Watts are eating steak!"

It was an outrageous remark, especially when directed at someone as loyal and devoted as Gladys, but then, Frances Liberace could be a completely outrageous person. Gladys, who was often left in charge of caring for her when Lee and I were out of town, was clearly upset. Fortunately, she was a wonderful woman with a tremendous capacity for forgiving arid forgetting.

While Frances lived in Vegas, Lee often asked me to take her to the Hilton so she could gamble. How she loved the slot machines! She may have been frail and old but she could spend five or six hours playing the slots. When she was feeling well I'd pick her up in the piano-key station wagon and drive her down to the Hilton. According to Lee, Barron Hilton was kind enough to have his staff rig certain machines for her so she had the pleasure of winning more than the average tourist.

She also spent a lot of time playing the slots in Lee's private casino in our house. On those occasions I'd be given the job of rigging them for her. I'll never forget the day she won so big that there wasn't enough money in the machine to pay her off. Frances was adamant. She wanted her winnings, *all* her winnings—then and there. Lee and I ran through the house collecting change from everyone, but we still didn't have enough for a full payoff. When we went to Frances and explained the problem she looked at Lee, smiled her sweetest, and said, "That's all right, son. I'll take a check."

It was indicative of their relationship that Lee got out his checkbook immediately. That was the kind of control she still exerted over him. We spent half the year in Vegas, doing shows and resting between tours, and while we were there Lee saw his mother briefly every day. He was the world's most dutiful, if not the most loving son, willing to do anything he could to make her happy, provided it didn't intrude too deeply into his private life. When it became obvious that the stairs in the White House were too much for her (Frances spent a lot of time in a wheelchair when she wasn't playing the slots) Lee bought a single-story condominium in the same building where he'd previously purchased a home for George and Dora. The new arrangement seemed to suit Mama Liberace and her hard-pressed nursing staff better. At least we heard fewer complaints in response to Lee's "How are you, do you need anything?" litany.

Strangely enough, although George and Dora now lived just doors away from Mama, I got the definite impression that I saw more of her than anyone else did. Angie, who was living in California, flew in to visit her mother occasionally. But it always seemed to me that Frances was cold and standoffish toward her other children. It was Lee that she loved and he came first right to the end.

I escorted her to see Lee's shows once or twice during a three-or four-week Vegas engagement. When she was sitting front row center in the showroom, Lee always made a point of introducing her to the audience. I always joined her after driving Lee onstage. The minute the spotlight headed toward our table Frances would perk up. No matter how poorly she felt she'd sit up straight, looking her regal best by the time the spotlight reached our table. Then she'd wave to the crowd with the royal aplomb of a queen. Clearly, she loved her moments in the limelight, loved being recognized as Liberace's mother. And I know he valued the opportunity to show her off. She'd become an intrinsic part of his image. How could anyone say or think anything bad about a grown man who took such devoted care of his mother? Who would suspect that the young man sitting next to her, in this case *me,* was really Liberace's lover? Frances was the perfect cover for our true relationship.

Frances rarely came backstage to visit, and she never commented on Lee's performance although we sat through many of them together. In fact, during her final years she was a somewhat silent lady who seemed to have a problem communicating verbally. But she effectively used gestures and facial expressions to convey her mood. A lot of things may have displeased her. But never Lee.

Being in Vegas and seeing her son every day did give Frances Liberace a new lease on life, but it proved to be a short one. By 1980 her stamina had decreased markedly. Clearly, her days were numbered. Lee, who'd always been uncomfortable during their visits, became even more nervous around her. He'd walk into her room, give her an obligatory hug, and spend the rest of the visit looking anyplace but at Frances. I think it was his way of blocking out the reality of her imminent death.

He'd gotten used to having his wealth and power shield him from life's unpleasant realities. If he couldn't buy his way out of a problem he used someone on the payroll, usually Seymour Heller, to deal with it. But no amount of money could prevent eighty-nine-year-old Frances Liberace from dying.

In view of his emotional distance from his mother, I thought Lee would have no trouble dealing with her imminent death. But he couldn't handle it at all. Instead, he ignored the situation. He didn't change his schedule to reflect his mother's now seriously declining physical condition. In fact, we were in Hollywood on vacation, staying in the penthouse, when we received word that Frances had died.

"Let me talk to my brother," Angie said abruptly when she called to give Lee the news. Angie was often abrupt with me so I didn't think anything of it.

As Lee spoke to his sister he gasped and shrank back, as though he were trying to avoid an unexpected blow. "When did it happen?" he asked.

Within seconds, he'd regained full control of himself. After hanging up Lee turned to me and told me Frances was gone. Tears filled my eyes but Lee, although he looked shaken, remained dry eyed. The first thing he did was to pick up the phone and call Seymour Heller to ask him to put an obituary in the appropriate newspapers. He returned to Vegas early the next day to make the funeral arrangements.

Lee played the dutiful son to the end. He picked out his mother's coffin—pink because it was her favorite color—had her properly laid out and prepared for burial, called Forest Lawn in Los Angeles where he'd purchased what was to be the family mausoleum, and made all the plans for the interment. It was a busy day and he wanted me by his side, giving what little support I had to offer, while he made those painful decisions. Lee, who had such an even-tempered disposition, showed very few signs of the stress he was under as he prepared his mother's final farewell. But those fingers of his fluttered nonstop as he played a silent concerto.

The entire family, including Angie, her children and grand-children, George and Dora, and Rudy's seldom-seen widow and children, in addition to all of Lee's people, Lucille Cunningham and her immediate family, the Strotes, Ray Arnett, the members of the band—everyone close to Lee was gathered at Forest Lawn for the funeral. Angie and Lee were stoical throughout the long day but George took his mother's passing very hard. He wept uncontrollably when he saw the coffin.

All the surviving family members were showing the strain by the time we adjourned to the penthouse after the burial. The old wounds inflicted during their childhood seemed to resurface. Grief, instead of making them closer, seemed to push them apart. George was virtually silent, clutching his wife's hand. But Angie, obviously distraught, began to boss me around. Lee intervened, saying, "For heaven's sake, Angie, leave Scott alone. Can't you see he's taking Mom's death as hard as anyone?"

As for Lee himself, he never shed a tear from the first phone call to the gathering after the funeral. He displayed emotion by snapping at people. Consequently, it came as a shock a few months later, when Lee wept buckets over the death of his favorite dog. Babyboy was the little poodle with the eye problem who'd played a part in bringing Lee and me together. Lee was absolutely inconsolable when the dog died of old age. For days afterward he moped around the house, breaking into uncontrollable fits of crying. I thought his heart would break. Seeing his distress, I couldn't help concluding that Lee loved his dogs more than he loved his family.

When Lee buried his mother he buried all his unresolved feelings about her. He'd loved her and resented her; but he'd never dealt with those emotions. And now he never would. Sometime late on the evening of the funeral, after everyone had gone, Lee turned to me and made the only comment he would ever make about his mother's death. "I'm finally *free*," he said.

Although we would live together for two more years, Lee seldom spoke his mother's name in my presence again. Liberace, the entertainer, made much of his *beloved* mother's passing while Lee, the man, put it behind him as he'd put so many other unpleasant things behind him. His reaction to Frances's death was a chilling example of his ability to close the door on the past, an ability that would one day serve him well with regard to me.

21

In 1977, shortly after I moved into the Vegas house with Lee, I came across a number of pornographic tapes that he'd left in the night table by our bed. When I questioned him about them he said he enjoyed watching porn and had a small collection of tapes and films. It was the only time I ever heard Lee minimize a situation. In fact, his collection was extensive and well used. Before my arrival he'd watched hard-core pornography as a steady diet.

During our first weeks together he showed me some of his films. They all depicted homosexual acts and, even at the age of eighteen, I found the movies offensive and boring. Sex, in the privacy of your own bedroom, can be thrilling, romantic—a real bond between two people. But sex on screen is just sad. The positions look awkward, the bodies unattractive, the photography poor. Worse, from my point of view, was the fact that homosexual pornography seemed embarrassingly *faggy*. The dialogue, what little there was of it, was so stereotypically gay as to be laughable. I believe a man should still act like a man, no matter what his sexual preference. But Lee's porn films often starred men who in the vernacular would be called "flaming fags." There are guys like that out there but they're not representative of the homosexual population as a whole.

I hated those films, hated the fact that Lee liked them so much and wanted me to watch them with him. They aroused him while they turned me off. Each time Lee viewed one of his tapes he'd want to have sex. The variety of sexual acts he saw on screen fascinated him. Nothing made him hotter than watching a three-way—three men in bed going at it. At the beginning of our relationship I was afraid his fascination with hard-core porn would cause a real problem between us. Fortunately, back then Lee cared more about me than about watching those movies. Since I disliked them so much he stopped asking me to view them with him and, to the best of my knowledge, stopped watching them himself.

Although sex was important to Lee and he liked a variety of sexual acts, it was never the most important thing in our relationship. That was fine with me and for a long time, it was fine with Lee too. He hungered for companionship. He couldn't stand to be alone and needed to know someone would always be there for him. That need fit perfectly with my desire to have a father figure. Lee became my father figure. I looked up to him; in fact, I put him on a pedestal. Considering the difference in our ages and his immense talent and charm, it's no surprise that I came to admire him so much. The public Liberace, the great entertainer, deserved all the admiration I could muster.

But the private man had traits and tastes that were less than admirable—foremost among them his consuming interest in pornography. Although I cared for Lee more than anyone I'd ever known and saw him through rose-colored glasses, there were times—more and more of them as the years went by— when ignoring or excusing his faults came hard.

When things went well we laughed a lot. The thing I remember most from 1977 to mid-1981 is laughter. In the privacy of our home, I poked fun at Lee, saying scandalous things that no one else would have dared say. He didn't mind me calling him an "old queen," teasing him mercilessly about his makeup, his clothes. I was probably the only person in the world who didn't treat him like a star twenty-four hours a day, kissing his behind at every opportunity.

But I began to sense a subtle difference in our relationship sometime in 1981. Lee didn't laugh at my jokes as much as he had in the past. I had to be careful not to anger him. He'd always been flirtatious toward other attractive young men, but now his flirting became so obvious that it embarrassed me. When he had a few drinks he'd come on to teenage boys as though I wasn't even there. I'm sure the other people who worked for him realized what was happening, even though I didn't at first. Lee was tiring of me. The plastic surgery and the weight loss that had drastically altered my appearance helped maintain his exclusive interest in me for a while. But underneath, I was still the same old Scott and, at twenty-two, past my prime for a man who liked younger, more malleable companions. Lee was a chickenhawk and he would soon be searching for new prey.

At first I tried to ignore the symptoms of his growing restlessness. When I couldn't we usually wound up fighting. Then I'd take a little cocaine to help me over the rough spots. As the frequency of our arguments increased, so did my drug usage. With the wisdom of hindsight I realize that my drug habit caused some of the difficulty between us. It made me less malleable and harder to reach. I'd been a kid when Lee and I met. His opulent lifestyle had been completely alien to me. So I followed his lead. By mid-1981 following his lead had lost its appeal. I'd become a man with opinions of my own, opinions I probably expressed too often. Now when Lee tried to tell me how to dress, what to eat, where to go, I often ignored him.

He resented it but, being Lee, he never openly expressed his resentment. Lee didn't confront his problems head-on. That wasn't his style. He kept quiet while his dissatisfaction ate away at our relationship. As a result he became more dictatorial and in turn, I became more rebellious. We were on an accelerating downward spiral and everyone seemed to know it but me. I kept on thinking, "This too shall pass."

Lee, who'd insisted on my being with him morning, noon, and night, began to give me a little freedom. It started with my taking Frances Liberace to the Hilton to gamble. Sometimes Lee went with us but more often he said he had errands to run. After Frances died I continued to do a few things on my own. Having time to myself, after being what I still think of as a "prisoner in paradise," made me so happy that I didn't question what Lee was doing when we weren't together. I made a few friends, tried my hand at songwriting with enough success to be encouraged. Looking back, I realize being Lee's favorite had gone to my head. I'd been given too much too soon. I didn't know how to handle my good fortune and my snorting coke didn't help. I had begun to think of myself as Lee's son, the power behind the throne, even as his *equal*. I felt I deserved to have my say and my way, at least part of the time.

That proved to be a mistake. Lee didn't want an equal, he wanted a subordinate—someone who'd jump when he said jump. There were still good times, enough of them that I didn't realize how close we were to playing out our string. Both of us were drinking more, smoking heavily; and we began to have serious disagreements about our sex life. Lee, who wanted more variety, tried to talk me into acts I found repugnant. "If you loved me, you'd do what I want," he complained bitterly.

"If you really cared about me," I replied, "you wouldn't ask me to do things I hate." The arguments became more acrimonious with every passing month. Lee wanted me to engage in anal sex and I hated even the thought. Our sexual encounters were creating even more tension between us.

During our last year together Lee and I made our annual pilgrimage to Fort Lauderdale, where he had a standing engagement. While we were there Lee renewed an old friendship. The two of them made me feel like a total outsider as they talked about the "good old days," people and places and incidents I knew nothing about. The man owned a string of adult bookstores and had supplied Lee with many of his pornographic films and tapes. We became a threesome for the next few days. Lee's pal kept on sniggering and telling me I ought to check out one of his bookstores. Obviously, Lee had already told him what I thought of porn.

"Try it, you'll like it," he insisted.

I didn't have any desire to and told him so, rather graphically.

But Lee had other ideas. "Boober," he said, "you're a goddamn party pooper!"

One night after we'd all had too much to drink I finally agreed to check the place out. The three of us piled into a car and

172

took off for one of Lauderdale's sleazier neighborhoods, where the so-called bookstore presented a blank, windowless face from the street. Inside, racks loaded with pornographic books and magazines lined the front of the store, while shelves of merchandise—whips, chains, other objects used in sadomasochistic sex acts, even dildos and other things I'd never heard of and had no idea how to use— were near the back.

Lee's eyes gleamed as he took it all in. There was a series of viewing machines, like old-fashioned nickelodeons, where you could watch sex flicks to your heart's content—heterosexual, homosexual, sex acts featuring animals or children; they had it all. Lee was soon going from viewer to viewer, grinning all over the place. The bookstore also had private cubicles in the back with what are known in the gay world as "glory holes." For a small fee a man could rent one of the cubicles, put his penis through the "glory hole," and wait for a response.

I was drunk when we arrived, a circumstance that prevented Lee from staying longer and enjoying the full use of the facility. We weren't there fifteen minutes before I threw up, making an unintended but valid commentary on my surroundings. Lee, who was thoroughly disgusted with my behavior, had no choice but to take me back to our hotel. The next morning I woke up with a killer hangover. But I made up my mind to have it out with Lee. A couple of aspirins later, I finally felt well enough to confront him.

"About last night," I said, "you're a well-known star and you're out of your fucking mind to go in a place like that! What the hell would you have done if someone, a reporter, had seen you in there? How would you explain that to all the little old ladies?"

Lee didn't have any answers. In the sober light of day he agreed he'd made a mistake. Never again would he insist on going into an adult bookstore, but his interest in pornography didn't end.

By 1981 Lee had tumbled from the pedestal where I'd rightly or wrongly placed him. I still loved him, dreaded the thought of losing him, but I no longer idolized him. Even then I recognized the fact that we both had problems. In the years to come, I would be able to analyze them realistically. Mine had to do with drugs. Lee's had to do with sex. Although his interest in sex was at an all-time high, his ability to achieve satisfaction had greatly decreased. Despite the silicone implant he had difficulty

173

achieving full arousal. Our sex life was diminishing, in part because Lee was much too proud to discuss his virility, or lack of it, with me. Instead, he used pornography to become aroused and ready for sex. Since I had no way of knowing why he did it, I interpreted his constant viewing of pornography as a complete lack of consideration for my feelings. We'd reached an irreconcilable impasse.

I didn't know where to turn or what to do. If I lost Lee—and I still refused to face that possibility—I'd be losing a lot more than a lover or a meal ticket; I'd be losing the person who meant more to me than anyone I'd ever known, the man who'd become my family. I knew Lee so well I could even hear a difference in the way he played piano as we grew further apart. He was more emotional; it showed in his eyes, his voice, but most of all in his performances. Looking back, I guess he too was going through some pain—and a lot of regret.

We still cared for each other, enough to try to resolve our problems. When Lee suggested that we experiment with an open relationship, I agreed. At the time I'd have agreed to anything that had a chance of stopping our arguments and keeping us together. An open relationship would have given Lee the sexual variety he needed, while we would continue to live together as friends and companions. It sounded reasonable. I wouldn't be losing Lee and he wouldn't lose me, we'd just be sharing a part of ourselves with other people.

Unfortunately, what sounded like a rational way to go on living together when we discussed it in the Jacuzzi turned out to be an emotional hell. I soon learned I couldn't stand the thought of Lee seeing anyone else, and he blew his stack the first time he saw me with another man, even though I explained that the man was a friend, not a lover.

"It's him or me," Lee declared.

We both realized that an open relationship wouldn't work for us. But we'd given each other one hell of a scare. For a while, it seemed we'd both learned a lesson. No matter what, we decided to stay together.

But, from then on, I felt I couldn't trust Lee. My response to his ever roving eye was to retreat further and further into drugs, using them to escape reality. Like most addicts, I still believed I

174

could handle drugs. When Tony Orlando tried to warn me that my habit was out of control, I refused to listen. It was a hell of a lot easier to rationalize taking drugs, to blame it on Dr. Startz or on Lee for causing my unhappiness, than it was to try to deal with my problems.

I don't mean to give the impression that I'd become an out-of-control drug addict. That wouldn't happen until I faced the reality of actually losing Lee. I could still go for days without taking as much as an aspirin. But gradually what had been a monthly habit became biweekly and then weekly. I continued to try concealing my cocaine usage from Lee, who—despite his own fondness for amyl nitrite, cigarettes, and liquor—professed to hate drugs. I never did coke around him, but he would have had to be blind not to know what I was doing.

At the same time, although I hadn't caught him with another man, I was convinced he was seeing someone. Weeks would go by without Lee initiating a sexual encounter, and I knew Lee too well to think he'd gotten hooked on celibacy. The pattern of fighting and making up accelerated.

When friends like Tony Orlando tried to talk to me about how much coke I was using, denial was the name of the game. "I'm not addicted, I can handle it, take it or leave it," I argued.

Then, of course, there were friends like Mr. Y, who were interested in seeing my addiction escalate so they could sell me more drugs. By late 1981 I was listening to all the wrong people. The more I used drugs, the more Lee pulled away from me. Although I didn't realize it then, he'd already started looking for a new "*protégé*." The casting call was out.

22

I'm not a psychologist, a social worker, or a doctor, but I believe that promiscuity is and always has been the most serious problem facing gay men and the gay community. Today everyone realizes that such behavior is a major factor in transmitting AIDS. But back in 1981 I was more concerned about what promiscuity might do to my relationship with Lee than about what it could do to my prospects for a long life. Too often gay men roam from partner to partner, indulging themselves in a series of one-night stands, acting like randy male dogs. Their code seems to be, "If it feels good, do it." From my own observations and experiences, I've reluctantly concluded that the gay male sex drive is so strong, so powerful, that even today—confronted with the possibility of contracting AIDS—some gay men seem willing to die just to have a new experience. Lee was one of them.

We'd agreed to have a monogamous relationship, but Lee's track record, coupled with his constant flirting, kept me from trusting him. I was always on the lookout for signs of trouble. Two of Lee's oldest and dearest friends served as a role model for the relationship I hoped he and I would share. Fred and Bob were a dance team, retired from their many years with Lee's show and living in Connecticut when I first met them in 1977. They'd been together two and a half decades and seemed completely happy. We visited them every time Lee had an East Coast engagement, and my esteem for them grew with each meeting.

When Lee decided to open an antique shop in his museum complex I immediately suggested Fred and Bob as prospective managers. They were well settled in their Connecticut home, and moving would mean a major upheaval in their lives, but they accepted Lee's offer out of their affection for him. I hoped their obvious stability, so different from most of the gay behavior that we saw day in and out, would rub off on us. Most of all, I hoped that Lee and I would have a long-lasting relationship like theirs.

But that wasn't in the cards. Lee's desire to have sexual variety with a younger lover, coupled with my drug problem, continued to drive us further apart as 1981 drew to a close. We had terrible fights, instigated by me when I caught Lee paying attention to a younger man, or by Lee when he thought I was stoned. We'd wind up in a shouting match that always ended with Lee calling me a "monster." Those words evoked memories of his final fights with my predecessor, Jerry O'Rourke. Lee had called him a monster too.

"I've created a Jekyll and Hyde," he sobbed when our fights threatened to become physical. And he was right. My years with Lee had turned me into a spoiled, pampered, cocaine-using jerk who no longer liked himself. Lee and I stayed together for a complex variety of reasons: habit, mutual dependency, caring.

There were still happy times, among them the day Lee was asked to play all the nominated musical scores at the 1982 Academy Awards ceremony. For Lee, that was the culmination of a lifelong dream. He wanted to be an actor, a star, to win an Oscar. Being asked to play at the awards ceremony—not just one nominated song but all of them—was the next best thing. A jubilant Lee looked forward to the evening of March 25, 1982, when he'd make his appearance at the Dorothy Chandler Pavilion before a star-studded audience. To Lee, it signified the acceptance he'd always wanted from Hollywood; at long last the film industry seemed to be taking him and his talent seriously. One of his last unfulfilled wishes was about to come true. I couldn't help being happy for him, but that happiness didn't last.

Early in 1982 Lee started paying a lot of attention to a kid named Cary James, an eighteen-year-old who was a member of the Young Americans, the singing and dancing troop that appeared with Lee. James was blond, blue-eyed; in fact, he looked a lot like me before my plastic surgery. James hung out around our dressing room all the time, and Lee often favored him with a private chat. Catching the two of them with their heads together, having what looked like an intimate conversation, drove me to a fury. But every time I brought up my suspicions Lee swore I was imagining things; his conversations with James were completely innocent.

Lee's people seemed to realize that change was imminent. In private, Ray Arnett would tell me that James was the most boring kid he'd ever known, but Arnett praised James whenever Lee was around. When so-called friends told me that Lee was buying James small gifts, clothing and the like, I forced a major confrontation.

"What the fuck's going on around here?" I shouted. "Why is that little son of a bitch hanging around our dressing room all the time?"

Lee played innocent. "Nothing's going on," he said. "The kid doesn't mean a thing to me. You're making a mountain out of a molehill."

I wanted to believe—how I wanted to believe him. I tried to take what Lee said at face value, but jealousy made me half crazy. I watched for any sign that he'd been lying to me. For the next few weeks James had the good sense to steer clear of Lee and me. Then, the third week in March, when we were appearing at the Sahara Tahoe, I got a phone call while Lee and I were in our dressing room resting between the first and second shows. My favorite foster mother, Rose Carracappa, had died.

The Carracappas were the first family to take me in when my mother had been hospitalized after we moved to California, and they were the last family I lived with before meeting Lee. If things had been different, if my mother had been willing to let the Carracappas keep me when I was little instead of reclaiming me, I probably wouldn't be writing this book. They were a good, dependable couple who would have given me a solid background, people who cared for me as much as the law, the welfare workers, and my mother had allowed. They represented the best the foster-family system can offer a kid and I'd never stopped caring for them, even though I hadn't followed their advice.

The news of Rose's death, coming in the midst of my emotional problems with Lee, tore me up. I asked him if it would be all right if he made his entrance for the second show without the car. I was too upset to come out onstage, all smiles, and play chauffeur.

"Sure, Scott," Lee said, patting me on the shoulder in his most fatherly way. "I understand just how you feel. You stood by me when Mom died and I'm going to stand by you now."

Those were exactly the words I needed to hear. Without the Carracappas, Lee was all I had left in the world. I grabbed the emotional lifeline he seemed to be extending. He was as good as his word. He not only permitted me to sit out the last performance of the evening, he arranged for a Lear jet to fly me to the funeral the next day. I was so grateful for his understanding and support that it never occurred to me that he might have an ulterior motive for wanting to get me out of town. It would be one of the few times since we became lovers that Lee and I spent a night apart. Knowing how much he hated to be alone, I regarded it as a sacrifice on his part. We were both solicitous of each other's feelings and needs as we said good-bye at the airport.

When I returned twenty-four hours later it was obvious that something had happened in my absence. Lee's people were looking at me differently, treating me differently, refusing to meet my eyes. I didn't trust any of them. But I did trust my sister Annette's husband, Don Day, who had a job working the concessions in Tahoe and who was staying with us, to tell me the truth. As soon as Don and I had a minute alone, I asked him what the hell was going on.

Don told me that Lee had invited Cary James over to the house while I was away and that James had spent the night with Lee in our bedroom. There was no way I could stay in control after hearing that news. How, I asked myself, could Lee do that to me, to us, while I was at Rose's funeral? The fact that I'd been away mourning the loss of someone I cared for doubled my sense of betrayal. Angry; God, I'd never been so fucking angry! If Lee had made the mistake of walking in at that moment, I think I'd have killed him then and there.

I cursed, shouted, tore our bedroom apart. I don't even know how long I went on like that. By the time I regained control the room was a disaster area of broken glass and furniture. Meanwhile, Lee was hiding downstairs, terrified of facing me. No way could I stay under the same roof with him. I didn't even want to be in the same state. I had to get away, try to cool down and think things through. So I tossed a few things in a bag and asked someone to drive me to the airport. The Lear jet was still there and I had the pilot fly me back to Los Angeles.

In L.A., not knowing where else to go or what to do, I took a cab to the penthouse. I couldn't shake the feeling that my life was over. Lee had been my whole world; if I didn't have him I didn't want anything else. The darkest thoughts ran through my mind as my emotions seesawed between anger and self-pity. Unable to face being alone, I called Mr. Y, the man I considered to be my best friend. He came over; we shared some cocaine and talked for hours.

By the next day I'd made up my mind not to call Lee. I wanted him to make the first move, to apologize for what he'd done. Then maybe I'd be able to forgive him and we could start over. While I waited for the phone to ring a note arrived. It was from Lee and said, "Love me or leave me!"—not exactly the abject apology I thought I had coming.

I stayed holed up in the penthouse, licking my emotional wounds, while Lee left Tahoe for Palm Springs. A couple of days later I got a call from the man who functioned as the majordomo of the Cloisters.

"For God's sake," he said, "what the hell is going on with you and Lee? Last night he had two French kids here with him in bed."

I couldn't believe it. I'd been sitting around like an idiot, waiting for Lee to call and the whole time he'd been amusing himself with a three-way. The anger I'd felt in Tahoe was child's play compared to the rage that shook me after learning that Lee had been tricking around as he'd done before we met.

I called him at the Cloisters, screaming into the phone, "How dare you? How dare you do that to me? I could kill you!"

Again, I couldn't face the night alone so I called Mr. Y and another friend who happened to be a former patient of Dr. Startz and who, like me, had become hooked on drugs. (As it turned out, this friend would later be my sponsor in a rehabilitation program.) This time cocaine didn't cool my anger or soothe my pain. I paced the penthouse, ranting and raving at my friends. Meanwhile, Lee was back in Palm Springs, convinced that I now represented a serious danger to his health and happiness. He was scared to death. Of me!

He was due in L.A. the next day to rehearse for the Oscar ceremony, and he intended to stay at the penthouse. Common sense should have dictated that Lee book a suite at L'Hermitage or some other luxury hotel, in view of my occupancy of the penthouse and the problems between us. But Lee had no intention of changing his plans because we'd had a battle royal. Once he set a course of action he was unstoppable, plowing forward regardless of the consequences.

There would be no time for me to cool down, to gather my thoughts and emotions—no time for me to decide what to do about Lee, about myself, no time to sort out the events of the last few days. Lee wanted me out of that penthouse so he could move in. Hell, I don't blame him. It was his property. He had a right to be there and, in his view, I didn't. But I can't help wishing he'd have changed his plans, just this once.

Instead he did what he always did when faced with an untidy problem that needed handling: he called Seymour Heller. He told Seymour I had to be removed from the penthouse no later than two o'clock the next afternoon. Lee himself planned to arrive shortly afterward and he didn't want me anywhere near him ever again. He told Heller that I'd threatened him, which was certainly true. But if everyone who has ever said, in the heat of anger, "I could kill you," carried out that threat, half the people in the United States would be in jail for murder. Right or wrong, Seymour regarded my threats as a serious danger to Lee's life. He made preparations to act with force.

When I first left Tahoe to take refuge in the penthouse Lee had asked Heller to have me watched. As I later learned, Heller contacted Jay Troulman, Liberace's business manager. Troulman subsequently got in touch with Tracy International, a private detective and security agency that had worked for Lee before. In the past, Tracy International had performed over a dozen investigations for Lee and provided bodyguards for him on special occasions. The firm, and specifically Tracy Schnelker who ran it, was given the task of keeping track of my comings and goings after I arrived in L.A. Schnelker would ensure that my departure from the penthouse was timely.

The night before the Academy Awards was one of the worst nights of my life. After my friends left I just couldn't get to sleep. The wreckage of my life with Lee stared me in the face. I knew he'd never take me back after the things I'd said and done. But, despite my anger over his infidelity, I couldn't stop loving him. It may have been wishful thinking but part of me thought if we could just sit down, face to face and man to man, we might be able to work things out.

I was still tossing and turning long after the television stations signed off. So I went into the living room and turned on the stereo. Lee had the lights rigged to respond to the music, dimming and brightening, and I finally dozed off early in the morning watching them. I would wake up a few hours later to find myself living a nightmare.

23

Lee woke up in the bed we had shared at the Cloisters on the morning of March 25, 1982, the day he would make his much-looked-forward-to appearance at the Academy Awards ceremony. As he'd done every morning when we were together, he kissed and cooed at the various dogs who slept in the bedroom, scolding them all if one had an accident during the night. Perhaps he even had a lover or two in bed with him that morning. By his own admission, he had continued to have the two young Frenchmen as his houseguests. Knowing Lee, I bet he'd already put the problem of what to do about Scott Thorson in someone else's hands. From that day on, Lee would do his level best to pretend I didn't exist.

From where he stood, it had been an exciting week. With the two Frenchmen he'd enjoyed the sexual variety he'd been craving and, in Cary James, he'd found a suitably youthful and malleable replacement for me. James would, in fact, become Lee's next companion. As Lee dressed for the day he was already concentrating on the evening ahead, anticipating the acclaim he expected to receive from the glittering Academy Awards audience. It was shaping up to be one of the happiest days of his life.

But it would be one of the worst in mine. As I caught a few hours rest after a sleepless night, Seymour Heller made plans to remove me from Lee's life—permanently. That morning, sometime after eleven, acting under Lee's instructions, Seymour Heller met private investigator Tracy Schnelker, and three of Schnelker's more imposing employees, in one of the offices on the ground floor of the penthouse building. Heller had also called my half brother, Wayne Johansen, asking him to be present during the meeting. While it may have made sense, from their point of view, to have my half brother present during a situation that could have been nasty, his presence is something I can never forgive. The subject to be discussed at that meeting: Scott Thorson and, more specifically, how to get me out of the penthouse before Lee arrived. Heller told everyone that I was in the penthouse using drugs, that Liberace wanted me fired from my job (I was on the payroll as a bodyguard-chauffeur-companion), removed from the premises, and, if possible, taken to a hospital where I could be treated for my addiction. He added the information that I carried a gun. Obviously, in Heller's view, he was certainly doing his job, but I felt hurt and bitter.

Any detective hearing such a description would conclude that Scott Thorson was a very dangerous character, to be approached cautiously and with all available force. Later testimony indicates that Schnelker came to exactly that conclusion while he listened to what Heller had to say. I'm sure that, as he and his men rode the private elevator up to the penthouse, they thought they were going to be in danger. When the elevator doors whooshed open they stepped out, ready for anything—except what they found.

The penthouse is enormous. But Schnelker and his men had no trouble locating me because two maids, already cleaning the premises despite the fact that I was supposed to be armed and dangerous, told Schnelker where to find me. I was, in fact, still sleeping on the sofa in the living room.

The first thing I remember was being roughly shaken awake. My immediate thought was that I was being robbed. I saw four men standing over me, none of them looking friendly. One of them had a hook instead of a hand, which he brandished in my face. My God, I thought, they're going to kill me. Desperate to escape, I began to struggle with Schnelker, ordering him to get the hell out of there or I'd call the police. That sounds ridiculous now, but I didn't know what else to do. During the ensuing brawl someone sprayed me with Mace but they missed my face. Somehow, I managed to shake free of them all. Looking back, it's almost comical. They were as afraid of me, and what I might do, as I was of them.

I sprinted through the penthouse wondering why the Pinkertons, who guarded the building and had spoken to me the previous evening, had let such dangerous characters inside. I could hear men pursuing me, knocking over furniture in their haste. Sometime during their pursuit I saw my half brother Wayne near the elevator. That brought me up short. My first thought was: What is he doing here? Why doesn't he help me, call the police?

Then the truth hit me. I'd been set up. No one got up to the penthouse without the express approval of Lee or Heller. The only way up was by private elevator and you needed a key to operate it. At that moment Wayne moved toward me, saying, "These are private investigators, Scott. They're here to get you to leave. Lee wants you to go."

I was outraged. Wayne and I weren't close, hadn't been close for years. And yet there he was, asking me to leave, on Liberace's behalf. "Who the fuck do you think you are, coming in here like this?" I shouted. "You have no right to be here!"

Then one of the four men, probably Schnelker, said he'd come to help get me to a hospital. The whole situation seemed unreal. There stood my brother Wayne, a man I rarely saw, and four hired goons, telling me I ought to go to a hospital. They tried to calm me down and I kept on telling them to "get the hell out," and asking for Lee. By then the maids had appeared from wherever they had been working and were taking in the free show.

While I faced Wayne and the detectives, Lee was enjoying a leisurely breakfast before dressing for the day. The sun was shining and he may even have taken time for a stroll through his beloved gardens at the Cloister, perhaps stopping in his private chapel for a brief prayer. By noon he was in his limousine, relaxing in total luxury as he made the two-hour drive into Los Angeles. His conscience was clear, his mind at rest, his hands clean; according to his way of thinking, he was in no way responsible for the events taking place in the penthouse. That would be his unwavering testimony in the years to come, although he would freely admit ordering my eviction. That day, Lee focused on his upcoming performance rather than the end of our relationship.

I didn't have that luxury. I'm a big guy, almost six feet three inches, and I weighed about 180 at the time, but in my pajamas and bare feet, I was clearly no match for four burly detectives who were determined to throw me out of the place I'd regarded as home for five years. My *only* weapon was anger. I couldn't have presented a real threat. Nevertheless, one of them maced me again, this time managing to hit me in the face. I guess they expected it to slow me down, but it only made me more desperate. I got past the four of them and raced for a bedroom, where I planned to barricade myself. As I ran, thinking myself in a life-and-death situation, I heard one of the maids screaming, "He has a gun."

At first I thought she was warning me that one of my attackers had a gun. Then, when I heard Wayne shout that I had two guns, I realized the warnings were meant for the detectives.

It is true that I had guns. Lee had insisted that I carry them and had obtained a permit for me from John Moran, a Vegas sheriff. But I'm not Dirty Harry. I didn't intend to make detective Schnelker's day. All I wanted to do was get to a phone, call Lee, and find out what the hell was going on.

Then I saw Seymour Heller, standing clear of the action but observing it all. Although I'd already been roughed up and maced, seeing him was the worst moment of the entire morning, because I knew Heller wouldn't evict me on his own. He would be thereonly if he was acting on Lee's behalf. And that meant Lee and I were finished.

I reached the bedroom ahead of my pursuers, locked myself in, and tried to think clearly. But my heart was pounding, my skin and eyes burned from being maced, and tears were pouring down my face. Meanwhile, Schnelker and Wayne kept on shouting through the door, saying that I ought to go to a hospital and that Lee would pay for my treatment. I didn't trust those bastards, not after what they'd done to me, and I still couldn't quite take the whole thing in. I was fired, they'd come to evict me. What did that have to do with me going to a hospital?

Obviously, I needed help. First, I called Irv Osser, an attorney I knew. I'm sure I must have sounded pretty incoherent as I tried to explain what was going on. Nevertheless, Osser told me to stay put, not to leave the penthouse under any circumstances. But that didn't seem a likely option in view of the fact that Wayne and Schnelker and God alone knows who else were standing outside the door, telling me I had to leave before Lee arrived—or else. It was the implied threat behind the "or else" that scared me.

I would have cried like a baby if I'd had the time. Lee and I had been looking forward to this day for months, planning what he'd wear, who we'd see, which parties we'd attend after the Academy Awards ceremony was over. Michael Travis had designed special costumes for the event and Anna Nateece had designed magnificent furs to go with them. How I wished I could turn back the clock, start the week over. I couldn't believe I wouldn't get to see Lee in those costumes performing the Oscar-nominated songs. I couldn't believe I'd never see Lee again, that he hated me enough to send detectives to the penthouse to forcibly evict me. But I knew no one else would have dared give orders like that; they had to come from Lee himself.

My next call was to Mr. Y, the underworld figure who had systematically insinuated himself into my life over the last year. I told Y what had happened and asked him to help me get out of the penthouse in one piece. My biggest fear at that moment was that Schnelker and his men would beat the hell out of me once I opened the bedroom door. Mr. Y warned me not to leave the penthouse with anyone, even if they promised to take me to a hospital.

"Do you know how easy it is to get rid of a body in the hills outside L.A.?" he asked. "Stay put until I can send help."

Believe me, I had no intention of moving after talking to Y. He promised to send some of his employees, men he trusted to handle any situation, to help me in any way I required.

More than anything, I wanted to talk to Lee, to ask why he was doing this terrible thing to me. I called through the door, asking to speak to Heller. When he got there I said, "Seymour, what the hell's going on here? Does Lee know what's happening?"

"Lee wants you to leave," Heller replied. "These are his wishes."

I felt he was telling the truth even though I didn't want to believe it. Despite all our problems I loved Lee and I thought he still loved me. This just couldn't be happening. "Let me talk to him," I begged.

Heller's voice seemed devoid of feeling as he said, "What would it take to get you to leave?"

I knew he was talking money but I didn't want money, I wanted Lee. "Just let me talk to Lee first and I'll go peacefully."

"You're sick," Heller said. "You should go to a hospital."

I felt he didn't give a damn about me or the state of my health. All the hospital talk was so much crap as far as I was concerned, a ploy to get me to open that door. Heller would follow Lee's instructions to the letter and Lee's instructions were to get rid of me, one way or another. The four goons outside my door were living proof of that.

"You can't talk to Lee," Heller repeated.

I was beaten and I knew it. Further resistance was useless. I had no choice but to leave the penthouse. I agreed to go and told Heller I wanted my clothes, all the things I'd brought with me when I left the Tahoe house. But time was running short. Lee was due within minutes. Heller wanted me out of the building before Lee arrived. One thing for damn sure, I had no intentions of leaving until I heard Y's men arrive. My clothes were in another room so there'd probably be no time to dress or pack after they showed up. When I heard new voices in the hall I opened the door, grabbed a fur coat and my jewel case, and headed for the elevator.

Mr. Y had sent four men, led by the manager of his gay nightclub. There was a lot of pushing, shoving, and shouting as they escorted me out of the building. Once we reached the parking lot I asked to be allowed back in to get my clothes, but one of Schnelker's men blocked access to the private elevator.

Losing what little self-control I had left, I began to shout obscenities and threats. The nightclub manager was trying to get me into his car when Pat Swanson, my real estate agent, arrived on the scene. I'd been looking at property with her earlier in the week and we were supposed to go out again that afternoon. Swanson would later serve as a witness to the day's events, but she wasn't much help at the moment.

There I stood in my nightclothes, wearing a coat and carrying the jewel case, wanting to return for my clothes and my money, while Y's men and Schnelker's had a Mexican standoff. Suddenly the whole thing seemed pointless. The one thing in the world that I cared about was Lee and I had the sick feeling I'd never see him again. The club manager, exhibiting a pretty cool head, got me in his car, and the next thing I knew we were driving down Sunset Boulevard, leaving my home, leaving everything I owned and loved behind.

Lee arrived at the penthouse a few minutes after my departure. By then the maids were hard at work, straightening furniture and sweeping up broken china, erasing the evidence of what had taken place so that Lee wouldn't have to face the harsh reality of my eviction by force. I suspect Heller spared him the more sordid and unpleasant details. Later I learned that the two men met out in the parking lot, where Heller reassured Lee I was gone.

Lee's two teenage French pals were with him in the limousine. I'm sure they'd had a delightful drive and were looking forward to the evening's festivities, whatever that might include. Lee was running late and didn't even bother going inside the building. Instead Schnelker, in his role as Lee's bodyguard, jumped into the front seat of the limo, and they all set off for the Dorothy Chandler Pavilion at Los Angeles's Music Center.

I learned later, from depositions, that not once during the thirty-minute drive did Lee ask the detective what had happened in the penthouse that morning. Heller had assured Lee that everything was taken care of in accordance with Lee's instructions, and that's all Lee needed or wanted to know. He was determined to put Scott Thorson behind him as quickly as possible. It was his way, his lifelong pattern.

Lee had his mind set on two things: the Academy Awards and the pleasure he would enjoy with his two houseguests later that evening. His cup was running over while mine had come up empty. Arriving at the nightclub manager's house in my pajamas, looking like someone who'd just escaped a tornado, did nothing to improve my mood. I began calling the penthouse at once, trying to arrange to get my money and belongings.

Meanwhile, the rehearsal at the Music Center went splendidly. Lee had a wonderful time mingling with the stars and playing the nominated scores. Rehearsal ended at three and he returned to the now-clean penthouse by three-thirty in time for a rest, a snack, and a pleasant visit with his new friends before he had to return for the Oscars at six. While Lee spent a euphoric afternoon in the penthouse, I made repeated efforts to contact him by phone. I knew we were finished, but I wanted to hear it from him, not from Heller or Johansen or some hired goon. It seemed the least Lee owed me. He had been my lover, my father, my confidant, and my best friend while I grew to manhood. He'd meant more to me than anyone in the world.

By throwing me out, Lee not only deprived me of emotional and spiritual support, he also took away my job and everything in the world I owned. I knew I would never get him back, but there wasn't any reason for him to withhold my personal possessions. When I couldn't get any answer to my repeated phone calls, I finally called the police and asked them to help. But they said that since I'd *voluntarily* left the penthouse, there was nothing they could do. I had no choice but to deal directly with Seymour Heller.

He finally agreed to permit me to return to pick up my belongings that night while Lee was at the Music Center enjoying his triumph. Not knowing exactly what to expect when I arrived at the penthouse, and fearing a repeat of the morning's assault, I took an armed guard and a dog with me when I returned. Heller met me on the ground floor and showed me into the small room he'd been using as his base of operations that day. It was crammed with green plastic trash bags which he said held my belongings.

I couldn't believe it at first. Lee was tossing me out like yesterday's garbage. Even more painful was the fact that my half brother, Wayne Johansen, was still on the premises and being treated like one of the family while I was told to take my trash and get the hell out of there. Heller made it very clear that I *must not* make any further attempts to contact Liberace; that it would be unwise for me to return to Vegas despite the fact that my house, my furniture, my cars, and the bulk of my clothes were there.

I left the building carrying those lousy trash bags, feeling a despair so deep that I can't even describe it. And yet I still couldn't believe what had happened. I was to have been Lee's son; he'd even had me made over in his image. I had a reasonable facsimile of his face, but I would never again have him.

24

In 1980, when tennis star Billie Jean King was sued for palimony by a woman who claimed to be her former lesbian lover, Lee and I joked about the much publicized scandal. Lee laughingly said, "Billie Jean—*what a guy!*"

And I rejoined, "You're next, Lee," in reference to the fact that, as his long-term lover, I could also sue him for palimony. At the time the thought of breaking up, of facing each other in a court of law instead of across the breakfast table, was so remote that we both laughed at the mere idea.

By the end of March 1982, the laughter had ended. I was torn up over the callous way Lee had had me thrown out of the penthouse. You'd think that after all the foster homes I'd lived in, I'd have become an expert when it came to handling rejection. But Lee's harsh eviction was the ultimate cruelty, the worst thing that had happened to me in my twenty-two years. It really hurt. I'll never forget or forgive the way it was done: the plastic trash bags, my half brother's presence, the private investigator with the arm that ended in a hook, being forced to leave the penthouse wearing pajamas, being told that any attempt to contact Lee or return to Vegas could be hazardous to my health.

Any lingering doubts I may have had about my position were soon squelched by my so-called friend, Mr. Y. He made it plain that my life might be in danger if I went against Lee's wishes. Heller had been quite clear the night he handed over my trash-bagged belongings. I was not to contact Lee, I was not to return to Vegas. "Do not pass Go, do not collect $200." Unfortunately, this was my life and not a game of Monopoly. My actions and reactions over the next few months were based on what I saw as a very precarious, even dangerous situation.

At first I stayed with the nightclub manager, Mr. Ys' employee. Everything I owned, except my jewel case and a few clothes, were out of reach in Vegas. My bank accounts, thanks to my own drug habit and friends like Y, who kept me well and expensively supplied with cocaine, were soon depleted. He and his friend, Joe, were to be my closest associates and advisers during the months that followed as I tried to sort out my future without Lee. Losing him in such a brutal way helped to accelerate my drug usage—which in turn deepened my problems.

My initial attempts at recovering my possessions met with failure. I'd asked a friend who owned a truck to drive up to Vegas and pick them up for me but he was denied access to both my tract house on Larrimore and Lee's home on Shirley Street, where I kept most of my clothes. I couldn't believe it when my friend returned with an empty truck. I'd been told repeatedly that Lee didn't want to see me, but no one had said anything about him keeping my belongings. I just couldn't understand why Lee had ordered his people to do that to me. Obviously I needed help—legal help—to recover all my possessions.

During my years with Lee, Joel Strote, who worked for Lee, had acted as my attorney. But Strote would now be my adversary. I needed to be represented by someone who had no connection with Lee, who would be unimpressed by Lee's fame and power. First, I asked a former foster mother to recommend an attorney. She sent me to two men who had handled her divorce. After a preliminary meeting with me, they concluded that the only means I had of paying for their services was with my jewelry. They asked that I hand it over, to be held in trust. It seemed like a good idea. I was staying with a known criminal, a man who supplied me with drugs. Clearly my jewelry would be safer in their hands than in mine.

I firmly believed, back in 1982, that attorneys were men of strict moral principles, men who were above suspicion. I'd been taught to look up to educated men like that. Consequently, when those two lawyers said they wanted to put my jewelry into some kind of trust account, I thought they would act in my best interests. Although I didn't realize it then, I was unconsciously looking for someone to replace the father role that Lee had filled in my life. Needing to trust and believe in someone made me vulnerable and careless. I turned the majority of my jewelry over to those two men and that's the last I ever saw of it. Their offices were ripped off before they could put my valuables into safekeeping—or so they told me. Exit my first attorneys.

At this point I asked Mr. Y to recommend legal counsel and he told me to contact David Schmerin. I called at once and made an appointment to meet with Schmerin at Joe's house, a place where Schmerin was a regular visitor. Schmerin readily agreed to represent me in my efforts to get my belongings, house, furniture, cars, and clothing. I was angry enough to discuss palimony and he agreed that I might have a case. After a couple of preliminary meetings, all held at Joe's home, Schmerin promised to contact Lee's legal representative, Joel Strote, on my behalf. Several of my friends suggested I get out of town while Schmerin made the preliminary moves.

It made sense to me. I knew Lee would be angry when he learned that I now had an attorney. In the past all of Lee's lovers had left quietly after he tired of them. But I was furious at the way I'd been treated and wanted to strike back, to hurt him as much as he'd hurt me. If that wasn't sufficient motivation, my home, my furniture, my cars, and my clothes were still in Vegas, a place I dared not return to without Lee's okay. I knew Lee wouldn't hesitate to use force to get rid of me; vivid memories of the scene at the penthouse offered graphic proof of that. I also feared that pushing Lee, getting an attorney to represent my interests, might make Lee decide to rid himself of me for good. Leaving town temporarily seemed like the better part of valor.

By then I'd learned that Lee had taken a number of steps to sever our ties and keep me from getting near him. Each one poured salt in my still fresh emotional wounds. I was told that the locks on all the properties we'd shared, including my own home, had been changed; the various phone numbers at all those properties had also been changed. I couldn't contact him in any way, short of going to Vegas, which I took to be risking a physical confrontation. But there was one way I could still get to him and I intended to take full advantage of that situation during the next few days.

Lee had neglected to cancel the joint credit card that we'd held for years. I used that card to finance my stay in Hawaii and, believe me, I checked into the best hotel and ate at the best restaurants. Sure, it was wrong; I know that. But doing it gave me a great deal of satisfaction. Lee was holding hostage my mail, my severance check, all my worldly possessions. I still had no more than the things I'd taken from the penthouse. But I did have that credit card, and I took tremendous satisfaction in every charge I made on it. I could imagine Lucille Cunningham's self-righteous outrage when she got the bills—and Lee's after she gave him a full report. Score one for my team!

I didn't return to Los Angeles until my attorney told me he was close to arriving at a settlement with Joel Strote. We continued to meet at Joe's house. Then, one evening in Joe's presence, David Schmerin told me that "Liberace was going to be a tough adversary, that he would litigate this thing all the way and that he had very deep pockets and could hire the best counsel."

I don't claim to be an angel; I'm more than willing to accept my share of blame in regard to my breakup with Lee. I know my drug use caused a problem. But the facts speak for themselves. Lee had known about my using coke for months and apparently accepted it. We didn't argue about drugs. Once, when Mr. Y left some cocaine in the house after a visit, Liberace actually asked when Y would return to pick up his "medicine." As I said before, Lee and I moved in social circles where marijuana and cocaine were as accepted as liquor. Although he may have abhorred my drug habit, Lee had not chosen to get rid of me until he'd found a suitable substitute in Cary James. Then and only then did Lee act. And when he acted he used force, assault and battery, and ultimately extortion, to rid himself of me.

Less than one month after I'd been tossed out of the home Lee and I shared, Schmerin told me that he and Strote had reached an accord, a meeting of the minds. Before Schmerin spelled out the terms of the proposal they had agreed on, he made sure I understood that I would not get my property, not one shirt or sock, not one thin dime, until I signed an agreement.

In anybody's book, withholding someone's property, especially when it's done to force them to do something, is illegal. In criminal cases it's called *extortion*; in civil cases, *conversion*. Although the legal document was twelve pages long and carefully couched in lawyer's mumbo-jumbo, the intent was simple. I was to get $75,000, three of my six cars, three dogs, and my clothes. I would be permitted to return to Vegas briefly to pick up my personal possessions. Seymour Heller would personally guarantee my safety and escort me through my house so I could pack my clothes.

In return for the money, the cars, the dogs, the return of my personal property, I would be required to sign over to Lee the title to my house on Larrimore, currently worth $200,000, and give its contents, which I estimated to have a value in excess of $50,000, to him as well. In addition, I would be required to sign over to Lee title to three cars, my Chevrolet van, an antique Cadillac, and an Auburn.

True, some of these things had been gifts from Lee. But they had been given to me freely. I held clear and legal title to them. There had never been any mention of the fact that they would continue to be mine only as long as Lee cared for me.

The agreement also specified that I would give up any other claims against Liberace—of any nature. I believe that was included in the text to ensure that I wouldn't sue for assault and battery or, more important, for palimony. Last but far from least, the document included a clause that prohibited me from revealing the true nature of my relationship with Lee.

The offer shortchanged me by about a quarter of a million dollars. But I was playing by Lee's rules and they were simple: I signed or I wouldn't get a thing. The agreement actually spelled out the extortion or conversion in subparagraph 6, where it said that Liberace would "tender to Thorson, as soon as practical after the date hereof, all the clothes and personal belongings now in the possession or control of Liberace." By admitting, in a legal document, that my personal belongings were in Lee's control and wouldn't be returned until I signed, Lee unwittingly admitted to the *conversion* of my property.

As we drove to Strote's Beverly Hills offices on April 22, 1982, Schmerin told me it was the best deal I could hope to get, that my drug addiction would make me a very unsympathetic witness should my dispute with Lee wind up in court. He talked about Lee's power, his money, his ability to carry on a legal battle no matter what the cost.

Back in 1982, I was desperate for money. I owed for drugs, and no one had to tell me what would happen if I didn't pay those debts. I had no place to live, few clothes, no car, no job. The agreement, in effect, was a legal gun held to my head. If I wanted any of my property returned, including my paychecks and all my personal documents and memorabilia, I would have to sign. I had no chance of beginning my life over until I did. So I walked into Strote's office and signed, even though I felt the document was unfair. I scribbled my signature and took that check from Strote's hand and thanked God I finally had some money again.

To my surprise the check was made out to both me and Schmerin. Since I didn't have a local bank account, Schmerin suggested that we drive to his bank to make the deposit. He said he'd give me my share of the proceeds when the check cleared. He'd been working under a contingency agreement and was to receive one third of the settlement, while I got the remaining two thirds.

A few days after the meeting in Strote's offices, I returned to Vegas and went through the house on Larrimore, accompanied by Seymour Heller, only to discover that many of my personal belongings had already disappeared. When I asked if there might have been a burglary, despite a newly installed security system, Heller nodded in agreement. In reality, later testimony would show that Lee had asked Gladys to pack my things immediately following our breakup. What happen to them after that is anybody's guess.

I came away from Vegas angry and upset, knowing I'd been ripped off, wanting to lash out and hurt Lee in any way I could. The period from Rose Carracappa's death to my return to Vegas seemed like a waking nightmare. Lee was at the center of it all. I'd loved him, trusted him, even at the very end. Now he had failed to live up to the terms of an agreement he himself insisted

I sign. It had never occurred to me that he would withhold some of my prized possessions: a valuable collection of porcelain flowers, a bronze sculpture, a television set, a favorite ring that commemorated our meeting. These were never returned. Apparently the papers we'd signed didn't mean a damn thing to Lee. As far as I was concerned the whole thing had been a con and I was the world's biggest chump for falling for it.

Lee had brushed me aside as easily and as thoughtlessly as he swatted a housefly. Like Jerry O'Rourke before me, I'd ceased to exist where Lee was concerned. But, unlike Jerry, I made up my mind not to take what Lee dished out without a fight. He wasn't going to be rid of me that easily.

25

On October 14, 1982, I filed suit against Liberace in Los Angeles County Superior Court. Much has been written about that suit, most of it inaccurate. It was usually described as a palimony suit, with all the overtones of a juicy sex scandal that such a suit implies. In fact, palimony was only one of thirteen causes of action. Most important was the cause of action based on extortion and conversion of my property.

The lawyers debate the legalities of my case far better than I can. But there was one unlisted cause of action, the most important one in my mind, that drove me into court. Six months after being thrown out of the penthouse I still hadn't stopped caring for Lee. I missed him in so many ways, like a child longing for a lost parent, a lover yearning for a loved one, a lonely man longing to see a friend. My entire life had been wrapped up in Lee; I couldn't figure out how to go on without him. While Lee and I lived together I had no idea how emotionally dependent on him I'd become. But I felt like a cripple without him.

I sued because it was the only way I could continue to be a part of his life, the only way I could ensure that he wouldn't forget me. Like a kid who prefers negative attention to *no* attention, I didn't care if the suit made Lee hate me, just so long as he didn't forget me. Anyone who has ever been rejected by someone they still love will understand my motivation. I just wasn't able to let go.

There were, of course, financial considerations as well. Lee had promised, time and again and in front of witnesses, to care for me for life, to have an exclusive and loving relationship with me. The fact that I'd been tossed aside for a younger man, a kid who looked much like me before my plastic surgery, infuriated me. I really wanted to hurt Lee. Anyone who says you can't love and hate a person at the same time is wrong. I loved and hated Lee in 1982 and I still feel the same way. Not a day passes when I don't think about him, sometimes with anger—more often with affection.

When I brought suit against Lee I was represented by another—my third—attorney, Michael Rosenthal. Rosenthal specializes in personal injury cases, not exactly the expertise needed for my problem, but I'd met Rosenthal through friends and he seemed to wholeheartedly believe in me and the merits of my case. We got along quite well.

My search for a competent, ethical, morally upright legal counsel reminded me of Diogenes's search for an honest man, and was to prove just as difficult. Rosenthal seemed to have my interests at heart rather than his own. He proved to be ambitious and energetic on my behalf, even if I occasionally disagreed with his strategies. After we had a series of interviews he concluded that the best way to get Lee's attention was through the press.

Lee went to great lengths during his lifetime to conceal his sexual preference from the public. Now, Rosenthal decided to blow the lid off the situation by notifying the media that he was about to file a multimillion-dollar suit on my behalf against my former lover—Liberace. Not unexpectedly, the ladies and gentlemen of the press were at the courthouse in force when I arrived with Rosenthal. Cameras clicked frantically, television lights blazed, and eager reporters begged for a statement as we walked into the courthouse. Being courted by the press felt wonderful after being ignored, for so many months, by the man I cared for. I felt important for the first time in a long time. It was virtually the first satisfying moment I'd had in the six months Lee and I had been apart. It would also be the last.

As it turned out, Rosenthal hadn't bargained for Lee's popularity and power. The torrent of publicity we received that day soon generated what I think of as the "war in the tabloids," a war that we had no chance of winning even though we struck the first blow. Rosenthal intended to use negative publicity to bring Lee to his knees and have him begging to settle the case.

After filing the suit his next move was to place a call to the *National Enquirer* offering them my exclusive story—for a fee, of course. Rosenthal negotiated a $32,000 deal, half of which he would collect for his services. The November 2, 1982, edition of the *Enquirer*, with a picture of Lee and me on the cover, bore the banner headline: "LIBERACE BOMBSHELL—BOYFRIEND TELLS ALL."

And I did.

The *Enquirer* article covered our homosexual love affair, the plastic surgery, the promises of lifetime support and the proposed adoption, Lee's new relationship with Cary James, and my subsequent eviction from the penthouse and from Lee's life. The story, which ran in two issues, was guaranteed to get Lee's attention. We expected him to ask for a settlement immediately. But we'd made a classic tactical mistake, that of using our best weapon first—full public disclosure—instead of holding it in reserve.

The night the story broke, Lee was appearing somewhere in the Midwest. Friends later told me that he was scared to death to go onstage, afraid his fans would hiss and boo now that they knew the truth. But Lee needn't have been concerned. When he walked out to face the audience they gave him a standing ovation. Either they hadn't believed the things I'd said in the *Enquirer* article or they could forgive Lee anything—including having sex with young men. That ovation brought tears to Lee's eyes and gave him the strength to face everything that lay ahead.

Predictably, he came out of his corner fighting. Looking back, everything he did after publication of the *Enquirer* articles was inevitable in view of his track record. I should have been smart enough to realize that Lee wouldn't take quietly being publicly branded a homosexual, that he'd fight my allegations with every weapon in his arsenal. He used the press to strike the next blow and, from then on, I was at his mercy in the media. By the time Lee finished with me I don't think anyone believed my story except my attorney.

Lee retaliated by giving an exclusive interview to another major tabloid, the *Globe*. Their November 2, 1982, front page bore the headline: "GAYS OUT TO ASSASSINATE ME, SAYS LIBERACE." The page-nine story began: "These vicious Lies— It's nuts, says star as gay sues him for $113 million." Lee was quoted as follows: "'This man is a former disgruntled employee. He was fired in 1982 because of excessive use of drugs and alcohol, because he carried firearms.

"'This is an outrageous [Lee's favorite word] and vicious attempt to assassinate my character.

"'We will fight this fully in the court. We will show that all of this is a fraud.'"

The article continued: "A source close to the superstar, who often speaks on his behalf [I suppose this was Seymour Heller's contribution to Lee's defense] says this is not the first time Liberace has been the victim of slander at the hands of the gays.

"'It's a battle he has had to fight throughout his career. Every time it's happened before, we've fought it and won. And we'll win this time—and every other time—too.'"

This quotation epitomizes the kind of thinking that prevailed throughout Lee's life. He simply refused to admit his sexual preference, even if by refusing he found himself slandering the very group of men who were closest to him, *gay men*. In my opinion his inability to deal openly and frankly with his own sexuality was a personal tragedy. Lee continued his pathetic charade right up to the grave, and then his people, Heller and Strote, continued the battle for him.

Back in 1982 the *Globe* article was a masterpiece of half-truths. The story detailed how well Liberace had treated me, saying, "Liberace gave him the best clothes, the best cars and spending money that was just out of sight." The reporter who wrote the article never questioned why Lee would have done all that for a mere chauffeur. The article closed with an interview with a hypnotist who claimed he'd been employed by Lee to help Lee overcome the pain of a broken love affair. The implication is the love affair had been with a woman; reality is, it was with me.

According to the hypnotist, Lee had said: "When negative people are around me, I say to them kvetch, kvetch, kvetch—and they usually snap out of it. If they don't, I avoid them in the future and keep them out of my life."

I can almost hear Lee saying those words. They certainly represented his philosophy. He would go to any lengths to put what he called "negative people" or "negative incidents" behind him. He'd done it with Vince Cardel, he'd done it when his mother died, and now he was determined to do it with me. Lee had made up his mind to bury me and he had the power and the influence to do it.

A major player in the next battle of the tabloid wars was Dirk Summers. He claimed to be a descendant of the Drew family that produced all the Barrymores. His biographical sketch also says that he was an associate producer on television's prestigious "Hallmark Hall of Fame," a producer for Sammy Davis, Jr., and the producer of sixty-five television shows and eleven motion pictures. And he was rumored to be screen actress June Allyson's former husband. It sounds impressive. But, in 1982, Summers's career as a television writer and producer had sagged.

On October 28, 1982, in response to my original "Bombshell" article in the *Enquirer*, Dirk Summers wrote a letter to Iain Calder, the publisher of the *Enquirer*, that said in part: "Rarely have I read such a scurrilous attack on an international figure. The issue is not Lee Liberace, but the greed and lies by your source, Scott Thorson.

"I have mand [the misspelling was part of the letter] many documentaries, and in 1975 I was preparing a documentary on prostitution—both male and female.

"We were *bombarded* by calls and letters from prostitutes, both male and female who wanted to be included in our production. One of the male aspirants was Scott Thorson, although he had one or two other names at the time.

"During the course of the interview, he told me of various 'johns' that he had 'turned on,' and of the kinky experiences (sexual) that he was involved in with numerous men."

The verbatim quotes are taken from depositions that became part of the court records. The letter, which continued to take potshots at me while singing Liberace's praises, wasn't written for Iain Calder's benefit. In my opinion, it was written to let Liberace know that Dirk Summers was ready, willing, and able to destroy my reputation by proving I'd been a male prostitute. Summers sent a copy of the letter to Seymour Heller, a man he would later describe as "Lee's alter ego," along with a cover letter stating that Summers would be more than happy to testify on Lee's behalf should my suit come to trial. In the cover letter, Summers claims to know that I was arrested for prostitution.

By his own admission, Summers had been deluged with letters and phone calls from male and female prostitutes back in 1975 when he was putting together a show on prostitution. He claimed to have interviewed me at the time, although he said I used an alias. Seven years had passed since that one so-called and admittedly short interview. I'd aged, had plastic surgery, and was using my own name, Scott Thorson, when Summers claimed to recognize me from my picture in the *Enquirer* as the kid he'd met years earlier. It shouldn't have taken too much intelligence to realize how unlikely it would be that Summers could have remembered me out of the many male and female prostitutes whom he describes as *bombarding* him with messages in 1975. Had Seymour Heller or Joel Strote taken the trouble to investigate Summers's claims, they would have learned that I was living with a foster family in 1975, as well as going to school. I was not, nor have I ever been, a male prostitute. But it didn't appear to me that Lee's people were interested in getting the facts. Their sole interest seemed to be getting a weapon they could use against me in the tabloids, a weapon Summers obligingly supplied.

Summers came to Lee's attention in the most favorable way. In the days that followed, Seymour Heller made direct contact with Summers, setting up a meeting at Summers's home on November 6, a meeting also attended by Joel Strote. At that meeting Summers said he had information about my supposed past activities as a male prostitute that could be helpful to Liberace.

On November 8, Summers was contacted again by Heller and Strote, who asked if he would be willing to tell his story to Mike Snow, a reporter for the *Globe*. The next day Snow called Summers, and the two men had a very lengthy conversation that resulted in a new banner headline for the *Globe*'s December 2 issue: WICKED PAST OF THE GAY SUING LIBERACE. The Summers interview began: "He [meaning me] told me he was turning 25 tricks a day." Since male prostitutes are often the doer rather than the do-ee, that would have taken a runaway libido; a man who can turn twenty-five tricks a day is a better man than I have ever been or will be. The *Globe* story went on to give lurid details of my supposed life as a boy prostitute.

Early in December 1982, Liberace promised to lend his name to a golf tournament Summers said he planned to hold on March 25–26, 1983, at the Dunes Country Club in Las Vegas. Having secured a top celebrity name, Summers was able to raise a great deal of money from would-be tournament sponsors. When the golf tournament failed to materialize, Summers ran into trouble with the law and with Liberace. Lee later claimed he had never given Summers permission to use the Liberace name.

Eventually, Summers came to my attorneys, volunteering to say he had never been sure I was one of the interviewees in his proposed prostitution show and that he now realized he'd been completely in error about the entire episode. By then we were suing the *Globe* for defamation of character and Summers's testimony would have been helpful.

One other person had played a major role in ruining my name—none other than my half brother Wayne Johansen. Next to the interview obtained from Summers, the *Globe* published an article attributed to Johansen and, again, written by Mike Snow. My half brother had invented a story about my wicked homosexual past, saying I had my first lover when I was eleven. He even soiled my relationship with the Brummets by claiming I had a homosexual affair with Mr. Brummet when I was fifteen. The Summers story had angered me. My half brother's sickened me. We hadn't been close for a long time but I never expected him to turn on me in such a cruel and vicious way.

By the end of 1982 Liberace had obviously won the tabloid wars. He had the money, the power, the popularity to make the public believe his side of the story. I don't begrudge him that brief happiness even though it meant that the public didn't believe the things I'd said. I don't even begrudge him his relationship with Cary James.

Lee would win the war in the tabloids and he would win almost all the legal battles, but he wouldn't win the final fight of his life: the battle against AIDS.

26

When I filed suit against Lee it didn't occur to me that I'd be unleashing a drama that would consume the next five years of my life. The Los Angeles Superior Court calendar is a crowded one. On average, it takes four or more years from the date of filing until a plaintiff has his or her day in court. In my case, trial would be set for early spring 1987. By then, the defendant would be dead. Today, the legal documents, summonses, complaints, cross-complaints, demurrers, depositions, copies of items in evidence, fill five large cartons. They represent countless hours of work on the part of a half dozen attorneys and court reporters, as well as many hours spent under oath for plaintiffs, defendants, and material witnesses. My own depositions, numbering more than a thousand pages, make a stack far thicker than this book.

Late 1982 saw Lee and me locked in battle in the tabloids, a war he won handily. From 1983 on we would be caught up in a series of legal maneuvers. As Lee threatened in his *Globe* interview, he was prepared to litigate forever if that's what it took to win. Joel Strote quickly emerged as Lee's staunch defender, a man who would stop at nothing to protect his boss. Since the most important part of my case was based on *conversion of property,* Rosenthal soon realized he needed an expert cocounsel, someone with an extensive background in business litigation.

All my other attorneys had been recommended by friends, but Ernst Lipschutz had been recommended by a prestigious New York law firm. He impressed me favorably during our first meeting. He was a soft-spoken man of medium height, with alert, inquisitive eyes. From day one, he looked, sounded, and acted like a polished professional. Lipschutz specialized in business litigation, focusing on business fraud.

At our first meeting he made it clear that he didn't believe in the kind of grandstanding and playing to the media that had resulted in massive tabloid coverage. Lipschutz said if he came on board he would refuse to conduct the case in the hot glare of media attention. There would be no more press conferences, no more exclusive interviews with the tabloids. He was, he informed us, a lawyer—not a circus master.

I had to agree that the publicity I had received thus far had resulted only in my being branded as a liar and a street hustler. Lipschutz insisted that, from then on, the case would be conducted with as much dignity as we could muster. The first item on his agenda, after agreeing to become cocounsel, was to urge me to drop the ninth cause of action involving the so-called palimony.

That came as a shock. The ninth cause of action was the one the media had focused on, the one that got all the headlines, the one that hurt Lee the most personally. By then I wanted to embarrass him as much as possible. Rightly or wrongly, I felt he'd ruined my life and I'd made up my mind to make him suffer for it.

As Lipschutz talked about the proper way to conduct the case I couldn't help thinking, Who the hell is this guy, coming in here and telling us what to do after one day on the case when Rosenthal had been handling it for months? The ninth cause of action, based on Lee's promises to adopt me, to care for me forever, was the most important one from a personal standpoint. Sure, money was a consideration; I'd be crazy to say it didn't matter. But exposing Lee to public ridicule, holding him up to the world as a liar, was even more important. Those promises had been made in front of a number of Lee's people. They knew the truth and, unless they perjured themselves, the public would know the truth when I had my day in court.

I also knew Lee would interpret dropping the ninth cause of action as a sign of weakness and I wanted him to know I was prepared to pursue the case as long and as vigorously as he was.

Lipschutz patiently explained his reasoning, saying that the judge was likely to dismiss the palimony cause on the grounds that a contract for sex couldn't be enforced; that Liberace, Strote, and Heller (who would be far better witnesses than I) would probably be believed if they said that Lee never made any promises to me about caring for me financially. Lipschutz added that, if a judge ruled against the ninth cause of action in a preliminary hearing, we'd be in the unfortunate position of starting the real trial looking like losers. He said our proof was much stronger in the other areas of the case and he wanted to do everything in his power to get us into court looking like winners.

Unfortunately, I wasn't thinking very clearly in those days. Logically, everything Lipschutz said made sense but, emotionally, I couldn't go along with it. I wanted to punish Lee and the best way to do that was to go right on reminding the public, through the palimony portion of the case, that Lee was gay. It was his Achilles' heel.

That proved to be a mistake. Predictably, one of Lee's attorney's pretrial activities was to file a summary judgment motion requesting the ninth cause of action be dropped. A hearing on the motion was set for February 1983. Disaster struck when Lipschutz had a heart attack a couple of days before the scheduled hearing. By then I was of the opinion that Lipschutz was better suited to handle some of the aspects of my case. Rosenthal asked for a continuance. But the judge refused to grant one, saying that as long as I had legal representation he saw no reason to delay. Just as Lipschutz had predicted, the judge dismissed the ninth cause of action on the grounds that a contract for sex can't be enforced.

Lee and his attorneys had won the first of the many legal battles. Then Lee, who'd already demonstrated his masterful use of the media, gave an interview to Neil Karlen of *Newsweek* concerning the results of the hearing. The *Newsweek* article said, in part: "In 1982 Scott Thorson filed a $113 million palimony suit charging that Liberace had promised to support the Las Vegas dancer in exchange for sexual services.

"'It didn't take the judge long to decide I was being exploited,' says Liberace of the case, which was thrown out of a Los Angeles court in February.

"'I could have stopped the whole thing before it started by paying off,' he remembers, 'but that would have been blackmail and blackmail never ends.'

"Today, the tabloid slander finally behind him, Liberace gratefully acknowledges his fans' willingness to forgive, forget or not care."

The article made marvelous reading for Lee's loyal admirers. But it was far from accurate. First, I had never ever claimed to be a Las Vegas dancer. Second, the case wasn't thrown out of court. The other twelve causes of action had yet to be settled and, despite many attempts to get them dismissed too, would still be pending when Lee became ill. Third, if anyone had been guilty of blackmail, it was Lee when he withheld my property. Fourth, there had been enough slander on both sides of the dispute to last a lifetime. As soon as Lipschutz was back on his feet, he filed a libel action on my behalf against *Newsweek* and Liberace.

My case spawned a number of corollary cases. The original suit included Schmerin, Schnelker, Strote, and Heller as Liberace's codefendants. Early in the legal maneuvering, Rosenthal decided to drop Strote from the suit to narrow the case's focus. But he didn't obtain a release from Strote. Strote filed a suit for malicious prosecution against Rosenthal and me. Liberace, Heller, and Schmerin filed countercomplaints. We filed a libel action against the *Globe,* Mike Snow, and Wayne Johansen. Marie Brummet sued the *Globe* to clear her husband's name.

Michael Rosenthal was suing Joel Strote for slander, claiming that Strote, in the presence of Rosenthal's father and others, said: "How is your love life with Scott Thorson? I understand that love blooms between the two of you. Which one of you is the husband and which is the wife?" It's an unfortunate fact of life that all my attorneys, *none* of whom was gay, would be subject to such speculation. Being a lawyer, Rosenthal struck back in court.

My battle with Lee resulted in two other suits. Tracy Schnelker sued Liberace for the part Schnelker had been caused to play in the whole affair. That case was still pending when Lee died. Last, a criminal case against Dirk Summers had been filed for Summers's part in promoting and taking money for the bogus golf tournament. By the end of 1983 we were all suit slaphappy. I lost track of the many times I had depositions taken.

We battled every step of the way. Simple things such as the place Lee would be deposed became major points of conflict. He wanted to be deposed in Las Vegas. Inadvisable, said Lipschutz, in view of the fact that the case would be tried in Los Angeles Superior Court. Then Lee insisted on being deposed in Strote's office. For psychological reasons, Lipschutz didn't want Lee questioned on what Lee regarded as friendly turf. After Lipschutz filed a motion to enforce a Los Angeles deposition, Lee agreed to be deposed in the Los Angeles court stenographer's offices.

The lawyers wrangled over everything, from permitting me to take cigarette breaks during my depositions to how to guarantee everyone's safety and privacy during the proceedings. Lee's people said they feared Rosenthal and I would turn the depositions into a media circus. My lawyers argued that I feared for my personal safety because of what I had construed as threats against my life from people associated with Lee.

Early in the case, Rosenthal and I decided we wanted Joel Strote removed as Lee's attorney of record because he'd acted as my counsel on a number of occasions in the past. Technically, we were right: it did create a conflict of interest. But Lipschutz argued that Strote, although a competent lawyer, was far from being the best in the business. Lipschutz feared that having Strote dismissed would result in Lee's hiring a heavy hitter. Again, we overruled Lipschutz's very sound advice. And Lee did just what Lipschutz predicted; he brought in Marshall Grossman, a senior member of one of the most powerful and prestigious law firms in Los Angeles.

From that day on, it was to be an uphill battle for my side. Grossman was tops and he had unlimited funds at his disposal. Lipschutz was tops, but hampered by my inability to supply him with funds and by a sometimes obstructive client. My continued use of cocaine didn't help me or my case. During my depositions, Grossman, who'd been thoroughly briefed on all my weaknesses, did everything in his power to upset me, to keep me off balance. And he succeeded. I didn't make a very good impression as a witness on my own behalf. To my surprise, neither did Lee. He tried to impress the court reporter by telling her how much money he made an hour and, in general, he seemed unprepared. I hadn't seen him for months and it was hard to control my emotions while I listened to him giving his version of how our relationship had ended. Looking back, the whole experience has a nightmarish quality.

Month after month and year after year, Lee used his money, his power, and his popularity to hammer away at us. I don't know why we didn't give up. I had no money to pay my attorneys, no money to hire investigators, no money to pay for depositions. The money from the original settlement had been quickly spent on lawyers' fees and cocaine. Getting a job wasn't easy because everyone in Hollywood knew, thanks to the tabloids, that I had a drug problem. I'd finally gone to work at United Postal Centers in West Hollywood, and worked there until I began this book, thanks to a very understanding employer named Carole Rosen. But I had no skills and it wasn't a high-paying job. I made barely enough to support myself, let alone fight a prolonged legal battle. Lipschutz covered almost all of the case's costs out of his own pocket. By 1985 I think he'd invested more than $10,000 in my suit. It had become a matter of principle for him, a David and Goliath battle.

There were occasional good days. In particular, one day before Strote's dismissal from the case, he was making an attempt to get the presiding judge to dismiss my entire suit. Strote asserted that once I had signed the original April 22, 1982, agreement—which stated I was not forced to sign it—I had no further right to sue.

The judge looked at him long and hard before commenting, "Are you saying you believe I could *force* you to sign an agreement not to sue by pointing a gun at your head—and you couldn't void the agreement by proving you weren't forced to sign it?"

Strote replied confidently, "Yes, your honor." The judge grimaced and said Strote could not convince him that that was the law of California. Lipschutz broke into a contented smile. But he seldom had much to smile about. I think he was probably the only man in the country who believed I'd told the truth about my past and my life with Lee. On his own, at his own expense, Lipschutz had traveled around California investigating my background, talking to people who'd known me when I was growing up. During his travels Lipschutz had come to know a very different man from the spoiled, drug-addicted, emotional mess who emerged from a five-year relationship with Liberace. Lipschutz had come to know the independent self-starter I'd been. More than anyone else, he'd learned how much I'd lost by loving Lee. Not money. Not cars. Not my home. What I'd lost was myself. Lipschutz knew it and I think that's why he fought so hard on my behalf. His motivation sure as hell wasn't the money.

While I slogged through each day, trying to get my head straight and usually failing, Lee had embarked on a relationship with Cary James similar to the relationship he and I had shared. Like me, James went everywhere with Lee. I occasionally saw them pictured together in some periodical and it hurt like hell at first. Gradually, the pain faded as I filled my life with other things. But it was never easy.

Early in 1986 Lee embarked on a powerful public-relations ploy. He began a book that would reinforce the bogus life history he'd been selling the public for so long. It would be published by Harper & Row in late 1986, and titled *The Wonderful Private World of Liberace.*

After all the scandal, all the gossip, Lee said he wanted to set the record straight. The second paragraph of the book states: "This latest effort deals with my private life, the offstage person few people know about." The text was classic Liberace: a mixture of truth, half-truth, and outright lies. On the first page Lee detailed the type of questions he faced when interviewed by the media.

To the query, "Have you had a face-lift?" he replied, "Not yet. But if you think I've already had one, it means I can still wait until my friend and authority on the subject, Phyllis Diller, tells me it's necessary."

In fact, Lee had had two face-lifts and a deep skin peel.

213

To the query, "Is that your real hair?" he replied, "The hair is real—but the color only my hairdresser knows."

In fact, the hair *was* real but it had grown on someone else's head.

The fiction continued. Lee, who'd always refused to discuss his sex life prior to my suit, titled chapter 16, "How I Lost My Virginity." In it he claimed to have been seduced at the age of sixteen by a blues singer named Bea Haven. Then he wrote, "The thrill of making it with an older woman diminished as I grew older. Younger girls started to represent more of a challenge, probably because of their innocence."

I was disgusted by Lee's lies. The text bore no resemblance to the things he'd told me, unless you substituted football player for blues singer, men for women, and boys for girls. Then and only then does it come near the truth. The book is larded with pictures, including one of Cary James, Lee, and Kenny Rogers, all standing with their arms around each other. James is simply labeled as "my friend." In other publications he'd been called a chauffeur, a secretary, a companion—all Lee's usual euphemisms.

Looking through the lavishly illustrated text brings back a lot of memories of the houses we bought and decorated together, the dogs we both loved, the Liberace family—and most especially Frances, who I had come to care for. Those photographs fill me with nostalgia. But the misrepresentations in the text are so blatant that I get angry every time I read it. The one that upsets me the most deals with Liberace's health.

By 1986 rumors about Lee's health were circulating throughout the entertainment industry and the gay community. I don't know for certain if he knew he had AIDS when he wrote the following words, but he certainly had to know he was a very sick man. For the first time in his life, Lee no longer had a weight problem.

He wrote: "He [meaning Lee's physician, Dr. Elias Ghanem] was concerned over reports that I'd lost thirty pounds on a—would you believe—watermelon diet? In subsequent testing, he discovered I'd robbed my system of essential nutrients, which was causing me to experience a letdown in my normal high energy level.

"Some of his testing required special equipment and had to be performed in a local hospital. As a result, false rumors started to circulate about my health. According to the gossips, you name it, and I had it.

"Let me assure you, I've never felt better in my life!"

These words ring with pathetic bravado now. They were written by a man who, in less than a year, would be dead of AIDS.

27

By the beginning of 1986 the legal battle was so acrimonious that my attorney, Ernst Lipschutz, and Lee's attorney, Marshall Grossman, had developed a bitter, adversarial relationship. Twelve of my suit's original causes of action had yet to be settled despite the fact that Grossman had done everything in his power, using every weapon in his vast legal arsenal, to get the rest of my case dismissed. Everyone involved, from principals to witnesses to counsel, had been sucked into the mud-slinging, name-calling mire of accusation and counteraccusation. I'd never anticipated that so much time, energy, and talent would be consumed by what had started out to be nothing more than a lover's quarrel.

There seemed to be no way to turn back. As Lee said in one of his depositions, he was caught in a "war he never made." There were times when I too wished I could forget the whole thing. But we'd long since passed the point of no return. The suit had developed a life of its own. By then our attorneys had an interest in winning that was so consuming that at times it seemed as if they were the injured parties.

I sat in on the first of Lee's depositions, feeling completely miserable every time I looked at him. Over the years it became easier to remember our relationship. I could look at him, even say a civil hello, without feeling torn by the desire to hit him or hug him. But we hadn't spoken in private and I didn't think we ever would. Cary James was still with him and, so far, Lee showed no signs of tiring of his new companion.

It came as a bolt out of the blue when Lee called me early in 1986. His voice sounded unchanged—still as familiar to me as my own. I remember thinking my imagination was playing tricks on me when I heard Lee say, "Scott, is that you?"

We'd been at war so long that I'd long ago given up any hope of reconciliation. But suddenly the four years since our last conversation disappeared. I felt as if we had talked just yesterday, as if all the bitterness, the anger had happened between two other men.

A part of me had been waiting for that phone call since the Academy Awards ceremony in 1982, and now that it was finally happening, I didn't know how to handle it. So many things ran through my mind. Had Lee called, after all that time, to say he was sorry about everything? Was he going to make a personal appeal to me to settle out of court? Did he hope to be friends again in spite of everything? None of those ideas sounded likely and yet I couldn't help hoping those were his reasons for telephoning. Hearing his voice made me realize how much I'd missed him.

"How have you been?" Lee asked, as if he'd been calling me every day and this was just another in a series of friendly conversations.

"Fine, just fine," I replied, knowing that he hated a kvetch, that he wouldn't want to hear I couldn't seem to get my life back together without him.

"And your health," Lee continued, with a tinge of anxiety elevating his voice, "how's your health?"

"I'm fine," I said again, although that wasn't quite true. I still used cocaine despite a dozen attempts to kick the habit. It kept me thin, nervous, and broke.

"Are you sure you're feeling all right?" Lee persisted.

"Sure, Lee, I'm fine," I reiterated, wondering why, after four years of silence, he would call to inquire about my health.

Then it hit me: the unspoken fear that hides in the dark corners of every gay's mind. Please, God, no, I thought, let me be wrong. Not Lee! Don't let it be happening to Lee. So far, unlike so many other members of the homosexual community, I'd been lucky. None of my friends had died of AIDS, even though the obits in *Variety* reported an increasing number of deaths among young, single, show-business males. It wasn't hard to read between the lines and figure out that many of those deaths were related to AIDS.

I'd even heard a few rumors about Lee. He'd lost weight in the last couple of months and gossip within the gay community had it that AIDS was the cause. But I'd ignored the gossip. Hollywood is often more successful at creating rumors than it is at making movies. There are always stories making the rounds. And Lee, by denying his homosexuality, had certainly alienated the gay community. No wonder they talked about him. But the stories were, I'd reassured myself, just vicious lies.

I could hear Lee clearing his throat. "Well," he said, "I guess you've heard that I haven't been feeling too well."

"Sure," I replied. "But I didn't take it seriously. Are you all right?"

Silence. The wire hummed with it. It seemed to last forever. My God, I thought, it's true!

Finally Lee said, "I just wanted to be sure you're okay, Scott. And I'm glad you are." He sounded genuinely relieved. We talked a little about mutual friends. I had a hard time keeping any hint of emotion out of my voice while we chatted. I knew that Lee had called me for a reason. I also knew he'd never be able to spell that reason out. We were still locked in a court battle and no matter what changes occurred in his life or mine, he'd never forgive me for suing him and publicly branding him as gay. But legal battles and personal vendettas aside, Lee wasn't a big enough bastard to let me go on living my life without warning me about his condition. It didn't take any special brilliance on my part to figure out what that condition was. I believe that Lee called me because he wanted to do the right thing, to warn me that he had AIDS. Then, despite his good intentions, he couldn't go through with it. So he'd concentrated on making sure I wasn't sick, knowing I'd put two and two together and go see my own doctor.

I sat still as a stone for a long time after hanging up, turning the brief conversation over and over in my mind, desperate to come up with some other reason for Lee to call. After all, I reassured myself, he hadn't really come out and declared, "I have AIDS." Maybe I was making too much of it, reading things into what he'd said that weren't there.

I felt scared, more scared than I'd been the day Lee had me evicted from the penthouse. God! I didn't want to think about Lee having AIDS because that meant there was a chance—a very good chance—that I had it too. I sure as hell didn't want to die, not at twenty-seven. Like most gay men, I'd read everything there was to read about AIDS. It didn't seem possible that Lee could have contracted it during the years we'd been together.

As far as I knew, we'd been faithful to each other right up until the last week. I had no proof of Lee's infidelity prior to our breakup. We were both too jealous to go along with the open relationship that Lee had proposed. There'd been a lot of flirting but I didn't think it had gone any further. While the AIDS virus had been leapfrogging through the gay community, Lee and I had been in a seemingly monogamous relationship—so how the hell, I asked myself, could we have gotten AIDS? No matter what, I still cared about him a lot; I always would. Lee had been my best friend, my mentor; we'd had some good times. I missed those times and I always will. I didn't want him to die.

I don't know how long I sat quietly, trying to deal with that phone call. Deep down, I knew Lee had AIDS. I couldn't help remembering the two Frenchmen who'd been a brief part of Lee's life back in 1982 when we broke up. During that period I'd heard other stories about the way Lee used his newfound freedom—stories of excessive behavior on his part. There'd been more than enough time in the years since we parted for him to have contracted it and, from things I'd heard, he'd been sexually active enough to have put himself at extreme risk. Damn Lee and his libido, his philosophy that "too much of a good thing is *wonderful*."

I knew he wouldn't have called for any other reason. But, as long as Lee continued to fight the suit, as long as he pursued his career, I couldn't be absolutely positive about his illness. It was easier to think Lee had called because of a whim, because he suddenly got lonely for old times and old friends. Nevertheless, I began to follow his career more closely, to check to see if he was playing Vegas or Tahoe or L.A. And I saw my own doctor.

Getting a clean bill of health was an enormous relief and reinforced my hope that I'd been way off base about Lee's call. At first, Lee's work schedule seemed relatively normal: he continued to play enough dates to allay my worries. More important, his attorney, Marshall Grossman, continued to pursue the case. Within a couple of weeks I'd almost managed to convince myself that I'd completely misinterpreted the phone call. When I heard, via the grapevine, that Lee would be making his long-dreamed-of appearance at Radio City Music Hall sometime in the fall of 1986, I felt sure he was fine.

Then one night in June 1986, I ran into him at a restaurant in the Beverly Center in Beverly Hills and, after getting a good look at him, denial was no longer possible. I hadn't seen Lee for a year and his appearance came as a shock. Lee had always been a stocky man with a barrel chest. He'd gotten increasingly overweight during the years we'd been together and we'd laughed about how much he loved food and hated dieting. Occasionally, he'd give lip service to the idea of losing weight but, when the time came, he just couldn't do it. There was always a new restaurant or a new recipe to try, or a favorite meal served up by Gladys. Lee couldn't deny himself the pleasures of the table any more than he could deny himself the pleasures of the bed.

Yet that night at the Beverly Center, it was obvious that he'd lost a lot of weight. I didn't believe the stories his people had been broadcasting about the famous "watermelon diet." Lee should have looked terrific, the way most people do when they drop an unwanted thirty or forty pounds, but he didn't! Under his makeup he looked pale, sick, and old.

We stood and talked briefly. I lied and said he looked great, that being thin became him. He asked about my health again and then again, staring at me almost as hard as he had the night we first met. The message was plain, if I had the guts to deal with what he *meant* rather than what he said. I didn't need to hear a doctor's diagnosis to know what ailed Lee.

In response to his queries I told Lee I'd seen my own doctor and felt great. I knew Lee would get my meaning. He smiled, told me he was happy for me, and we parted. By then the entire world knew that Rock Hudson had died of AIDS. I expected it would just be a matter of months before the public knew Lee had the same disease. Poor Lee. He'd spent a lifetime denying his own homosexuality in public, fighting the papers, the tabloids, fighting me for daring to tell the truth. Soon everyone would be able to judge his personal honesty for themselves. Heller couldn't handle this problem for him. The best medical minds in the world couldn't. It would take a miracle to help Lee now.

Sometime in early autumn 1986, Ernst Lipschutz called to say he'd been advised that Lee had dismissed Grossman as his attorney of record. A new attorney, Toni Bruno, had been hired in Grossman's place. "In my opinion," Lipschutz said, "that can only mean one thing. I think they're going to try and settle out of court. They know Grossman and I have become adversaries, in every sense of the word. So they've brought in someone else to work out an agreement."

Lipschutz's intuition turned out to be right on the money. Toni Bruno raised the topic of an out-of-court settlement almost at once. I asked Lipschutz to try to find out if the offer was motivated by Lee's deteriorating health, but Bruno stonewalled the question. According to her, Liberace had never felt better. When asked if there was a special reason why the settlement offer came this late in the game, she replied that Lee just wanted to put an end to our dispute.

I didn't believe Bruno for a minute and neither did Lipschutz. I'd told him about the phone call and the chance meeting in the restaurant. He knew what I suspected. The offer to settle out of court merely confirmed my suspicions. But three more months would pass before the scheduled court date for a voluntary settlement conference.

Meanwhile Lee was making preparations for his appearance at Radio City Music Hall. The show, which climaxed his career, would run more than two hours and Lee had agreed to do a total of twenty-one performances. The demanding routine would have taxed the strength of a young entertainer. But for Lee, sixty-seven years old and suffering from AIDS, it was damn near suicidal. Common sense dictated that he cancel the appearance. I'm told he didn't consider it, not for a second. He came from the "show must go on" school of entertainers. Lee had a brush with death back in 1963, but he'd continued performing during his

Hershey, Pennsylvania, Holiday Inn booking despite the fact that his kidneys were shutting down. His will was as strong in October 1986 as it had been twenty-three years earlier. Lee had dreamed of appearing at the Music Hall for years and made his first appearance there in 1984. Now nothing, not even the grim reaper, would be allowed to keep him from repeating the success he'd had in 1984.

Lee hadn't told any of his people that he suffered from a fatal illness. He talked about being overtired and anemic instead. To this day, some of them refuse to accept the fact that he died of AIDS. I understand their reluctance. He seemed larger than life to everyone, filling our hearts and minds as easily as he filled a stage. He'd become a living legend—and legends don't die. It seems impossible, even now, that anything could have killed him.

But he was already a dying man when he stepped on the Radio City Music Hall stage that October. Doing so took great courage on his part. He had no way of knowing if he'd be able to complete the agreed-on number of shows. If he faltered, in front of John Q. Public, he must have known how hard it would be to go on keeping his final secret. With nothing more than his own fighting heart, Lee held his illness at bay and put on the show of his lifetime. Although I wasn't fortunate enough to see his final appearances, friends tell me Lee was at the top of his form, full of energy and good spirits, for each performance. He held the sophisticated New York audiences in the palm of his hand from the overture to the final curtain.

The show opened with motion pictures of Lee's homes projected on a screen at the back of the stage. Their opulent luxury set the tone for the entire show. Then the scene dissolved to a picture of the New York skyline at night while wisps of smoke billowed over the stage, creating an atmosphere of beauty and mystery. Lee made one of his more spectacular entrances, flying across the stage wearing a harness under his costume that enabled him to soar as easily as Superman. Such apparently effortless flying is in fact one of the most physically taxing theatrical tricks, requiring great stamina and agility. Lee could have conserved his energy by being driven on stage in one of his many Rolls-Royces. But this was to be his swan song as an entertainer and he wanted to give his unqualified best.

I still shudder when I think what that cost him, flying across that stage night after night. He'd land in the wings, get out of the harness, and make his entrance on foot to thunderous applause. Knowing him, I suspect it was the applause that kept him going, that fed his soul after his body had begun to fail. No matter how bitterly we'd fought in the tabloids and then in court, there are no words to express my admiration for what he did in those twenty-one magical shows at the Music Hall.

No one guessed that he was terminally ill, not his audience, not his closest associates. Ray Arnett, a man who'd been a part of the entourage for years, later told me he didn't suspect. Perhaps he didn't want to. Lee put on the act of his life for all of them. He was living his final dream and he intended to live it full throttle. That takes one hell of a man.

He made his final entrance near the end of the show in a red, white, and blue Rolls while the Rockettes marched in perfect precision, banners swirling, and the orchestra reached a crescendo. The two-hour performance concluded with patriotic flag waving. Night after night, Lee took his final bow to a thunderous ovation. No performer deserved it more.

It was nothing short of a miracle that Lee made it through all twenty-one shows. I've been told he couldn't have made it through a twenty-second. His strength gave out as he took his final bow on November 2, 1986. It was the last time any audience would have a chance to share the special fun and wonder of a Liberace show. Had Lee been able to choose the time and place of his final curtain call, I think he would have chosen the one God or fate or whatever power you believe in gave him.

He came home in November to celebrate his last holiday season. Lee invited his closest friends, the nearest and dearest of his people to share Thanksgiving and Christmas. But I'm told that he still refused to share the truth about his health. Lee always hated a complainer. It's to his eternal credit that he didn't permit himself to be one either. As far as anyone knew, he was suffering from a combination of overwork and excessive dieting. Because they all wanted to believe it, they did. It's that simple and that sad.

While Lee prepared for the season of "peace on earth, goodwill toward men," our legal drama was playing out its final scenes. On December 3, 1986, the interested parties, or their attorneys of record, met in Los Angeles Superior Court to work out their differences. A compromise met, we signed an agreement a few days later. Lee and I were finally finished with our war.

Knowing what I did about his health, I could have refused the settlement and fought on in the future against Lee's estate. And I might have won. In refusing the many motions to dismiss the case, the courts seemed to indicate that it had some merit. But my argument was with Lee; my anger had been directed at him. I could not, would not, battle it out with a dying man—or his heirs. And, to be honest, I needed the money the settlement gave me. It's always been that way with me and I'm afraid it always will.

Bit by bit, from 1982 to 1986, I'd been saying good-bye to Lee. Signing the agreement meant the relationship had ended. I'd loved him and lost him. Now the world would lose him too.

28

On Tuesday, December 20, 1986, on page 14 of the *Los Angeles Times* a headline declared PALIMONY SUIT AGAINST LIBERACE SETTLED. Five years of litigation had gone by and the media still couldn't seem to get the facts straight. It was not—I repeat, *not*—a palimony suit! Had the headlines been required to read correctly CONVERSION OF PROPERTY SUIT AGAINST LIBERACE SETTLED, I doubt the paper would have bothered to publish the story.

I never expected to hear from Lee after we signed the agreement. The last tie between us had been severed; he would go his way and I would go mine. My biggest concern was to stay off drugs, to build a new life. I'd been angry at Lee for a long time, feeling he'd cheated me out of whatever happiness I could hope for. But now, feeling gut sure he had AIDS, I couldn't help being grateful that we'd broken up when we did. Fate had dealt me a better hand, in March 1982, than I'd realized at the time. Leaving Lee in 1982 may have saved my life.

Despite a stipulation that the parties to the final settlement would never reveal its terms, the *Los Angeles Times* printed an accurate estimate of the financial arrangements. But stories about the settlement would soon be replaced by stories about Lee's health as rumors ran wild through the entertainment communities in Los Angeles and Las Vegas. Lee had taped an interview with Oprah Winfrey for her 1986 Christmas show, and makeup couldn't hide the fact that he looked almost as bad as Rock Hudson had during Hudson's final public appearances. One of the tabloids had already learned that, for the first time in Lee's forty-three-year show-business career, he had no future bookings. It didn't take the media long to put two and two together and, in this case, it added up to AIDS.

While the rumors about his health escalated, Lee remained in seclusion in his Palm Springs home. He no longer felt well enough to see his closest associates, men such as Ray Arnett and Bo Ayars. They would not be permitted to share his last weeks, a fact that makes them, in my opinion, the lucky ones. I never expected to see Lee again either. After all, we'd settled our suit and I didn't think we had anything more to say to each other. But Lee had one last surprise in store for me.

He telephoned a few days after Christmas and, just as with the call months earlier, his prime concern seemed to be my health. I did my best to reassure him; however, he couldn't or wouldn't take my word for the fact that I was in the best of health. Lee, who'd always been so unflappably even tempered, sounded agitated as he repeated his questions. Then, almost abruptly, he said he had to go but that he'd call again.

I was half hoping he wouldn't. Lee hadn't sounded well on the phone—mentally or physically. If I had my choice, I preferred to remember him as he'd been before we parted, not old and sick and failing as I feared he was now. His next call, about a week later, deepened my concern. He wanted to see me, he said, to make amends. I tried to tell him there was nothing to make amends for, that we'd both made mistakes and that I hoped he forgave mine as I forgave his. But he was insistent, he *had* to see me.

I didn't want to make the trip to the Cloisters. For one thing, I knew Lee's people would resent my presence. Lee might have forgiven me for suing him, but I felt damn sure they hadn't. Going to see him on his home turf would be the equivalent of walking into the lion's den, and I wasn't that brave or that foolhardy. I told Lee I didn't think seeing each other was a very good idea, but he kept on insisting. Sick or well, he had the tenacity of a bulldog when it came to getting his way. I made him promise that any meeting between us would be as private as possible, that no one else would be in the house beside Lee and the person who would let me in. He agreed to my terms and we set a time for our meeting.

It takes two hours to drive from Los Angeles to Palm Springs and I almost turned around a half dozen times. I was still afraid of Lee's power, his ability to hurt me without even meaning to. He'd sworn, again and again under oath, that he hadn't meant me any harm when he'd told Heller to get me out of the penthouse all those years ago. No matter what Lee's intentions, I'd been threatened, roughed up, and maced. To this day, I don't think he actually asked anyone to do that to me. But when he gave the orders that set the wheels in motion, he must have known my eviction from the penthouse might turn nasty. And he hadn't hesitated.

I had no idea what lay waiting for me at the Cloisters— reconciliation or renewed warfare. Lee could easily have people there who would be less than friendly when I showed up. Emotionally, I wanted to trust him, to believe him when he said he wanted to make amends. Logically, I felt that going to see him was one of the dumber things I'd done in the last five years.

The desert is spectacular in January—lush, warm, and sunny while L.A. is foggy and damp. But the gorgeous scenery and delightful weather didn't calm my anxiety as I exited the interstate and headed toward Palm Springs. Would Lee keep his word, I worried, or would he take this last opportunity to make me regret suing him and publicizing his homosexuality? As I pulled up in front of the high stucco wall surrounding the Cloisters and got out of my car, the estate looked just the way it had the last time I'd been there. A wave of nostalgia washed over me as I took in the tiled CASA DE LIBERACE sign. I drew a deep breath, rang the bell, and waited for the heavy wooden gate to swing open.

A maid let me into the compound, and it soon became apparent that Lee had kept his word: no one else was there. The house looked deserted except for a few of the smaller dogs who greeted me ecstatically, cavorting at my feet and trying to lick my hands. The fact that they still remembered me after all that time brought tears to my eyes. Despite their enthusiasm it was a far different homecoming from the one I'd hoped for five years earlier when I'd dreamed of returning to this, Lee's favorite house. The house looked the same but everything else, my life and his, had changed.

Lee was waiting for me in the bedroom and seeing him was a terrible shock. I don't think he weighed more than a hundred forty pounds. With his gaunt face and wasted body, he looked like a scarecrow. A heartbreaking mixture of fear and despair filled his eyes. I walked over to him to give him a hug, but he stopped me. "I don't want you to touch me," he said.

If I'd had any guts, I'd have hugged him anyway. But seeing him like that scared the hell out of me. I backed off and concentrated on patting the dogs instead. Lee seemed to want to talk about the past, the good times we'd shared, and I let him reminisce while I struggled to get used to his frightening deterioration. It was one thing to hear stories about how terrible he looked, how sick he was. None of those stories prepared me for the reality. AIDS had a death grip on Lee.

I could see it wasn't going to be a long visit; he just didn't have the strength, and a part of me couldn't wait to get out of the house. Seeing Lee like that had to be one of the most frightening experiences of my life. He told me that his sister, Angie, and his old friend Tido Minor (the ex-wife of Don Fedderson, who'd discovered Lee) were practically the only people he saw anymore. I could understand why. One look at him and you knew he was dying, no matter how many stories his publicist put out about his just needing a long rest. This rest was going to be permanent.

I wanted to cry but I knew that wouldn't do Lee any good. Laughter would have helped both of us, but I couldn't think of anything funny to say. Fortunately, it didn't seem to matter. As we talked, there were times when I felt as if Lee's illness had affected his mind as well as his body. He rambled, lost his train of thought, skipped from one topic to another. It took him a while to get to the point. But he finally looked at me and said, "I'm not going to make it." Tears filled his eyes. "I don't want to be remembered as an old queen who died of AIDS."

I tried to reassure him, to tell him he would always be remembered as a great entertainer. Nothing I could say seemed to help.

"Promise me you won't talk to anyone about this visit," he said, "or how bad I looked."

Not trusting my voice, I nodded.

"Scott," Lee said, "I asked you here because I wanted you to know you made me the happiest." Then he gave me a ring that had belonged to his mother and one of his own that he always wore during his shows. "Just a little something to remember me by," he said, smiling with something like the old sparkle in his eyes.

Lee knew I loved jewelry almost as much as he did. Nothing he could have given me would have pleased me more. I remembered his telling me how he'd given away so many of his treasured possessions back in 1964 when he thought he was dying, and a terrible feeling of longing and regret washed over me. This time there would be no miraculous recovery. Lee and I had been through a lot together, not all of it good. But I wouldn't have wished AIDS on my worst enemy. Seeing him like that was rough. I just hope it gave him a little peace. Before I left he gave me one last parting gift—a big panda bear much like the one I'd seen on his bed ten years earlier, the first time I walked into his bedroom in Vegas. Then our brief visit was over. Driving back to L.A., I knew I'd never see him again.

On January 14 the *Las Vegas Sun* ran an editorial that was, in part, an appeal to "one of entertainment's brightest stars—to face reality with courage and determination, to lick the disease if there is a way. He has all the money in the world and he should be experimenting, not only for his own life but for the sake of others."

It didn't take a genius to read between the lines and figure out that the paper was talking about Lee, even though they didn't come right out and name him. Predictably, Seymour Heller rose to the challenge and immediately issued a vigorous denial, saying that Lee didn't have AIDS, that he suffered from emphysema, heart disease, and anemia. That was to be the party line for the next few weeks.

When Heller was asked why Lee didn't have any future bookings he quoted Lee as saying, "Seymour, I have these lovely places and I never take time to enjoy them. What's the sense in having them if I don't take the time?"

In reality Lee's time had almost run out. His last few weeks would deteriorate into a Roman circus with the media playing the lions while Lee and his people played the Christians. The worst thing, in my opinion, is that the circus would never have happened if, at any time in the past, Lee had admitted to being homosexual. Instead of treating him sympathetically, the press seemed determined to catch Lee in the lie of a lifetime. They began to gather outside the Cloisters, where the death watch had begun.

Again the *Vegas Sun* scooped everyone when its January 24, 1987, edition bore the headline LIBERACE VICTIM OF DEADLY AIDS. The day before, Lee had checked into the Eisenhower Medical Center in Palm Springs, where he would spend three days in isolation. As he fought his deadly illness his worst fears were realized. He had lived his life flamboyantly and his final days would be equally attention-getting.

Liberace and AIDS were a major story, to be told and retold in the papers and on all the newscasts. Seymour Heller fought a last-ditch effort to keep Lee from being branded, on his deathbed, as an aging queen dying of AIDS. Heller built a solid wall of denial that the press didn't breach until Lee's death. Everyone associated with Lee, including his private doctor, told the same story. Lee had heart problems, complicated by anemia and emphysema. When Lee left the medical center, the people closest to him were quoted as saying he was feeling better. In fact, he left because he wanted to die at his beloved Cloisters rather than in unfamiliar surroundings.

He would not be alone during his final days. The man who lived his life surrounded by other gay men would spend his final days being ministered to by women. Angie, Gladys Luckie, and another housekeeper, Dorothy MacMahain, would keep a constant vigil by his side while round-the-clock nurses gave Lee the best medical care available. But all their efforts would prove useless against a disease for which there is no known cure.

Outside the Cloisters, the media maintained their own vigil. Curious bystanders, perhaps drawn by the television cameras, began to keep the vigil too. Any hope that Lee could die with dignity disappeared. Everything that happened during those final

230

days became fodder for the tabloids. Lee's last hours were described in infinite and often inaccurate detail. No element of the story seemed too personal to publish.

There were accounts of how Lee asked to say good-bye to his dogs, how the day came when he no longer recognized them, how he had conversations with his mother or his two deceased brothers as he lapsed in and out of a coma. Lee's last words are contradictorily quoted as being "Babyboy, I'll soon be there to feed you," and "I'll soon be with you, Mother." Although the official death certificate places February 4, 1987, 2:05 P.M., as the date and time of his death, insiders are reported to have said that he died at 11:30 A.M. There would be other discrepancies.

Lee's personal physician, Dr. Ronald Daniels, listed cardiac arrest due to cardiac failure as the cause of death. Technically, I guess he was correct, if not strictly forthcoming, in that everyone dies of heart failure. At 2:50 P.M. one of Angie's sons-in-law stepped outside the Cloisters to announce that Lee was gone. At 3:20 P.M. a plain gray hearse was admitted to the Cloisters compound and Lee's body, encased in a black plastic body bag, was placed inside. As the vehicle exited the grounds, heading for Los Angeles, where the body would be prepared for burial at Forest Lawn, cars full of reporters and even a television helicopter gave chase.

The next day, shortly after Lee's body had been embalmed, the Riverside County Health Department formally rejected Dr. Daniels's death certificate and ordered an autopsy. California law requires that an autopsy be conducted when there is a suspicion that someone has died of a contagious disease. According to the Riverside coroner, Raymond Carillo, there were more than enough grounds for suspicion. But Carillo would be handicapped by the efforts of Lee's friends to protect his reputation. Heller and Strote vigorously protested the need for the autopsy, citing Dr. Daniels's death certificate. They would deny Lee's AIDS with their last breath if need be. Because Lee had already been embalmed, it would be necessary to take tissue samples and to get the medical records, including blood tests, from his recent stay at the Eisenhower Medical Center. Carillo would eventually be forced to subpoena them.

All of this kept Lee's name on the front pages. Lee's Palm Springs memorial service at Our Lady of Solitude served as a media event rather than a last farewell. Reverend William Erstad's earnest plea: "Let us not judge our fellow man. . . . Everyone needs forgiveness," went unheeded, as did a telegram from President Ronald Reagan saying that Liberace "will be remembered in many ways, but most importantly as a kind man who lived his life with great joy."

I sat in the church that day, listening to the well-meaning words, knowing they would be ignored by the press. Lee, having spent so much of his life trying to conceal his homosexuality, would now be remembered as the second famous entertainer to die of AIDS. By denying his homosexuality, by trying to conceal his AIDS rather than going public as Rock Hudson had done, I felt Lee had set the entire gay movement back a decade. Back in 1982, during the tabloid wars, Lee had said, "The gays are out to assassinate me." In a bizarre way that no one could possibly have foreseen—his prediction had come true.

Epilogue

Lee's illness and subsequent death shook me up more than any other event in my life, made me take a serious look at where I was and where I seemed to be headed. A few months after I began to suspect Lee had AIDS, I finally managed to kick my chemical dependency. I joined an AA drug program where, coincidentally, my sponsor turned out to be a recovered addict who had also been introduced to hard drugs by Dr. Jack Startz. Staying clean is a battle I fight every day, and it's never easy. But it's essential to my survival.

Job-wise, I'm not doing as well. Being Lee's former lover isn't something I can put down on a résumé. Today, because of the AIDS epidemic in Hollywood, employers are reluctant to hire known gays. Sometimes I feel as if the deck is stacked against me, even though I'm the damn fool who shuffled the cards. I've been through tough times before and I've always survived. I plan to survive this one too. Putting this book together has helped me to see things—myself, Lee, the effect we had on each other's lives—more clearly. In the months following his death Lee continued to be the subject of controversy, discussion, and legal action. He was mourned, lamented, hated, and loved, just as he had been in his lifetime—but not forgotten.

One day in April 1987, I got a pathetic phone call from one of Lee's people, a man who'd been with Lee through thirty years of performances. "I woke up this morning," he said, "and the damnedest thing happened. I completely forgot that Lee was gone. And you know, Scott, it's the time of year when we always go on tour. So I picked up the phone to call Seymour Heller. I was going to chew him out for not telling me when Lee and I would be leaving town."

The poor guy's voice was quivering as he said, "Then it hit me. We'll never be going on the road again; there won't be any more tours." Like me, this man couldn't come to grips with the fact that Lee was dead. Like me, he seemed to be wondering what to do with the rest of his life now that Lee wasn't part of it. I could sympathize with the guy but I couldn't help him. I'd faced the same problem five years earlier and I still hadn't come up with a good answer for myself.

Everyone associated with Lee had to learn to deal with his death. It affected them all differently. The first of several disputes over Lee's estate made headlines in March 1987. Rudy's four children, who'd been excluded as heirs by a new will written just weeks before Lee's death, appeared in a Las Vegas courtroom to contest the will's validity.

Then, on May 12, 1987, Joel Strote, now the executor of Lee's estate, filed a claim for unspecified damages against Riverside County, claiming that Lee's reputation had been damaged by the county coroner who publicly linked Lee's death to AIDS. It would seem that Strote was prepared to fight one last futile battle on Lee's behalf, to keep Lee from being identified, publicly and for all time, as a homosexual male. I admire Strote's loyalty, although his actions were ultimately futile. Perhaps he too was having trouble accepting Lee's death; perhaps he was trying to do what he thought Lee would have wanted. I've never been able to figure the guy out. In any case, the court denied the claim and, in July 1987, the Riverside County coroner made his final findings public. The coroner concluded that Lee *had* died of an AIDS-related cause.

While the survivors argued among themselves, Lee's estate went into probate. Lee had earned hundreds of millions of dollars in his lifetime, but he'd spent lavishly. I have no way of knowing how much money he left, but the events that followed his death seem to indicate that the estate is cash poor. On May 24, 1987, Christie's of London, one of the world's most prestigious auction houses, announced that it would hold a three-day auction in the Los Angeles Convention Center in mid-April 1988, to dispose of more than twenty thousand items belonging to Lee, ranging from dozens of trademark candelabra to mirrored pianos to Rolls-Royces. Bit by bit the things Lee loved, including most of his homes, are being offered for sale.

Lee's sister, Angie, has made a public plea for funds to save Lee's Vegas house from the auction block and turn it into yet another Liberace museum. As of this writing, the Shirley Street house is still on the market and I guess it will sell one of these days.

More recently, in August 1987, I heard that Angie, Gladys Luckie, housekeeper Dorothy MacMahain, and Cary James were all bringing suit because Lee's new will, written by Joel Strote and signed just days before Lee's death, didn't fulfill the promises he'd made over and over to them during his life. It all has a terribly familiar sound. As they say, "What goes around comes around." It's sad but predictable that the people closest to Lee would quarrel now that he's gone. He was the glue that held them all together.

The only thing that now seems to unite them is a determination to keep me from writing this book. With few exceptions, they have refused interviews, turned down requests for pictures, used Lee's vestigial influence to keep places such as the Vegas Hilton from helping me, and threatened a suit should this book be published. Those who have cooperated, fearing reprisals from Strote and Heller, have asked that I never reveal their names. But I have two powerful reasons for writing this book. As you may have guessed, I need the money. The settlement I got at the end of the lawsuit went for legal fees and to set up my own apartment. More important, I believe that Lee's story—his true story rather than a carefully concocted fairy tale—deserves to be told, for his story can teach all of us a lesson. It serves best as a cautionary tale whose moral is: Too much of a good thing, be it sex, booze, success, or fame, *is not wonderful*. In fact, it can kill you.

Afterword

Beyond the Candelabra

At the close of the time period covered by *Behind the Candelabra*, I was a young man, but a young man with the life experience of someone much older and more experienced than is typical for my age. Lee's money, age and dominating role within our relationship had resulted in my meeting and coming to know people with considerable influence in a wide range of pursuits—movies, television, Vegas, nightclubs and organized crime, primarily the drug trade.

And I had possessions. My famous lawsuit against Lee was not terribly successful, but during my time with him, I accumulated considerable assets—not just hard assets like cars, houses and jewelry, but also investment in businesses. And the businesses with the biggest impact on my life going forward were nightclubs.

In the best of times, the nightclub business attracts investors with less than the most altruistic motivations. With my luck, I found myself in partnership in a number of clubs with a man who went by the alias "Eddie Nash." Nash's primary occupation was acting as kingpin of the drug trade for organized crime throughout Southern California, among other areas. In his overall enterprise, our nightclubs' primary purpose was to launder money being thrown off by his drug business. We were scrubbing huge amounts of drug money. Nash's success in the drug trade attracted the attention of and created envy in smaller, less disciplined drug traders, particularly a wild group known throughout the Southland as the Wonderland Gang because of the location of their operating headquarters on Wonderland Avenue in the Laurel Canyon section of Los Angeles.

In one of the most sensational cases of the 1980s, Nash colleagues butchered four members of the Wonderland Gang in their hangout in retribution for their break-in at his mansion and theft of drug inventory, massive cash reserves, jewelry and other valuables. Nash gained knowledge of the perpetrators of the theft by torturing John Holmes, a pathetically drug-addicted porn star who frequented both Nash's mansion and the Wonderland Gang hangout in his search for drugs. The federal government had leverage on me because of my shared ownership of the money-laundering clubs, so my testimony at trial about the torture of Holmes was regarded as very helpful in the conviction and sentencing of a major mob figure, and into the federal Witness Protection Program I went. But now I was penniless. Federal confiscation of my club ownerships was just the starting point. The government ended up with all my jewelry, real estate and other belongings of any value. But they gave me a new name, life history and social security number. Hello, Jess Marlow.

Witness Protection works by changing pretty much everything about you to hide you among the population. I was sent to rural Florida and became an employee of an evangelistic church with a significant outreach program. Only God could have arranged for me to meet Him under circumstances that I would truly respond to. It was here that I quickly became a born-again believer and developed a reputation for my "testimony." In short order, the pastors learned that I could move an audience with my preaching and I became part of their itinerant preaching program. I was actually becoming something of a hot commodity in the television and radio evangelism scene, flying in private jets to speak at events held by respected preachers, including an appearance at a Billy Graham Crusade event. The Witness Protection marshals warned me, I will give them that. My service in sharing God's Word was raising my profile throughout America, including prisons, and Eddie Nash was able to pierce my veil of protection.

I went to the door of the motel where I was staying in Jacksonville, Florida expecting a pizza. Instead I got five .38-caliber slugs—three in the abdomen (one striking my spinal column), one in the chest, and one in the head. The hit men left me for dead, and indeed I was technically dead for several minutes based on medical definitions. But I was rushed to University Hospital and revived, at least into a coma state. A coma that would last six months.

During my preaching career, my messages had particularly affected a young divorcee in Maine. She felt moved by the Lord to pray for me and visit me in the hospital. Due to the circumstances, my room was guarded and a number of similar-minded people were turned away by law enforcement. In one of those coincidences that make it hard to believe in coincidences, my soon-to-be benefactor found herself on a business trip to Florida and able to walk straight through the entire hospital and directly into my room without any contact whatsoever with any official personnel. And so we were reading Scripture, and praying, and eventually she offered me shelter in her home in Maine.

From 1991 to 2005, I lived in Maine with someone who had nothing but my best interests at heart. But my heart wandered continually, causing me to seek drugs and to leave her in Maine for more than just a few days at a time. For fourteen years, I always came back to Maine and to her and to the large group of dogs she had allowed me to bring into the house as pets. (To this day, I believe that, had I not met Liberace, a career with animals either as a vet or trainer would have been my best course.)

In any event, in 2005, I could no longer resist the temptation to return to something like the life I had had with Lee. The problem was there was no Liberace. I had to finance my own lifestyle, and all I knew from a practical standpoint was drugs. I threw myself headlong into the crystal meth scene. After three separate stints in Delano and Corcoran California state prisons, I now find myself on disability (the heritage of one of the .38-

caliber slugs against the spine) with the added plague of the same type of anal cancer that recently took the life of Farrah Fawcett.

I hope to see the movie made based on *Behind the Candelabra*. Matt Damon plays me, and Michael Douglas is Lee.